on track ...

Jimi Hendrix

every album, every song

Emma Stott

SONICBOND

sonicbondpublishing.com

Sonicbond Publishing Limited
www.sonicbondpublishing.co.uk
Email: info@sonicbondpublishing.co.uk

First Published in the United Kingdom 2022
First Published in the United States 2022

British Library Cataloguing in Publication Data:
A Catalogue record for this book is available from the British Library

ISBN 978-1-78952-175-7

Typeset in ITC Garamond & ITC Avant Garde
Printed and bound in England

Graphic design and typesetting: Full Moon Media

on track ...

Jimi Hendrix

every album, every song

Emma Stott

SONICBOND

sonicbondpublishing.com

Would you like to write for Sonicbond Publishing?

We are mainly a music publisher, but we also occasionally publish in other genres including film and television. At Sonicbond Publishing we are always on the look-out for authors, particularly for our two main series, On Track and Decades.

Mixing fact with in depth analysis, the On Track series examines the entire recorded work of a particular musical artist or group. All genres are considered from easy listening and jazz to 60s soul to 90s pop, via rock and metal.

The Decades series singles out a particular decade in an artist or group's history and focuses on that decade in more detail than may be allowed in the On Track series.

While professional writing experience would, of course, be an advantage, the most important qualification is to have real enthusiasm and knowledge of your subject. First-time authors are welcomed, but the ability to write well in English is essential.

Sonicbond Publishing has distribution throughout Europe and North America, and all our books are also published in E-book form. Authors will be paid a royalty based on sales of their book. Further details about our books are available from www.sonicbondpublishing.com. To contact us, complete the contact form there or email info@sonicbondpublishing.co.uk

I ain't finished yet, brother… I got more to say.
Jimi Hendrix

With love and thanks to my other favourite guitarist, Dad.

on track ...

Jimi Hendrix

Contents

Introduction

Curiously, for an act who omitted the question mark from the title of their ground-shaking debut *Are You Experienced*, The Jimi Hendrix Experience were a band of powerful punctuation – guitar work that declared, interrogated and exclaimed; drumming that bracketed and divided like commas, and bass lines which pounded out intriguing ellipses. And that's what *really* testifies on each listen. The threadbare cliché that Jimi Hendrix made his guitar *speak*, really misses the point: Hendrix himself speaks, coaxes, boasts and teases in an unmistakeable baritone, but the guitar gives it meaning. Think of the question-exclamation riff that announces 'Purple Haze'; the asterisk-ampersand frustration and ecstasy of 'Foxy Lady's' explosive solo; the big interrobang of 'Can You See Me?'

In 1966 – the year Hendrix began recording in London – the French author Hervé Bazin created six new types of punctuation, consisting of marks for love, acclamation, doubt, irony, authority and conviction. Hendrix was doing the same for the guitar, developing bends, trills and vibrato that would give new intention to song. Progressing beyond the biff-bang-pow of garage and the po-faced purity of blues echoists, Hendrix's music has flares of pop art's punctuation, knowingness and an appreciation for the ready-made; even a measured banality and, similarly, he drew on American and British influences, eschewing elitism. In the extraterrestrial '3rd Stone From The Sun', the very terrestrial cobbled stones of the *Coronation Street* theme are resounded; numerous songs include Hendrix clearing his throat; Rover the dog is name-checked; Superman becomes a motif of ironic masculinity. For someone feted to be extraordinary, the ordinary often peeps through. Yet, at the same time, the notes that splash, splurge and splatter from his Fender Stratocaster evoke abstract expressionist canvases, with 'strange, beautiful' patterns in the crafted chaos.

If his guitar did speak, it wasn't in any existing language, but was formed of borrowings, coinages and intonations of remarkable force. The Creation's guitarist Eddie Phillips (The Creation gave 'Hey Joe' a try in 1966 too) declared their own music to be 'red with purple flashes', but Hendrix's sound is purple, with gold, rose, misty blue and lilac radiation.

At the risk of sounding trite and nostalgic, much of the music of the 21st century seems to be looking neither back nor forwards and is strangely neutered. Little seems to acclaim; to doubt, to love. And who is creating a new musical language? Hendrix's guitar sound remains synesthetic, leaving a shadow of texture and colour and flavour. In 'Love Or Confusion', Hendrix asks: 'Must there be all these colours/Without names, without sound?' He gave them sound. The sound gave them meaning. And he did it with only a handful of albums.

Jimi Hendrix

It seems like a sort of nominative destiny – four years after Hendrix's birth (27 November 1942 in Seattle, Washington), his father Al altered Hendrix's first names from Johnny Allen to James Marshall. James Marshall Hendrix: a man who would challenge the world through his Fender guitar and Marshall stack. After a somewhat nomadic childhood (Hendrix and his brother Leon lived with various relatives after their parents' divorce, whilst his father struggled to find work), Hendrix would undergo other name changes as he strived to build a musical career. Firstly, he was Private Hendrix when he spent a year in the 101st US Airborne Division in California. Reportedly obsessed with his guitar, Hendrix was a distracted and uncommitted paratrooper, and it's likely that his discharge over an ankle injury was highly convenient and probably apocryphal. It's rumoured that Hendrix faked mental illness and homosexuality to get himself thrown out, such was his antipathy towards being a soldier. Nevertheless, his time in the army did bestow two blessings – he experienced 26 parachute jumps: a feat that must've contributed to the vertiginous lyrics and soundscapes to come. He also met his future bassist Billy Cox, who would play with Hendrix in the army band The King Kasuals, contribute to Hendrix's first recording session in 1962, and later be part of the Band of Gypsys.

In 1964, after gigging around the Chitlin' Circuit (a problematic and divisive term taken from the dish of chitterlings – pig intestines – a meal frequently offered to black people in place of finer cuts; the term referred to venues that welcomed performers of colour at a time of racial segregation), Jimmy Hendricks backed the Isley Brothers, adding irrepressible guitar to their joyously unrestrained 'Testify (Parts 1 and 2)': 'So glad I got some soul, woo!'. The track also declared, 'I know James is a witness/Go ahead James and testify!' Despite this being a name-check for James Brown (Stevie Wonder – who later jammed with Hendrix – and Jackie Wilson are invited to testify too), it seems to predict the musical avowals to come from Hendrix himself. He can also be heard on the Isley Brothers' energetic 'Move Over And Let Me Dance', developing the polyphony he would later master, though his scribbly trills are lost behind the dogmatic brass. Another song that came in two parts like 'Testify' was Ray Sharpe's 'Help Me (Get the Feeling)' – Hendrix brought it a tight rhythmic riff, but was again overpowered by the horns. Unfortunately, the song's first part fades out just as the trim solo begins. 'Part 2' fades in on this and reveals it to be an almost shy performance. Nevertheless, the song has the vibe of Them's 'Gloria', which Hendrix would later cover with some outright rude and crude playing and singing!

Unsurprisingly, there then came a stint backing Little Richard (later, Reverend), under Hendricks' new moniker Maurice James. His snaking riffs can be heard on 'It Ain't Watcha Do (It's The Way How You Do It)', which has a shiver of 'Gypsy Eyes' from *Electric Ladyland*. The lines 'Well, if the shoes don't fit you/You better not force it' could apply to the combination of two of rock's most flamboyant figures sharing a stage. Little Richard was said to be annoyed – even threatened – by Hendrix's ostentatious dress and stagecraft. Notwithstanding, Hendrix backs him with unassuming guitar on the rueful

'I Don't Know What You Got, But It's Got Me', where Richard sing-speaks in a way that his guitarist would later adopt. 'Whole Lotta Shakin' Goin' On' is Hendrix's messiest recording, with lots of ideas, from bends to trills to runs, but none of them executed cleanly. Nevertheless, Little Richard said of him in a 1973 documentary: 'At times, he used to make my big toe shoot up in my boot… he didn't mind looking freaky.'

However, Little Richard did seem to mind this, and by the end of the year, Hendrix had moved on and was playing with Curtis Knight and the Squires, but not before a curious detour that found him providing backing to cuts by actress Jayne Mansfield – star of the rock 'n' roll vehicle *The Girl Can't Help It*, which also features an exuberant Little Richard. Mansfield's 'As The Clouds Drift By' cannot exactly be deemed a hidden gem, but in truth, is no worse than many frothy ballads of the time, and its dreamy minor-key fade-out is not a million miles from later floaty psych tracks. Its B-side – co-written by Hendrix's first manager Ed Chalpin – is daft and jazzy in faux beatnik style à la Miss X's 'My Name Is Christine': 'It makes my knees freeze/It makes my liver quiver!' The slick guitar licks and jumpy bass lines (both supposedly delivered by Hendrix) promise the more symbolist playing to come.

In *Jimi Hendrix and the Making of Are You Experienced*, Sean Egan writes: 'The various musical adventures in which he took place (before forming The Experience), comprise the most inauspicious preamble'. This is an overstatement. Like The Beatles and indeed Led Zeppelin, Hendrix had to serve as a novice, and his varied apprenticeship made his music all the more kaleidoscopic. It cannot be asserted that anything pre-Experience is its equal, but there are enough highlights to make seeking out these tracks worthwhile. It also challenges some of the hyperbolic discourse that sets Hendrix as a *sui generis* phenomenon. In truth, that doesn't elevate his brilliance, which he strove to achieve, but rather removes it from the man and his own experience. He was undoubtedly remarkable, but as has previously been stated, was also a man within as much as without his times. Furthermore, Hendrix was not only an innovator in terms of composition, but was an interpreter of genius. It is hard to deny that two cover versions ('All Along The Watchtower' and, yes, even 'The Star-Spangled Banner') rank amongst his most significant, powerful and famous accomplishments. Whilst nowhere near his greatest work, 'Hey Joe' is nevertheless an astonishing and encouraging interpretation. A man removed from his context would not have been as sensitive, knowing or responsive enough to put forth these recreations.

Where The Beatles' covers – and even those of The Rolling Stones – are frequently the least interesting cuts of their *oeuvre*, there is a compelling argument that Hendrix's reworkings are part of his quintessence, and certainly of his legacy. Would he have been as adept an interpreter without supporting other acts? And if we're looking for inauspicious beginnings, then his predictable first live set with The Experience seems even less remarkable: 'Land of 1000 Dances', 'Midnight Hour', 'Mercy, Mercy' and 'Hey Joe'. Yet these songs would inform his own writing and playing beyond the Experience and all the way into Band of Gypsys and beyond.

Returning to Hendrix's stint with the Squires, we have him lending restrained support to the pleasant instrumental 'Station Break': a menacing riff to the buzzy Dick Dale-esque 'Hornet's Nest' (where on this Hendrix co-write, his guitar and Nate Edmonds' organ, work particularly well together, giving a little promise of 'Voodoo Chile'), whilst 'Gloomy Monday''s fusion of pop, soul and rock showcases Hendrix on assured backing vocals too. But this work is still embryonic, and the newly named Jimmy James now formed his own band: The Blue Flames. But previously to this significant step forward, Hendrix also appeared on another important track: 'Mercy, Mercy' by Don Covay. Covay had worked with Little Richard and would go on to write for Aretha Franklin. Hendrix's guitar-playing is understated (as is his contribution on a less successful Covay track 'Can't Stay Away') but has a suitably pleasing tone that gives the song its character and would be partly revived for Hendrix's own 'Remember'. The song also opens with a rueful but ear-catching riff, and Hendrix would develop this for 'Hey Joe'. Furthermore, the song so impressed Stax guitarist Steve Cropper that he recorded a version with Booker T. & the M.G.'s, and asked Hendrix to show him how he'd played it. Don Covay and the Goodtimers' version of 'Mercy, Mercy' (sometimes known as 'Have Mercy') became an instant R&B standard, despite only reaching number 35 on the Billboard chart, and The Rolling Stones covered it on *Out Of Our Heads*. It was to be a bridging song for Hendrix; one he performed with the Squires, The Blue Flames and during Mitch Mitchell's audition for The Experience and at some of their early gigs.

The Blue Flames started out as a trio with bassist Randy Palmer and drummer Dan Casey, performing a blend of blues, pop and soul. Intriguingly, a second guitarist was added: future Spirit member Randy California, who impressed with his slide playing. Rumour has it that Hendrix would later feel upstaged by some of California's performances and, subsequently, California turned down Hendrix's invitation to join him in London. Yet other sources attribute it to California's parents considering him too young to go, which seems the likeliest story as he was only 15. Regardless, California learnt much about distortion from Hendrix, and would later cover 'Red House' and 'Look Over Yonder'. Hendrix nicknamed him California because of the other Randy in the band: Randy Palmer, who became Randy Texas. However, Randy's given name was the unfortunate Randy Wolf – sounds almost like the title of a Hendrix track! We can get a sense of how The Blue Flames were looking more towards Hendrix's future sound in this reminiscing by Bob Kulick: sometime guitarist for Kiss, Alice Cooper, Meat Loaf and Diana Ross. He told *Classic Rock*:

> In 1966, I was 16, and my band The Random Blues Band, played at the Café Wha? club in Greenwich Village. One day we were told this guy was coming down to audition, and the name of his band was Jimmy James and The Blue

> Flames. So we watched as this guy came in and started to set up his gear. He was asking about using two amp cabs together, and we all looked at each other like, 'What? How do you do that?' On stage, he had all these pedals, and I thought, 'This should be interesting.' He had a very interesting look. He looked like a star. The band started playing what sounded like a prototype of a 'Third Stone From The Sun' kind of song, and within one minute, you knew that the guy wiped the floor with everybody we'd ever seen play. By the end of his set, when he played solos with his teeth that nobody could play with their hands, we knew this guy was a sensation.

The Blue Flames' take on Bo Diddley's 'I'm A Man' displays Hendrix in a lower, growling register, but complete with ironic 'Look out babies' to announce its spiky solo. By then, they were a quintet with guitarist and harmonica player John Hammond swelling the ranks. It was this group that The Animals' bassist Chas Chandler watched perform 'Hey Joe' at New York's Café Wha? in the summer of 1966 after Linda Keith's persistent recommendations: astounded, Chandler subsequently offered to manage Hendrix. One of the first questions Hendrix asked Chandler was if he knew Eric Clapton. Indeed, Chandler felt his friendship with Clapton – and his promise that Hendrix would impress Clapton much more than the other way around – was what really convinced Hendrix to fly to England and accept Chandler's offer.

Lamentably, Hendrix had previously committed to a deal (in 1965) with Chalpin's PPX Enterprises for exclusive recording rights. But in the excitement of becoming Jimi Hendrix – and a month later, The Jimi Hendrix Experience – this was forgotten.

The Are You Experienced Singles

Legend has it that Hendrix settled on his final and most famous moniker on the plane flying to Britain. An airborne baptism does indeed seem fitting. The Experience tag has been attributed to Chas Chandler, or sometimes to Mike Jeffery: The Animals' manager who co-managed Hendrix with Chandler. Jeffery would be killed in a mid-air collision in 1973, but his troubling reputation has endured, with allegations of financial mismanagement, punishing work schedules, a bizarre kidnapping of Hendrix, and even involvement in his death. Whilst some of these claims are unsubstantiated, condemnation of Jeffery has been consistent from Hendrix's bandmates, friends and biographers over the years. Many of these biographers have also sometimes taken exception to what they consider to be sexist Hendrix lyrics, yet it's hard not to consider that the guitarist's yearning to be 'stone free' might often have had more to do with Jeffery's restraining deals that tethered Hendrix's career than outright misogyny.

Yet Hendrix was blessed by Chandler's support, and he was to step away from managing Hendrix to focus on producing him, meaning Chalpin was necessary. Chandler, too, has sometimes been described as tyrannical, and the dual roles of producer and manager usually do result in the artist feeling constrained (see also The Rolling Stones and Andrew Loog Oldham), but Chandler's discipline, tenacity and professionalism undoubtedly helped to realise the Experience's sound. Furthermore, he also coached Noel Redding in bass techniques and encouraged Hendrix to use his voice rhythmically and confidently. Another boon was the involvement of Kit Lambert and Chris Stamp, who set up Track Records to provide a label for Hendrix, and would allow him his greatest creative freedom so far.

When Hendrix arrived in England, he not only desired a sympathetic label, but he also needed a band. Curiously, Chandler first tried out Hendrix with organist Brian Auger, who introduced him to Marshall amps. This is a tantalising idea – as Hendrix might have gone on to develop his sounds with piano and organ augmentation – but surely, two lead players of such potency would neutralise each other. As this wasn't to be, Chandler and Hendrix then began to seek musicians to form a band with Hendrix, although at this stage, it still wasn't decided whether Hendrix would be the singer or frontman.

There were two likely candidates for drums: Mitch Mitchell and Aynsley Dunbar. Dunbar had played for The Mojos and would go on to work with John Mayall, Frank Zappa and David Bowie. The story goes that Dunbar lost on the toss of a coin.

Ealing's Mitch Mitchell had picked up his drumsticks after a career as a child actor and had worked in Jim Marshall's (he of the amplifier) music shop. Despite Mitchell's contribution being underplayed at times, he features in *Rolling Stone*'s top 10 drummers, with Queen's Roger Taylor commenting insightfully that Mitchell played 'riffs'. Notwithstanding, being barely 20 when he met Hendrix, Mitchell had played with numerous acts, including The

Pretty Things, The Riot Squad and The Who. His rock and pop experience was augmented with jazzier influences by backing Georgie Fame and then joining The Soul Messengers, who included a saxophonist. Playing with an instrument of such sustain proved effective rehearsal for complementing Hendrix's fluidity.

Completing the trio was Noel Redding, whose first instrument had been the Jew's harp, and his first song was the murder ballad 'Tom Dooley', which recounts a knife killing to parallel the *crime passionnel* of 'Hey Joe'. Redding then moved on to the violin, the mandolin and finally the guitar, though he would be nudged on to bass for the Experience. He gigged around with The Lonely Ones before enjoying a stint with The Loving Kind, releasing the non-charting 'Love The Things You Do'. As Redding was auditioning for The New Animals, Hendrix admired his use of blues techniques (and his impressive hair!) and offered him a place alongside Mitchell. Despite being dismissed at times as the luckiest backing band in rock, Mitchell and Redding were crucial additions, with Keith Shadwick explaining in the compelling *Jimi Hendrix: Musician* that Hendrix thought 'Mitchell was Elvin Jones… Redding was his Jimmy Garrison'. Garrison and Jones were jazz musicians who worked with John Coltrane, amongst others. Perhaps this overstates Redding's skills a little, but his playing is often suggestive rather than merely rhythmic, with something of Garrison's good taste; Elvin Jones' rich timbres certainly influenced Mitchell's sound and technique. Chandler put it more succinctly and pragmatically in the *The Making Of Are You Experienced* video: 'That's what delivered the money. Them three.'

Within a few weeks, The Experience had recorded their first single, 'Hey Joe'. Buoyed by performances on *Ready Steady Go!* and *Top of the Pops*, it peaked at number six in the charts. In between touring, Hendrix was working on his original compositions: 'Hey Joe''s self-penned follow-up 'Purple Haze' was released in the spring as the trio were working on their debut collection. *Are You Experienced* soared into the charts in the middle of May 1967, just as the Summer of Love was blooming. But the album was more than a change of season: it was an electric manifesto that galvanised fans and peers; its aftershocks are still being felt. All this from an album that took around ten days to record and cost approximately £1,500.

Yet some weren't ready to be experienced. The album was met with criticism of both the music (though revealingly not of Hendrix's playing) and lyrics. And even Hendrix himself was already frustrated by how he was being represented. The UK album cover caused him some misgivings too, and indeed the US version is superior. The UK visual shows Mitchell and Redding peering from Hendrix's cloak like Ignorance and Want in *A Christmas Carol*. Aside from being unintentionally comical, it does seem to sideline the musicians in a way that Hendrix himself never did: his hand-drawn sketches for the cover's design give space to all three. In contrast, the US cover by Karl Ferris uses a fisheye lens to imbue an otherworldly quality, with the trio looking as if they've been locked in a paperweight, and Hendrix was reputed to have been thrilled with

Ferris' results. The innovative infrared technique mirrors Hendrix's inventive use of colour in his lyrics, and in the way he described the sounds he wanted to achieve when talking to Chandler and South African engineer Eddie Kramer. Moreover, the image emphasises Hendrix's large, illustrious hands, foregrounding his expertise.

The UK and US versions of *Are You Experienced* not only have different covers, but different track listings. The UK version is going to be considered here, and the singles will be explored separately: tagging them on the end of the album weakens their power. 'Purple Haze' is a single in the 'Strawberry Fields Forever' mould in being a complete statement, and feels unfairly anticlimactic after the album tracks. After all, 'Purple Haze' is the Experience's fanfare.

'Hey Joe'/'Stone Free'

Personnel:
Jimi Hendrix: Guitar, vocals
Mitch Mitchell: Drums
Noel Redding: Bass
Recorded at De Lane Lea Studios, October–November 1966
Producer: Chas Chandler
Engineer: Dave Siddle
The Breakaways (Margaret Stredder, Gloria George, Barbara Moore): Backing vocals
Chart placings: UK: 6

'Hey Joe' (Billy Roberts)

The debut single of The Jimi Hendrix Experience is at once a curious and logical choice. Listening to cuts like 'I'm A Man' by Jimmy James and The Blue Flames (Hendrix's previous band) proves there's a sauntering assuredness that can also be found in 'Hey Joe'. Hendrix's half-spoken/half-sung vocal style must've made another blues standard seem like a natural choice to launch his next endeavour – especially in the UK, where the song had yet to garner the attention it had drawn in the US in various incarnations by different acts. Furthermore, Chas Chandler had hit the big time with The Animals' reworking of the folk song 'The House Of The Rising Sun', and had shown the pop potential of brooding regret. Yet, 'Hey Joe' is a cod-blues folk song by Billy Roberts (Hendrix described it in the *Are You Experienced* notes as 'a blues arrangement of a cowboy song') that takes the form of a duologue between a cuckolded would-be murderer who'll soon be on the run, and a supposed confidante, but the song just doesn't quite make it in any of its many recordings. Hendrix excises the opening verses, straight into enquiring where Joe is going 'with that gun in your hand', and shows the join between the frenetic version by The Leaves and the lamenting sound of Tim Rose. Hendrix keeps the admonishing backing vocals of Rose – a rare incidence of female vocals on a Hendrix track, here supplied by The Breakaways (an earlier Hendrix cut features an unknown group) who can be heard on recordings by Petula Clark and Dusty Springfield – whilst realising that the propulsive walking bass of The Leaves is its most gripping ingredient. But this is the problem – listening to 'Hey Joe' is the aural equivalent of a patchwork quilt: the joins are evident. Some of Hendrix's more committed live versions take this further by embroidering the song with licks borrowed from The Beatles: notably 'Day Tripper' and 'I Feel Fine'.

The first take – available on the excellent *The Jimi Hendrix Experience* box set – touchingly reveals Hendrix being surprised at his own voice and asking for the backing track to be augmented to drown him out! Sometimes Hendrix would sing in darkness or facing away from others, such was his self-consciousness regarding his singing voice. Not only does this take show his lack of confidence in the recording studio, but it displays the incongruous backing vocals and is testament to the transformative effects of Hendrix's guitar: this is threaded and weaved around a dated backing, but the track becomes three-dimensional. In short, without the virtuosity, it would be an almost tedious listen. An early live version in Paris is a misstep, showing Hendrix still working out the embellishments, and it's an uncertain performance, with Mitchell's drumming hesitant in its punctuation, and Hendrix not really inhabiting the swaggeringly defiant persona of Joe. Only Redding's bass line is constant and assured. But, returning to the first studio version, Hendrix must've been inspired by the *idea* of ethereal backing vocals, as he'd reuse this to thrilling and unnerving effect on 'Purple Haze', and then to add a warmth to 'The Burning Of The Midnight Lamp'.

Hendrix's true debut/manifesto is to be found on the B-side 'Stone Free'. Nevertheless, there's an almost sepia quality to the instrumentation and vocals of 'Hey Joe' that is thrown into relief by the technicolor of the following singles, and the pensive solo still impresses every time. Also, Hendrix would begin tentatively to establish part of his signature sound, with the use of the ascending chromatic scale creating an exciting suspense. Really, this is the sound of Hendrix 'looking through the bent-backed tulips' before redesigning the landscape with 'Purple Haze'.

The Experience performed 'Hey Joe' for the penultimate episode of *Ready, Steady, Go!* on 16 December 1966, alongside The Troggs, Keith Relf, Marc Bolan, and The Merseys. The close of *Ready, Steady, Go!* is often seen as symbolising the shift from pop to rock music, and indeed, Hendrix's performance caused waves. Tony Crane – singer and lead guitarist with The Merseys – told Andy Neill for *Ready, Steady, Go! The Weekend Starts Here: The Definitive Story of the Show That Changed Pop TV*:

> When we did *RSG*, we caught up with Noel (Redding had been on tour with The Merseys when he was in The Burnettes), who told us he was now playing bass with this new band. We said, 'But you're a lead guitarist – what are you

> doing playing bass?' He said, 'You haven't seen this guy play. If you were in his band, you'd be playing bass as well!' Noel introduced us to Jimi Hendrix, and he was the quietest guy you could ever meet. And then when he went on, playing his guitar with his teeth, our mouths were wide open!

Marc Bolan – whose comments are collected in the same publication – also found Hendrix's performance remarkable:

> Everyone else used to use backing tracks, but he was going to play live because they got him on the show the same day. I was in the control room with the producer, just sitting about, when they started 'Hey Joe', and this old lady really freaked out bad and said, 'Turn the backing track down!' Because it was really loud. All the machines were shaking. And they said, 'But there is no backing track!'

Future glam rocker Bolan was performing the weirdly brilliant 'Hippy Gumbo'. According to Carl Ewens' *Born to Boogie: The Songwriting of Marc Bolan*, Hendrix was impressed, and predicted that Bolan would make it big. Whilst Bolan was no novice when it came to self-mythologising, 'Hippy Gumbo''s narrative about meeting an enigmatic stranger – 'In the morning with the sun he pulled an automatic gun/He blew my soul, he blew my brain' – would probably have appealed to Hendrix. Bolan had also briefly been a member of John's Children, whose destructive stage act involved them flagellating each other with chains. And just like Hendrix did when supporting The Monkees, they would incur the fury of The Daughters of the American Revolution – not with their stage act, as Hendrix did, but by naming their debut album *Orgasm*.

Although Hendrix's theatrics would go on to define his legacy, it's clear here that what first astounded was his sound: and even on a track that was already becoming a bit of a cliché.

'Stone Free' (Jimi Hendrix)

The ersatz nature of 'Hey Joe' calls to mind the 'Stone Free' observation of those who 'try to keep me in a plastic cage'. This B-side builds on the 'I'm A Man' proclamation 'I'm a rolling stone!' to assert Hendrix's love of liberty. The chugging rhythm motors through and his vocal has a compelling impatience that combines to give the free stone a rollicking – rather than rolling – action. There's also powerful use of one of Hendrix's musical fingerprints – the expectant augmented-9th chord – and the relentless tolling of the cowbell looks ahead to the defiant piano of 'Are You Experienced': a metronome to keep the speaker on the run. Redding employing *obstinati* adds to a sense of paradox – dynamism and stasis: a texture that would recur in many of Hendrix's recordings. But the track looks back as well as forward – the intro riff is a slower boogie, and if we sped this up, there would be the essence of Little Richard: Hendrix nodding at his legacy so far. Chandler claimed the song was recorded in little more than an hour, and there's a palpable urgency in its mix. The producer was later to be frustrated by how long Hendrix would deliberate over his recordings, and it's hard to deny that the painstaking workmanship paid off, but this recording is evidence of immediacy being just as powerful.

Most Hendrix writers feel duty-bound to bemoan the casual sexism of the lyrics, and then to extend this observation to Zeppelin, The Stones and the whole hypocrisy at the heart of the so-called *swinging* sixties. It's certainly an observation that needs to be made, and a debate that must be developed. But whilst rock, blues, pop etc. are not exactly crucibles of gender equality (and let's not forget that men are derided as little red roosters, hound dogs, or *celebrated* for their big ideas and little behinds too), often the constraints of relationships are a protean – if unoriginal – metaphor for social constraints in general in pop music, and for eschewing a society that ties us to parents, teachers, presidents and employers, possibly even more than to partners. Hendrix himself was certainly oppressed by the political system he was born into, but also seems to have been inhibited more by paternal control, the force of the military or the rules of his bandleaders than by his relationships with women at this point in his life. Romantic relationships appeared to mature into metaphors for segregation later in Hendrix's work too. In fact, he was to live for only two more years after the Supreme Court declared segregation to be unconstitutional. In this context, it's more difficult to view 'Stone Free' as simply a complaint about 'woman here, woman there'. Politically speaking, the implications of being black and itinerant go much deeper, as black people were more likely to be arrested for vagrancy. Being stone free is a radical act in this context.

More personally, Al Hendrix said he was imprisoned in an army stockade the night Hendrix was born, as the officers feared that a new father would go AWOL to visit the child: Hendrix junior seemed to be in the shadow of that stockade for much of his life. In some ways, the words simply propel the music all the way to racing fade-out, a sound that would be echoed by Pink Floyd's *The Dark Side Of The Moon* and Giorgio Moroder's disco recordings. There is a good argument for Hendrix's lyrics being almost dispensable on a number of tracks, or at least seen more as a selection of complementary sounds. After all, how could the words consistently compete with the playing? The free vowels of 'stone free – ee!' echo the scream of the guitar rather than the other way around. That is, the words reply to the sounds, not vice versa, which moves on from the call-and-response playing of the early blues. Hendrix later lamented to his PR man Keith Altham: 'The words are so bland that nobody can get into them.' Whilst this isn't always the case, the lyrics are mostly subservient to the sound.

A more valid objection than one based on the politics of relationships is that Hendrix would recycle this metaphor and produce paler and paler versions of it throughout his career, starting with the 'Purple Haze' UK B-side '51st Anniversary'. Indeed, Hendrix was thinking of releasing 'Stone Free' as a single in its own right in 1969, almost as a reset action. The track was re-recorded in New York with The Experience and Family's Roger Chapman, with Amen Corner's Andy Fairweather Low providing fervent backing vocals. The take is poised; swaggers more than sprints but, unsurprisingly, lacks the spontaneity of the original. The re-recording is available on the *The Jimi Hendrix Experience* box set and the *Valleys Of Neptune* compilation. (See entry under *Valleys Of Neptune* also.)

'Purple Haze' (Jimi Hendrix)

Personnel:
Jimi Hendrix: Guitar, vocals
Mitch Mitchell: Drums
Noel Redding: Bass, backing vocals
Recorded at De Lane Lea Studios and Olympic Studios, January–February 1967
Producer: Chas Chandler
Engineers: Dave Siddle, Eddie Kramer
Chart placings: UK: 3, US: 65

Whether 'Purple Haze' is a paean to epiphany or a keening on bewilderment lyrically, musically it's indubitably eye-and-ear-opening. And here's the Hendrix chord: E7#9. The Beatles and Cream had already utilised variations on this chord in rock, whilst jazz musicians John Coltrane and Wes Montgomery had included it in their work. However, its quirkiness vanishes under Hendrix's rule, becoming at once subversive, exciting and disquieting: it's a feral blast. Moreover, it's married to the tritones that announce the song, and these were known as 'the Devil in music', resulting in the church banning the interval's threat of dissonance in the Middle Ages. The intro implies a conversation already begun, and challenging and uneasy conversations yet to come: an uncanny sound to fill the airwaves of the Summer of Love. Yet, for Hendrix, the unresolved and homeless nature of the tritone is the perfect metaphor for his peripatetic spirit. Miles Davis' version of the Richard E. Carpenter composition 'Walkin'' (supposed: the track's pedigree is as complex as 'Hey Joe's!) employs tritones in the intro to arresting effect too, and Hendrix is thought to have admired the piece. Keith Shadwick also notes that the Hendrix chord can be heard in Henry Mancini's 'Peter Gunn' theme, which similarly makes evocative use of *obstinati*. This was one of the earliest pieces that Hendrix learnt to play, and he would often segue into it when a take of one of his own compositions faltered. Indeed, 'Purple Haze' is said to have been written after Chandler overheard Hendrix experimenting with a riff in the dressing room of the Upper Cut, and urged him to form it into a song. However, its lyrical inspiration is quite different – Hendrix is said to have been influenced by dreaming of being under water: a trope that would recur in '1983… (A Merman I Should Turn to Be)'. (Hendrix also said he'd been inspired by a dream to write another song at about the same time: the mysterious 'First Look Around The Corner'.) The sensation of everything slowing as one pushes against the current is evident in his cover of Bob Dylan's 'All Along The Watchtower' too, and didn't just inform his lyrics but his musical lexicon. Hendrix began to work out a template whereby the chord sequences might be quite simple, but the augmentation of these would be innovative and elaborate.

On 'Purple Haze', he's fretting the chords differently so that unusual voicings or patterns can be played around them, heightening the track's uncanny feel. (Hendrix essentially begins the song in a medieval style before launching into psychedelic blues rock, mirroring his updating of the blues itself. But for Hendrix, updating meant trailing the roots behind him.)

This feeling of disorientation is further enhanced by Hendrix's pioneering use of the Octavia effect pedal, designed by electrical engineer Roger Mayer whom Hendrix first met at London's Bag O' Nails club, and who would eventually accompany him on tour. More accurately speaking, it wasn't quite the Octavia that Hendrix would use later, but an earlier version known as Evo1 that worked along similar lines. Hendrix explained the device to *Music Maker*: 'It comes through a whole octave higher so that high notes sound like a whistle or flute.' This is a redolent description but is also revealing of how Hendrix often strove to recreate sustained sounds like brass or woodwind instruments, with him frequently being compared to saxophonist John Coltrane in his vision and invention. This disconcerting sound is apparent in Hendrix's original lyric where he positions himself 'Down on the ceiling looking up at the bed': an Escher queasiness that the Octavia continued in its almost 3D sound. Interestingly, the lyric evolved from an initial exploring of obscurity (the original first line being 'Purple Haze, Jesus saves') to one of emerging revelation and wonder. This aura of awe is enhanced in the solo, where the notes spark and spiral off from the melody as if from a Catherine wheel, and the backing vocals go into slow motion, reminding us of that underwater drag. Hendrix had been experimenting with different effects whilst still a backing musician, and is said to have been intrigued by Elmore James' innovations with electric pickups on acoustic guitars, and 'Purple Haze' was finally the perfect vehicle.

Whilst pulp sci-fi also helped Hendrix imagine a landscape of purple haze, there is the influence of shock-rock original Screamin' Jay Hawkins too in 'That girl put a spell on me'. Hawkins' track 'I Put A Spell On You' was truncated for radio airplay as its grunting fade-out caused offence, which is referenced slightly in Hendrix's coughs and grunts on 'Purple Haze'. As Hawkins would rise from his coffin on stage, we can see a thread of the rock spectacular leading us to Hendrix's immolation of his guitar and even the shredding of 'The Star-Spangled Banner'. Whilst much of the commentary about 'Purple Haze' has understandably focused on the musicianship, less has been said about the vocal, which does evoke the testifying style of Hawkins. Hendrix was not only fortunate in his pairing with Chandler, but in finding an engineer as sympathetic and responsive as Eddie Kramer. As is evident in the *The Making of Are You Experienced* video, Kramer is still thrilled by Hendrix's sound, and demonstrated that reverb augmented the vocal. The reverb thickened the sound, but also meant that the vocals could be further back in the mix – Hendrix was always requesting that his voice be turned down, but here it's perfect for implying the haze taking over. When Kramer isolates the vocal in the documentary, the power and clarity are astonishing and shows Hendrix's conviction in his singing abilities leaping ahead from 'Hey Joe'. The vocals on the fade-out – Mitchell's higher lines and Hendrix's deeper drawl – pan from right to left, creating a wooziness until the flickering solo at the close: a high octave, flashing through the fog.

Kramer also had the ingenious idea to double the speed of Hendrix's guitar at certain points in the song, so that the ear never takes for granted what it's hearing on the track. 'Hey Joe' had been recorded at De Lane Lea studios with Dave Siddle engineering, and work on 'Purple Haze' had begun there. Yet, Chandler felt that studio wasn't the right home for The Experience and they moved to Olympic, which had just relocated to a newly designed building in Barnes. Chandler explained: 'A great asset was that it seemed you could play louder than other studios.' Blessedly, it also meant they were introduced to Kramer, who'd studied classical piano as well as violin and cello in Cape Town.

However, the recording was not an entirely harmonious experience, with tempers erupting after Chandler asked Hendrix to turn his guitar down as he was using his twin Marshall stack to its full might. This had often been a source of contention when Hendrix was a backing player in his pre-Experience days. When he remarked that there was no point in recording if he couldn't do it his way, Chandler offered Hendrix his passport and told him to 'piss off'. Thankfully, Hendrix didn't.

But the song does seem to link to Hendrix's status as being new to London. Surprisingly, the song title occurs in Dickens' *Great Expectations*, describing Pip in a boat on the river:

> There was the red sun, on the low level of the shore, in a purple haze, fast deepening into black; and there was the solitary flat marsh; and far away there were the rising grounds, between which and us there seemed to be no life, save here and there in the foreground a melancholy gull.

This is a painterly description with touches of Hendrix's signature colour imagery and an echo of his later line 'There ain't no life nowhere…' ('I Don't Live Today'). Whilst this might seem a negligible connection, in *Jimi Hendrix: The Man, The Magic, The Truth*, Sharon Lawrence reveals that Hendrix owned a second-hand copy of *David Copperfield* and was reading it on the flight over to the UK. The phrase 'purple haze' might more readily conjure a sci-fi landscape, but it could apply to a legal alien: the nomadic far-from-home musician. Author Philip Norman notes that Philip José Farmer's 1957 novel *Night of Light* was a likely source, which recounts an event every seven years where the inhabitants of a distant planet experience a transformative and brilliant light: a radiance so intense that many can't bear it (an apposite metaphor for stardom also!). The light leads to redemption for some, destruction for others. Although Hendrix never mentioned the novel directly, this metaphorical use of light and epiphany does seem to be continued in the 'Purple Haze' lyric and musical textures.

More surprisingly, the phrase is sung by Elvis for romantic effect too – 'Of holding hands and red bouquets/And twilight trimmed in purple haze' – in his tender 1968 ballad 'Memories'. An ill-advised take on 'Purple Haze' called 'Hooray For The Salvation Army Band' by Bill Cosby with Hendrix on the backing track includes the (in hindsight) worrying line: 'Got some chicks on the run'. The Travelling Wilburys reference it in their philosophical 'End Of The Line' – 'Maybe somewhere down the road a ways/You'll think of me and wonder where I am these days/Maybe somewhere down the road when somebody plays 'Purple Haze'', which eventually found its way into a complicated gag in the finale of British sitcom *One Foot in the Grave*. But for the most sobering reminder of how the counterculture is inevitably pulled into the mainstream current, listen to June Whitfield chirruping 'Purple Haze' in the 'France' episode of *Absolutely Fabulous*.

Figures from the past were also intrigued – American singer-songwriter Dion recorded a laid-back acoustic version of 'Purple Haze' for his 1968 comeback album. The Cure's 1993 interpretation turns it into a hung-over anthem, whilst The Kronos Quartet clarify it into what could be the score for a film by French director Henri-Georges Clouzot. And for further confirmation of Hendrix's reach into the classical world, Nigel Kennedy's fascinating *The Kennedy Experience* album takes several Hendrix songs – including 'Purple Haze' – as inspiration. Kennedy is backed by an eight-piece orchestra, and his interpretation has shades of jazz violinist Stephane Grappelli, and Hendrix's hero, jazz guitarist Django Reinhardt. Moreover, on his live 'Purple Haze', Kennedy includes a hint of Sinatra's 'Strangers In The Night': something Hendrix had added to his own concert renditions. In an interview with Mark Coles for the Radio 4 Today programme, Kennedy asserted: 'I think he (Hendrix) was possibly more akin to Franz Liszt or Chopin. He was more like one of those figures – a great composer and player of his instrument who made music in a totally new genre.' 'Purple Haze' was the start of it.

Though there is an argument that there are parallels between Hendrix's work and 20th-century Austrian composer Arnold Schoenberg. Schoenberg believed in the importance of traditional music but combined this with radical ideas, just as Hendrix did with the blues. Schoenberg realised that innovation was – almost paradoxically – the way to maintain traditions and prevent them from degenerating to the level of the platitudinous. As blues purists were preserving the sound, Hendrix was regenerating and reforming its language – we might call this track an example of his 'purples'; a blending of the psychedelic and the blues. Schoenberg's experiments with developing variation can also apply to Hendrix's later and longer works.

'51st Anniversary' (Jimi Hendrix)

This is the kind of solid, swaggering song that Hendrix would rewrite countless times, again on the theme of being put 'on a chain'. In Harry Shapiro's tellingly titled biography *Electric Gypsy*, he reveals that Hendrix often signed autographs with the motto 'Stay free'. It's as if he's signing off his singles and later his albums similarly, but there is something already repetitive and a little predictable about it. In the song's first half, he presents a celebratory view of marriage. But the second is spent changing the mind of his lover, who's keen to wed, by describing a marriage with a wife who is a 'louse', and a husband 'down at the whiskey house'. Some commentators have taken exception to Hendrix's patronising tone as he tells his wannabe spouse, 'You must be losing your sweet little mind.' Casual sexism is undoubtedly a feature of many pop lyrics, but there could be more to this. Hendrix's advice here seems heartfelt and mutual:

> So now you're seventeen
> Running around hanging out, and a-havin' your fun
> Life for you has just begun, baby

Hendrix's mother Lucille had been 17 when she gave birth to him, and would eventually have six children, but died aged only 32 of complications brought about by alcoholism. In this context, the song is more of a cautionary tale than simply about a braggadocio longing to shirk responsibility. Revealingly, when Hendrix was feeling constrained by The Experience towards the end of their tenure in the summer of 1969, he explained to *Beat Instrumental*: 'It's like being married with me, Mitch and Noel. Real happily married when we get our thing going without a single hang-up.' The song reflects the unity, but also the indifference that can come from being in any close relationship. In the end, The Experience had too many hang-ups to continue together.

Returning to '51st Anniversary', the changes in rhythm hold the attention from the marching opening to the on-the-run thrum of the verses. But just as the anniversaries 'roll around', this imagery would become monotonous with Hendrix's plea to 'Let me get back in my groove' unfortunately reinforcing that lack of freedom would become something of a thematic rut; yet there looks like a sly humour is at work as the outro lick repeats like a stuck record needle, and the discordant guitar phrases change as the lyric's cynicism deepens. It's a piece showing a remarkable amount of attention to detail, despite the lyrical repetitions, especially for a B-side.

'The Wind Cries Mary' (Jimi Hendrix)

Using colour imagery as a metaphor continues on the US 'Purple Haze' flipside, with the wry detail 'The traffic lights turn blue tomorrow' signalling the ending of a relationship, whilst the ascending chords of the opening mimic 'happiness staggering on down the street' and away from the speaker. In many ways, this is the perfect B-side for 'Purple Haze' as it displays a rounder persona: both the vaunting peacock and the tender-hearted balladeer. This was an older song than its US A-side – perhaps reflected in the insecurity of the lyrics – and had been performed by Hendrix's earlier band The Blue Flames.

'A broom is drearily sweeping up the broken pieces of yesterday's life' is one of the song's more neglected images, but may have an unexpected origin. Hendrix's younger brother Leon told the *Guardian*'s Ed Vulliamy in 2016:

> I was there when Jimi was a boy, and he'd play with a broom, his first guitar. And Pa would come home and see the straw and shit from the broom on the floor, because Jimi'd been doing acrobatics with his broom-guitar, and Jimi'd get a whuppin'.

Furthermore, in the blues, the broom is often a symbol for moving on, as in Robert Johnson's 'I Believe I'll Dust My Broom'. In the same breath, Leon talks of Hendrix's inspiration being 'in the wind'. It's curious that he should've placed these images together. As has been said, Hendrix desires to escape frequently in his songs, but it seems much more complex than simply slipping the leash from suffocating romances. Al Hendrix was a strongly disciplinarian father – Jimi's siblings were in care and he was offered two forms of institutionalisation (prison or the army) after he was caught riding in a stolen car. His girlfriend Kathy Etchingham lived with him at 34 Montagu Square – a property owned by Ringo Starr, who, as landlord, often had to field complaints about noise from the neighbours. In her book *Through Gypsy Eyes*, she related that the track came from a spat over her cooking:

> Having rows never worried either of us much; I guess we had both listened to enough of them throughout our childhoods not to take them too seriously. When I returned, the next day, having cooled down, I asked him what he had done while I was away. 'I wrote a song,' he said, and handed me a piece of paper with 'The Wind Cries Mary' on it. Mary is my middle name, and the one he would use when he wanted to annoy me.I didn't feel the least bit appeased.

It's not surprising if Hendrix had included a name designed to irk her. But 'Mary' also connotes motherhood, linking this lament to Lucille as well. Furthermore, Hendrix had a younger sister – Kathy – who had been born blind, and he might have felt the name was inappropriate.

Some reports have suggested that the tune already existed in skeletal form, but domestic discord could've reminded Hendrix of other stern talks around the dinner table, and perhaps he was more bothered by these disputes than he seemed. Whilst the themes might've been percolating for years, Kramer and Chandler said the song took barely 20 minutes to record.

It's a striking track, and here, the meditative soloing style of 'Hey Joe' finds the right setting: almost as if the guitar is shaking its head, or at least its neck! There are five guitar overdubs, as Hendrix kept being inspired to add lines, as though other gusts kept blowing. One guitar is a bluster of rhythm, and other lines breeze in and out. Hendrix also played some rhythm guitar as he recorded his vocal, because he found it difficult to sing without the assurance of the instrument in his arms. But the vocal is secure and effectively understated, with a hint of mourning. The wind progresses from whispering to crying to screaming in the lyric, and the guitar lines keep up with this intensity. Hendrix's sci-fi knowledge means he might've been influenced by the Ray Bradbury story 'The Wind', which postulates that the eponymous force is made up of the voices of its victims. Interestingly, the story's mother collection *The October Country* also includes the story 'Jack-in-the-Box' ('After all the Jacks are in their boxes') – a tale about a sequestered child – and marks the emergence of nursery symbolism that inflects other tracks in Hendrix's canon. Alternatively, Etchingham recollected that the clown image came from the BBC test card. Whatever, the 1960s gave birth to a number of 'dollhouse songs' – creepy in unspecified ways, with a stilted, dusty feeling as in Pink Floyd's 'Matilda Mother', The Beatles' 'Cry Baby Cry', and Family's 1968 debut album *Music In A Doll's House* which closes with an anticlimactic blast of 'God Save The Queen'.

A more unusual source of inspiration for the song comes from art historian Stephen Eisenman, who detects a similarity between 'The Wind Cries Mary' and William Blake's poem 'Mary' which closes with the following stanza:

And thine is a Face of sweet Love in Despair
And thine is a Face of mild sorrow & care
And thine is a Face of wild terror & fear
That shall never be quiet till laid on its bier

The poem reflects on how the feminist Mary Wollstonecraft was not of her time and was suspected and rejected by the society in which she lived. It also uses the motif of the whore/virgin dichotomy, and its angel imagery and lyrical description of how Mary moves, may well have influenced 'Little Wing', 'One Rainy Wish' and of course, 'Angel'.

Eisenman explores Blake's influence on Bob Dylan too. Dylan later said he complimented Hendrix specifically on 'The Wind Cries Mary', telling him it was his favourite along with the opposing 'Dolly Dagger'. The former track certainly has a flavour of Dylan's symbolist lyrics too. Moreover, these tracks seem to be mirror images: the innocent and the experienced.

'The Wind Cries Mary' has been a popular track for covering, with versions by Seal, Sting and… Pat Boone. The best tribute is Miles Davis' 'Mademoiselle Mabry' from 1968, which builds a similarly pensive and rueful piece around Hendrix's opening riff.

'Highway Chile' (Jimi Hendrix) (B-side of 'The Wind Cries Mary')

Hendrix's clarion riff triggers the track, like starting a race: a feeling often evoked by his on-the-road songs. And this sibling of 'Stone Free' sprints along, with Hendrix describing the title character in the couplet 'I know you'd call him a tramp/But it goes a little deeper than that' – essentially summing up the itinerant desires still to be explored on the subsequent album, but also reflecting Hendrix's life on the road so far. Richard Wright notes in the foreword to Paul Oliver's *Blues Fell This Morning*, 'Though constant reference (in the blues) is made to loved ones, little or no mention is made of the family as such.' Hendrix is continuing this tradition, eschewing a sense of belonging. Yet Wright also commented that this can be linked back to the difficulties of family life under slavery, thereby elevating this desire to keep on moving, from simply being about irresponsibility, towards a whole group of people being denied roots; of their family being seen as a piece of machinery. Not conforming to family values, then, is a much more complex and rebellious act.

The most noteworthy point of the cut is Hendrix declaring, 'He's a – ,' and his guitar squawking out the answer in the opening riff before Hendrix echoes 'Highway Chile!' Here, we have the guitar as the main voice again, with Hendrix's vocals a translation, not the other way around. We're also being introduced to the pattern of Hendrix enquiring before giving us the answer in shredded notes and howled chords. Dylan's 'Like A Rolling Stone', with its rhetorical chorus line 'How does it feel?', was much admired by Hendrix, and its central questioning became a recurrent device.

Redding's bouncy bass harmony must be mentioned too, as it thrums beneath like a motorbike engine, counteracting some of the more hissing drum rhythm patterns that don't fit the determination of Hendrix and Redding's playing.

Are You Experienced (1967)

Will it burn me if I touch the sun...

Recorded at De Lane Lea Studios; CBS; Olympic
Producer: Chas Chandler
Engineer: Dave Siddle
Jimi Hendrix: Guitar, vocals
Mitch Mitchell: Drums
Noel Redding: Bass
Chart placings: UK: 2, US: 5
UK Order. Side A: Foxy Lady, Manic Depression, Red House, Can You See Me, Love or Confusion, I Don't Live Today
Side B: May This Be Love, Fire, 3rd Stone from the Sun, Remember, Are You Experienced
US Order. Side A: Purple Haze, Manic Depression, Hey Joe, Love or Confusion, May This Be Love, I Don't Live Today
Side B: The Wind Cries Mary, Fire, Third Stone from the Sun (US Spelling), Foxey Lady (US Spelling), Are You Experienced?

'Foxy Lady' (Jimi Hendrix)

Aside from its famously lascivious riff, Hendrix's throat-clearing and lip-smacking define the song and continue the kind of *vocal vérité* that is threaded throughout his work, and which particularly befits a song declaring unbridled desire. Beginning with a tremor of warning guitar (a trick Mick Ronson nicked for David Bowie's 'Width Of A Circle'), the song stalks like a panther with its paralleling of the Hendrix chord: the sound of innocence bending to experience. It's the perfect motif to bridge the album to Hendrix's true debut single ('Purple Haze') and to hint at the exploration of experience to come.

The vibrato that opens 'Foxy Lady' and is echoed towards the coda lends it a trembling excitement, further developed by the fuzz box giving each note a dangerous electrical halo. Hendrix had been experimenting with the fuzz box since his Café Wha? days when The Fugs' guitarist Pete Kearney gifted him one. Certainly, this track seems its natural home, much more than on R&B covers. Hendrix's lead and rhythm-playing form a skilful hybrid, especially with that variation of the Hendrix chord, and they exhibit his mastery of this combined playing style or polyphony.

'Foxy Lady', 'Love Or Confusion', 'Can You See Me' and 'Third Stone From The Sun' were worked on at CBS Studios and also at Olympic. In Mick McStarkey's article for *Far Out* – 'Behind the Album: Jimi Hendrix's Debut Masterclass, 'Are You Experienced?' – CBS engineer Mike Ross explained that Hendrix asked for the microphone to be positioned 'about 12 feet' from him, which contributed to his signature sound as though he's decrying from a mountain top or, as in the case of this track, like a distant siren enticing the foxy lady. The whispered backing vocals add to a sense of the illicit, and could be mistaken for the sighing of something that sounds more like 'fuck's sake' than foxy. The earlier version on *The Jimi Hendrix Experience* box set reveals that these vocals were originally clearer, though still breathy, so Hendrix definitely opted for the more ambiguous tone. Furthermore, the run down the guitar neck at the close is similarly ambiguous: either a sigh of exhaustion or thwarted lust in the manner of Eddie Cochran's 'Twenty Flight Rock'.

There's no denying the track's voluptuous carnality, but this doesn't have to mean it's sexist. Rock writer Charles Shaar Murray has Hendrix perceiving the foxy lady as a 'strutting bimbo'. For all we know, it could be Foxy Lady PhD. Whilst great love songs are celebrated, great lust songs can be perceived as divisive, but there's an undeniable corporeal glory here. Furthermore, Hendrix said of this track to *Record Mirror*: 'I can't write happy songs. ('Foxy Lady') is the only happy song I've written.' Heather Taylor – model and now wife of Roger Daltrey – is often cited as the foxy lady of the song. But Lithofayne Pridgon – also known as Apollo Faye – an early girlfriend of Hendrix's, is another likely muse. She claimed he told her the song was for her, and Hendrix also recorded a private blues for her, which she played to *Guardian* journalist Chris Campion in 2015. Pridgon – best friend of American singer Etta James, and a songwriter herself – wrote in the notes for James' *Blues To The Bone* album, a tribute to James, saying they were 'liberated, modern-day, black females'. Certainly not a strutting bimbo. In the interview for the *Guardian*, Pridgon identifies Hendrix as her 'type', and her type was 'skinny, raw-boned, over-fucked, underfed-looking guys'. In the same interview, love letters from an infatuated Hendrix are described as reflecting the romanticism of his lyrics with one revealing quotation: 'As I write more and more, I feel myself grow so very weak under the power of you.' Pridgon didn't want to be only Hendrix's girlfriend, and continued her other relationships and friendships with men. Hypocritically, Hendrix did indeed try to uphold his own freedom whilst being jealous of Pridgon's, but that doesn't mean that the subject of his song is automatically weak-willed. Ultimately, it sounds as if the 'Foxy Lady' isn't 'all mine'. There could also be a sly pun at work here, with Hendrix the hen in danger of the predatory fox. And anyway, Pridgon emerges in the *Guardian* interview as strong, articulate and funny as hell. In fact, as desirable as 'Foxy Lady' celebrates.

Hendrix's live versions – particularly at Miami Pop in 1968 – illustrate the importance of the backing vocals, as there's something a little hollow about it without them. The slight lag between the beats of the riff heighten the anticipation on the record, whereas live, it's rushed and the hint of hesitancy and expectation is sadly lost. Long solos also undercut the premature climax of the song. Frankly, it's much more potent as an explosive quickie. Yet the version from *Saturday Club* on *The Jimi Hendrix Experience BBC Sessions* is superb.

It's little wonder then that Paul McCartney – the man who encouraged Hendrix's booking at the Monterey Pop Festival – has taken to seguing into

'Foxy Lady' at the end of his 'Let Me Roll It': two songs with angst-ridden riffs that bemoan amorous frustration.

'Manic Depression' (Jimi Hendrix)

This track is a thrilling band performance, illustrating that Redding and, in particular, Mitchell, were not making up the numbers. Hendrix summarised the trio for *Open City*: 'One of us is in a rock bag (Redding), another is jazz (Mitchell), while I'm on the blues.' This is somewhat of a simplification but does explicate their unique blend, especially at a time when blues and jazz purists were keen not to dilute their identity. From the declamatory opening chords onwards, the drumming provides a perfect demonstration of the lyrics, bolstered by its insinuating gallop that cannot progress, pounding on the spot. Although Hendrix's playing is compelling – especially when his guitar mimics his vocal line, and the vertiginously bent notes introduce the solo – the relentless misery of the rhythmic punctuation is its most undeniable element, right down to the cymbal that gasps in relief at the song's close. Seal and Jeff Beck's otherwise fine cover is let down by some timorous drumming that doesn't even try to compete with the original.

In 2012, Mitch Mitchell explained to *Drum* magazine that he was inspired by Ronnie Stephenson's drumming on Johnny Dankworth's version of 'African Waltz' (composed by Cannonball Adderley) in 1961. There is a similar sense of restlessness, and of beats 'hitting the ceiling', but Mitchell's sound is angrier, threatening to 'break love'. The jazz influence is even stronger live, especially on a version from an Italian show where Mitchell's drum solo – a much more relaxed shuffle – audibly delights the audience. However, the album version is where the real innovation is: a jazz-blues fusion that the trio could call their own sound.

The title was attributed to Hendrix's frustration at not being able to 'make love to music', as stated by 'Music, sweet music/I wish I could caress, and kiss, kiss…' The unusual waltz rhythm is no longer romantic or wistful, but is an ironic restriction recalling the queasy sway of The Beatles' similarly frustrated 'Baby's In Black' – albeit that was in 6/8 compared to 'Manic Depression''s 3/4, but the technique is much more successfully realised here, with the rotations indicating a grinding mourning and melancholy. It sounds like the inside of a melomaniac's head! A few months later at the Monterey Festival, Hendrix attached a poem to the back of his scorched guitar before launching it into the audience. The poem read:

> frustration wracked
> feelings – of not
> being able to
> make true physical
> love to the
> Universal Gypsy Queen
> True, free expressed music

What 'Manic Depression' stammers around, is made explicit here!

More soberly, Love's Arthur Lee recounted an incident to John Einarson for *Forever Changes: Arthur Lee and the Book of Love* that illustrates the instrument's value to Hendrix:

> He pointed to his guitar case on the floor. Then he opened it up. I thought he had a stash in there, but as he stood up, he pointed to it again and said, 'This is all I have.' I couldn't figure it out at first, but then it hit me. He was telling me that the white Stratocaster guitar and the case were his only possessions. I felt kind of sad for him. It's as if the guitar was a companion to him.

Hendrix's guitar was almost an extension of his nervous system but was also the one constant love of his life, and 'Manic Depression' broods on his perceived inability to serve it as well as he desired.

Hollywood Vampires – the supergroup comprised of Alice Cooper, Johnny Depp and Joe Perry – include a cover of 'Manic Depression' on their eponymous 2015 debut album, with Joe Walsh and Zak Starkey also appearing on the track. Whilst powerful, it's another reminder of the 'strange beautiful' chemistry of the Experience, as their sonic unease yet again has the edge.

'Red House' (Jimi Hendrix)

'Hey Joe's' cod folk-blues and tale of woe is surpassed here in an authentic Hendrix 12-bar original that competes with Willie Dixon or Albert King. Instead of the 'little red rooster' roaming, it's Hendrix who's gone walkabout and is now locked out of the red house after a bust-up with his baby. However, Hendrix doesn't despair for long, confessing that if his 'baby don't love' him anymore, her sister will, giving it a lyrical shimmer similar to the bathos of 'Drive My Car' and the revenge fantasy of 'Norwegian Wood'. Opening with a diminished-7th in the style of many blues songs – but notably and ironically Robert Johnson's 'Kind Hearted Woman Blues' – the initial four-bar intro implies a nonchalant stroll, before Hendrix is disabused of his partner's patience and loyalty. Then it's a fabulously eloquent but lachrymose solo, offset by the weary seen-it-before nodding of the bass. According to Redding's memoir *Are You Experienced? The Inside Story of The Jimi Hendrix Experience*, he didn't actually play a bass guitar on the track, but a tuned-down hollow-body electric guitar. Whilst he explained this had been down to his lack of experience with the bass, it lends an earthier sound. This is apparent too in Hendrix's habit of laughing in song, being continued with a cartoonish 'Ha! Ha!' All told, 'Red House' is an affecting blues of remarkable maturity and displays some of Hendrix's most disciplined playing. Unsurprisingly, the track was much admired by John Lee Hooker.

Charles Shaar Murray traced the song's inspiration to Albert King's 'Travelin' To California'. The melody and guitar trills are certainly similar, but there's a development here too, especially in Hendrix's slinking intro – like someone walking home at dawn, dragging their coat through the dirt behind them, which would again be implied both musically and lyrically in 'The Wind Cries Mary'. King's notes are short and unequivocal, but Hendrix's often groan with a shiver of pleasure at his desolation. King's lyric confesses, ''Cause I'm a travelin' man, I say I'm a travelin' man/I don't want to lose this groove, I got to move'. Hendrix develops the groove of freedom, finding abandonment thrilling. Yet Harry Shapiro suggests another origin of the red house symbol: in Hopi legend, rising through the storeys of the red house was the path to enlightenment. Why then is the speaker dispassionate about being denied admission? Perhaps this is a disavowal of a fixed sense of enlightenment or experience. More crudely, the red house could be a euphemism for the female anatomy (there is also lock-and-key imagery), similar to the equivalent little red rooster, and quite simply, other red houses are awaiting the wanderer.

Hendrix's own peripatetic lifestyle meant he lived at many addresses. When he stayed at Linda Keith's New York apartment in his Café Wha'? days, they would refer to it as the red house and play each other blues records. Hendrix might have seen this fertile environment as something of a womb: a place where some of his blues inspirations gestated. Furthermore, one of his first girlfriends – Betty Jean – lived in a house with her sister Maddy, which they also referred to as the red house. Hendrix painted his second guitar – a Danelectro – red and named it after Betty. Leon was dating Maddy, which may have further helped to inspire the song's romantic intrigue.

'Travelin' To California' is obviously a root source, but T-Bone Walker's (Walker also perfected playing his guitar behind his head) weary 'Call It Stormy Monday (But Tuesday Is Just As Bad)' might also have been in mind, as Hendrix remarked in Arnold Shaw's *Honkers and Shouters: The Golden Years of Rhythm and Blues*: 'When I first heard T-Bone's single-string solo on "Stormy Monday", it drove me crazy. I could never believe a sound could be that pretty on an instrument. T-Bone has a way of using 9th chords nobody's ever done yet.'

Hendrix uses the 9ths for an unusually arch tone in 'Red House', and created a resigned but wryly amused lyric in a similar fashion too. The horn blasts after Walker's 'Lord have mercy!' are echoed in the dampened, frustrated notes following Hendrix's 'key won't unlock this door': the aural equivalent of asterisks in place of curse words. Hendrix would often further emphasise this point in live versions too. In fact, it's one of the songs he performed most frequently and would often showcase some of his cleanest licks and most doleful singing. But at times, the live song becomes somnolent, with Redding's bass continually gearing up for a punchline that is indefinitely deferred. Yet the version from a live set in San Diego in 1969 is first class, showing Hendrix not only as a master of the blues, but experimenting with jazz tones and looking ahead to funk riffs, with Redding and Mitchell solid throughout.

Robert Wyatt of Soft Machine – who supported Hendrix on an American tour – commented about 'Red House' to Charles Shaar Murray: 'Night after night, after he had thrown everything at everybody, the high spot of the night would be 'Red House', where everybody would go quiet, he would go quiet, he would sing and play and he wouldn't even need a band.'

Whilst much of the critical attention for *Are You Experienced* focused on 'Purple Haze' and 'Foxy Lady', 'Red House' was in some ways the album's instant classic. Yet it was left off the US version as the record company alleged there was no audience for the blues. However, American issues often favoured collecting singles rather than new recordings on albums, and 'Can You See Me' and 'Remember' were also omitted.

But 'Red House' still became a firm fan favourite and was also much admired by other musicians. Buddy Guy's respectful cover is cool and controlled, but the more fuzzy tone seems out of place, giving the guitar an ineloquent feel in opposition to the coolly knowing tone Hendrix achieved.

'Can You See Me' (Jimi Hendrix)

Here's the upswing from 'Manic Depression': confident, assured, somewhat arrogant. Hendrix is enquiring if his lover can ever see him being pinned down. The bend in the note after he asks, 'Can you see me?' mimics an incredulous inflection that answers 'No!' This track also makes evident Mitchell's almost evaporated drum sound, with the beats dry, the fills crisp – only the cymbals splashing now and then. This control is an effective counterpoint to Hendrix's protesting licks, with the rhythm determined and implacable like an interrogation. The alternative version on *West Coast Seattle Boy* has the vocals almost below the guitar, undermining the cocksure tone. Yet Hendrix's giggles are also audible, lending an interesting irony.

The influence of the track is clear on Cream's 'Swlabr', which was the B-side to their better-known Hendrix tribute 'Sunshine Of Your Love'. Pete Brown's lyric makes humorous use of a Hendrix motif too – the rainbow: 'But the rainbow has a beard'!

'Love Or Confusion' (Jimi Hendrix)

There's an Eastern flavour to this track, with a spidery, chiming guitar intro resembling a sitar, and then Hendrix holding down a droning note in the first verse contrasting with his 'reeling' mind. The change in rhythm after the second chorus is jolting and creates an unease, enhanced by the minor rhythm strokes, looking forward to 1970s Deep Purple. Having the vocals deep in the mix lends a shiver of the confessional, and the indecisive riff that twitches behind the chorus is suspenseful. 'Is that the stars in the sky/Or is it rain falling down?' ponders the lyric – an exploration of romantic uncertainty; an ambivalence mirrored by the false endings and an implied lack of resolution. The reverb on the vocal implies a distance between Hendrix, his ideas and his audience too, giving a sense of aural estrangement.

'Love Or Confusion' was suggested as the follow-up to 'Hey Joe', but once 'Purple Haze' had been captured, 'Love Or Confusion' was understandably displaced. However, its drone effect reappears on the next track and the final one, creating a thread of unease.

A lesser-known gem from *Are You Experienced*, it's regrettable that the song was only ever recorded once more: The Experience laid down a committed performance for the BBC radio show *Saturday Club*.

'I Don't Live Today' (Jimi Hendrix)

'Like I'm living at the bottom of a grave', laments Hendrix in this *Revolver*-influenced cut. Indeed, *Revolver* is a useful frame of reference for understanding the Experience's debut album and early singles, as The Beatles' masterpiece rotates between different styles, hence revolver. Hendrix spins from rock à la 'Taxman' in 'Purple Haze' (The Beatles' opening track employs a variation on the Hendrix chord) to an elegy in 'The Wind Cries Mary' that recalls the melancholy of 'Eleanor Rigby', to the raga rock of 'Love Or Confusion' and 'I Don't Live Today' that each evoke 'Tomorrow Never Knows', also forging a brooding proto-metal atmosphere.

Hendrix usually dedicated 'I Don't Live Today' to American Indians and 'all minority depression groups', with the live versions making the link clearer by using a drum pattern recalling Native American rhythms. Hendrix's paternal grandmother was of Cherokee heritage; his mother also had Cherokee ancestry, and as part of the 40th-anniversary commemorations of Hendrix's death, his estate donated some of his belongings to the National Museum of the American Indian.

This is unique on the album in that it sounds like genuine frustration and despair, and might have led to Jon Landau's tin-eared review in *Rolling Stone*: 'Above all, this record is unrelentingly violent, and lyrically, inartistically violent at that.' Violent is a difficult description to use because the sounds are not destructive but, rather, rousing. Unrelenting is a better fit, and is not to be mourned. Whilst Hendrix's lyrics are less incisive than his sounds, they are often an accent in the mix. Thickets of poetry couldn't flourish in these soundscapes, but his 'livin' at the bottom of a grave' analogy is one of only a handful of undeniably pessimistic – or perhaps nihilistic – images, supported by a feeling of weight in the music and jump-scares of lashing, discordant licks. Redding's nervy bass lines complement with a defiant but anxious throbbing, like a heart full of dread. The solo quotes that of 'Purple Haze' but uses similar notes not to voice euphoria but restraint, illustrating the fluidity of Hendrix's guitar language. Yes, it could be violent, even destructive, although the defiant little riff after the chorus deflects this. But this track is balanced by the bursting fireworks and fizz of so many others. Moreover, the fade-out is a rich example of Hendrix's trademark – controlled cacophony attenuated by a wry humour. Hendrix undercuts his own severity with the false endings, like ironic resurrections, suggesting he's living today and tomorrow and tomorrow… and this reminds us of Chandler's impatience with the misconceptions of 'Jimi as a tortured artist'. The mumblings about *experience* as the slow knock… knock heard at the fade-out, look ahead to the album's final (and title) track. And that metronome – first suggested in 'Stone Free' – is still keeping him on the run.

'May This Be Love' (Jimi Hendrix)

British band Blur reference the dreamy opening of 'May This Be Love' on *Parklife*'s 'Far Out'. This Hendrix song is a sharp change of mood from the dejected 'I Don't Live Today'. It's a strange but effective cocktail of the Hawaiian mele joined to an almost military drum rhythm with Mitchell playing tom-toms, making it simultaneously stimulating and soothing. Hendrix gets his guitar to *croon* and to serenade his 'waterfall'. It's like a cooling hand on the fevered forehead of the previous track.

Hendrix never performed the song live, with Mitchell commenting that this was because it was an album filler. But it points towards 'Little Wing': a sublime song that Hendrix also rarely played live. Possibly, the fleeting nature of the beauty in these tracks – the 'misty breeze' – made them hard to replicate on stage.

The title may be another question or the granting of a desire, and this uncertainty is raised by the sudden escalation of rhythm in the middle eight before there's a trembling and then a return to the languid verses. Liquid notes in the gentle solo are more like summer rain than a waterfall, but they shimmer, lending the piece an iridescent quality. Delay is used too, to create a dreamy underwater sensation. Here, the violence has not only relented, but has changed element too.

'Fire' (Jimi Hendrix)

And then this song crashes in, with Hendrix as a sorcerer in elemental control yet again, and a swing from water to fire. The track burns brightly but briefly and is a lot of fun. Critics have rolled their eyes at how 'sixties' the cut is, but that is no reason to label it as a failing. The lead and bass display a superior chemistry and Hendrix's joyous and Little-Richard-esque 'ooing' to mimic his guitar's yelp is a little treat in the fade-out too. Alice Cooper covered it on *Classicks*, but it lacks the original's sense of humour, and for all its stridency is dull, attesting that Hendrix's magnetism is often as important as the chord structures. Moreover, this is the only Hendrix track bar 'Purple Haze' to use the Evo1, bestowing its tones with a unique timbre.

The story behind the track is well known: an exhausted Hendrix asking to warm himself beside Redding's mother's hearth, which was being guarded by her German shepherd – though its meaning in the song is not as innocent. It has drawn comments that, as a metaphor for sex, it's confused, but then these things shouldn't be examined too closely or we'd never get past banging gongs, squeezing lemons and wanting to be sledgehammers. Regardless, the song must've been thought to have commercial potential as it was eventually released as a single in the UK in 1969 with the somewhat opportunistic and inaccurate re-titling: 'Let Me Light Your Fire'. Backed with 'Burning Of The Midnight Lamp', it unfairly failed to chart in either the UK or the US.

Hendrix frequently played the song live and embellished one performance with: 'Old Mother Hubbard went to the cupboard to find her poor dog a bone/ But when she bent over, Rover took over, because Rover had a bone of his own! Shakespeare, page 35!' Perhaps we have Hendrix to thank for the career of Judge Dread.

'3rd Stone From The Sun' (Jimi Hendrix)

This cut looks forward to the *Axis: Bold As Love* concept of alien interaction and a higher power at work, by narrating an extraterrestrial visit to the third stone (Earth), and their disrespect for all but the 'majestic and superior cackling hen'. The ETs obliterate Earth, and crow, 'You'll never hear surf music again!' On one hand it's barmy, laughable nonsense ('May I land my kinky machine?'), but on the other, it's glorious. It's hard to imagine many of today's bands loosening up enough to seem almost ludicrous or to take joy in splashing around in sound like a child throwing paints on paper. Yet, when the seemingly bizarre images are closely examined, their importance shines, as in author Harry Shapiro's linking the hen to Louis Jordan's 'Ain't Nobody Here But Us Chickens', which was backed with future Hendrix cover 'Let The Good Times Roll'. Various origins have been posited for the phrase, with one attributing it to a joke about foxes in a chicken house, as in Jordan's lyric. However, it's also been suggested that it refers to those who refused to fight in the American Civil War, lending the image of 'chickens' a problematic ambiguity. Hendrix says hen – the female, a superior in the model of 'Little Wing''s muse perhaps. Although, it might be the majestic Hendrix, of course.

Chas Chandler believed the track was influenced by George R. Stewart's *Earth Abides.* The novel follows Ish as he tries to survive after a disease obliterates most of humanity. Significantly, Ish finds a mixed-race partner and has children with her; the children know nothing of the old America. Chandler commented that both he and Hendrix were dedicated sci-fi fans, and much of the imagery Hendrix employed with The Experience certainly reflects this.

After the annihilation in the song, the earthlings are taunted with 'You'll never hear surf music again'. Whilst Hendrix admired surf instrumentals, he was said to have less time for the frothier examples of surf pop (he described The Beach Boys to *NME* as 'a psychedelic barbershop quartet'), and indeed a shift was occurring as youth culture moved from Venice Beach to San Francisco. However, on an early version, Hendrix follows his pronouncement with 'Sounds like a lie to me…' The line is thought to be in tribute to Dick Dale, who played a right-handed white Fender that had originally been strung for a left-handed player. In the liner notes to *Better Shred Than Dead: The Dick Dale Anthology*, Dale remarked that he thought Hendrix was responding to a rumour about his supposed imminent death. It's also difficult to imagine that someone so obsessed with imagery of the sea and what was beneath would find little to enjoy in this genre. Interestingly, '3rd Stone From The Sun' is in mixolydian mode – a triumphant anthemic mode closely associated with blues, funk and jazz – whilst Dale's most famous piece 'Misirlou' uses the phrygian mode (heavy with foreboding), so Hendrix might be having fun with a bit of a musical battle, or simply representing the victory of the aliens. Indeed, he uses the vibrato arm to hair-raising effect, creating a feeling of a sucking vortex.

The version of '3rd Stone…' on *The Jimi Hendrix Experience* box set is delightful as we eavesdrop on Chandler and Hendrix practising their respective parts as traffic controller and space pilot, with each corpsing repeatedly. Chandler's Geordie accent juxtaposed to Hendrix's languorous tones is amusing, giving a hint of what a psychedelic *Auf Wiedersehen, Pet* might've been like. Another ITV programme linked to the song is *Coronation Street,* or rather its Eric-Spear-composed theme. Hendrix evokes it in his octave riff, and his girlfriend Kathy Etchingham claimed him to have been a fan of the soap: in particular, hair-netted harridan Ena Sharples. The theme was originally titled 'Lancashire Blues', and uses a cornet solo to educe the broad, plangent sound of the industrial North. Hendrix uses the melody here similarly to convey a sense of technological innovation redesigning the landscape.

In terms of the elemental journey the album sets us on, we've moved into air now with Hendrix's floating licks. These are anchored by Redding's bass throbbing behind like an impatient spacecraft engine, and this driving force is evocative of Giorgio Moroder and Pete Bellotte's 'I Feel Love'. The fade-out recreates a dogged pursuit, and that train-like knocking sound from 'I Don't Live Today' is audible again, as if Hendrix can still hear his train a-comin'…; the seconds ticking away, even in this space fantasy.

Nigel Kennedy's version is a 14-minute opus, beginning quietly, like strangers landing in a strange land, seeming to gain their bearings before joyously breaking out into the main riff – given real timbre by the violin's sustain – a sophisticated yet rambunctious interpretation. It also makes use of the dobro: a resonator guitar designed to be louder than a standard acoustic. The dobro is also used on another Hendrix cover: The Corrs' version of 'Little Wing'. One can't help but wonder how Hendrix himself might've employed this instrument.

'Remember' (Jimi Hendrix)

We now have a palate cleanser, with a track that could've been a Northern soul favourite. The tables have turned, and Hendrix's lover has gone roaming. However, what Hendrix characteristically misses most is the birdsong that has silenced since, and it's more a love song to song itself. It would have benefited from an injection of gusto in the middle eight, but shows that Hendrix could keep it understated and still have something to say. It's the closest to his pre-Experience sound and displays a softer, more controlled vocal of the type that would flower on the *Electric Ladyland* title track. Mitchell was disregarding of 'Remember' in his book *The Hendrix Experience*, commenting, 'There were a few we didn't do live, such as "Remember" and "May This Be Love", because in all honesty, they were album fillers.' Whilst nowhere near as strong as other cuts, 'Remember' does widen the album's range, and the mockingbird symbol is thought-provoking.

His mockingbird may have been inspired by the Inez and Charlie Foxx classic 'Mockingbird', which Hendrix went on to sing with Dusty Springfield on her eponymous show in 1968. Only the soundtrack remains, but shows that Springfield and Hendrix made a favourable team. Moreover, the track is based on the southern lullaby 'Hush Little Baby', linking it to Hendrix's songs of childhood. Intriguingly, the mockingbird is symbolic of innocence: another motif in Hendrix's 'innocentia'. This term was first applied to Hendrix in Sheila Weller's 1969 *Rolling Stone* article 'I Don't Want to be a Clown Anymore', where Weller recounts a conversation in a car with him 'of puppies, daybreak, other innocentia'. It's a great label for a set of symbols that thread through his songs and that contrast with the wild man of rock persona imposed upon him. Mockingbirds, hummingbirds, jack-in-a-boxes, zebras and moonbeams are the images of the nursery, and seem to suggest a longing for childhood.

On the BBC's *Look of the Week*, Austrian classical musician Hans Keller opined that the loudness of Pink Floyd was 'a little bit of a regression to childhood. But after all, why not?' There is some unexpected insight here – 1967 was a year redefining innocence and experience and casting its children of the revolution. William Blake's *Songs of Innocence* – printed in 1789 and coinciding with the French Revolution – is rarely perceived as infantile, despite its ingenuous outlook; why shouldn't *Are You Experienced* and *Electric Ladyland* stand as statements on both of these conditions? As Blake delineated his philosophy through the symbolism of both the guileless lamb and the red-blooded tiger, Hendrix split his own work into febrile sound explosions and elegant elegies. He too was writing in the shadow of revolution: the civil rights movement and the sexual revolution. There was a quiver in the air like that of the expectant 'Foxy Lady' intro. *Are You Experienced* could be a sexual invitation, but might also be asking about how *aware* one is. And as Blake's generation would see progression turned to destruction, the revolutionaries for race and gender equality would not be without casualties.

Hendrix's sound is at once portentous, celebratory and lamenting. Perhaps there is a violence in that after all, but then we have to ascertain what the violence is directed at. There is a hint of a child scrawling colourfully on an empty page – part in the joy of creation and part in denial of the existing scrawls, lines and boundaries. It can't be suggested with a completely straight face that Hendrix – or any other artist who wrote of childhood at the time – absolutely intended direct comparisons with Romanticism, but there are interesting and important parallels. Are Hendrix's sound representations of innocence and experience as significant as Blake's? But after all, why not?

'Are You Experienced' (Jimi Hendrix)

After being initiated into the Hendrix sound, we're finally asked the album's main question. Questions are a tic of Hendrix's lyrics, and he certainly seemed more at ease asking them himself and replying in sonic innovation than he did being asked them in interviews, where he revealed, 'I can't explain myself like this or that.' Indeed, the track opens with a flapping sound like airborne wings that can't quite get off the ground.

Hendrix invites his listener to join him in a new perspective: 'Come on across to me/We'll hold hands and then we'll watch the sun rise from the bottom of the sea'. But he needs to know if we've been experienced first. There is an echo of the Sylvia Plath poem 'The Applicant' – which opens 'First are you our sort of person?', and progresses through a satirical interview where suitability for marriage is determined. Whilst there may be no direct link between the two works, it does kindle the connection between experience and the standard job interview question. Is Hendrix satirising the language of these transactions and its connotations of daily grind à la '51st Anniversary'? In his book *Crosstown Traffic: Jimi Hendrix and Post-War Pop*, Charles Shaar Murray quotes the below to illustrate that Hendrix's tone is that of a 'pimp': 'But to who in your measly little world/are trying to prove /That you're made out of gold /and can't be sold?' However, this may be a lyric misquote. The printed lyric reads, 'But who in your measly little world are trying to prove that/You're made out of gold and can't be sold' – in which case, the address is not simply to a naive or vulnerable lover, but could be a comment on the Madonna/whore dichotomy, and the 'measly' seems less patronising as it applied to the society around her.

Kramer described this song as one of his favourites. He explained that the piano notes that toll like a call to worship are A-flat octaves that put the rest of the track effectively off kilter. He also admired the lead and rhythm-playing that Hendrix moves seamlessly between, creating a dynamic polyphony. It's the first time he tuned his guitar lower to make manipulation of the strings easier, but also to give a looser sound. The bass on the track is nebulous and without its definite anchor, it's as if the escape that Hendrix has been straining for happens here in the finale, as the bass often represented a type of running on the spot in his previous work. This is audible on the version on *West Coast Seattle Boy* where the bass just tips the track too deeply into the murk.

In the superb *Psychedelia and Other Colours*, Rob Chapman comments that 'Are You Experienced' '…builds its rhythmic pulse on the bold premise that the coda to 'Strawberry Fields Forever' was a starting point, not a fade-out'. Also taking inspiration from The Beatles' 'Tomorrow Never Knows', it's built around a drone, which some critics have felt imbues an Indian feel. Native American music similarly uses drones, and there's a comparable timbre between this track and 'I Don't Live Today', which Hendrix dedicated to Native Americans. Indeed, 'Are You Experienced' subverts the former song because experience *is* living the day, thereby redefining innocence as stasis.

For Hendrix, experience is 'Not necessarily stoned, but beautiful…' Whilst not exactly coherent lyrically, the music pulls its weight with this. The backwards guitars are like an indecipherable rumour – you know something is happening, but you don't know what it is exactly, to paraphrase Dylan –

although Hendrix *was* definite regarding the solo, taking the tapes home to practise his 'moves'. The chorus leaves the ground with a piano tolling like a cowbell, adding a sense of morning-after inertia. Simultaneously, there are peaks of euphoria before the closing chord leaves his question unresolved. Regrettably, Eric Burdon and the New Animals answered the track with their 'Yes, I'm Experienced': a tedious blend of Dave Brubeck and LSD from the film *The Producers.*

In the beautiful *1967: A Complete Rock Music History of the Summer of Love* by Harvey Kubernik, the singer Gary Stewart remarked: 'I look at the rock 'n' roll of the '60s as puberty. The birth of the form happened in the '50s, and that was great. But the most interesting phase – and the richest period of any movement – comes after that formative period, when the possibilities inherent in growth exploration and experimentation get realised.' Hendrix knew this, and *Are You Experienced* is the definitive comment on that shift of innocence moving towards awakening; its blend of dissonance and harmony reflecting both states, yet definitively choosing neither. And would innocence be harmonic or dissonant anyway?

Are You Experienced is an extraordinary debut – at once accomplished and promising, and undeniably one of the greatest. Indeed, the excitement sometimes comes from what it hints is still to flourish, and the working out of the Hendrix lexicon. But truthfully, the experience as a whole is padded out with rewrites and moments of self-plagiarism too, and the musicianship is miles ahead of the songcraft. Many have argued that Hendrix's work dwarfs the other colossi of 1967: *Pepper*; *Disraeli Gears*; *The Doors*; *The Who Sell Out*; *Something Else*; *Forever Changes*. In terms of melody, coherence and incisive social observation, this idea isn't entirely accurate. Considering virtuosity, sonic innovation and an intangible sense of 'what the hell?!', it *is*. Actually, it's absurd (even ungrateful!) to set these works against each other anyway – giants standing on the Pierre Cardin shoulders of giants standing on Marshall stacks! Writing in the CD booklet for the 1997 *Are You Experienced* remaster, Dave Marsh notes that it's 'the musical equivalent of the big bang'. The work doesn't stand as an origin story in general, but it's an evolutionary leap in the ascent of rock, and it's exceptional that The Experience crafted a work of such intense dynamism within months of forming. Hendrix told *Record Mirror*'s Peter Jones: 'We don't want to be classed in any category. If it must have a tag, I'd like it to be called free-feeling. It's a mixture of rock, freak-out, blues and rave music.' If we judge the album by Hendrix's own intentions, then it's a victory.

The *NME's* review of it, summarised with 'a one-man assault on the nerve cells'. Whilst completely ignoring the bolstering but sensitive and responsive contributions of Redding and Mitchell, it's a lazy statement: the music attacks, insinuates, seduces and entrances too. Looking back on the album two years later, Hendrix said he was bemused by some it, but explained to Keith Altham: 'The way I write things, they are just a clash between reality and fantasy. You have to use fantasy to show different sides to reality.'

It's easy to see how Hendrix would quickly tire of the 'fantasy' – his presumed primitive stage persona – and, probably, more precisely, become weary of others constructing it from only a shade or two of his vast rainbow palette. One of the most beautiful and insightful comments on Hendrix's innovation is from David Stubbs in *Jimi Hendrix: The Stories Behind Every Song*. He asserts the sound is 'sculpted – liquid and fire expertly shaped in mid-air as if by a glassblower'. And that is exactly the power of Hendrix – the unifying of those elements that seem incompatible with the fires of passion and lust and the quenching waters of tenderness. Furthermore, this sonic sorcery was to be continued on *Axis: Bold As Love*: his *second* album of 1967.

Axis: Bold As Love (1967)

And I come back to find the stars misplaced…

Personnel:
Jimi Hendrix: Guitar, vocals, piano, recorder
Mitch Mitchell: Drums, backing vocal, glockenspiel
Noel Redding: Bass, backing vocals, lead vocals
Roy Wood: Backing vocal on 'You Got Me Floatin''
Trevor Burton: Backing vocals on 'You Got Me Floatin''
Graham Nash: Backing vocals on 'You Got Me Floatin''
Recorded at Olympic Studios
Producer: Chas Chandler
Engineer: Eddie Kramer, Terry Brown, George Chkiantz, Andy Johns
Chart placings: UK: 5, US: 3

The man in fiery orange, straddles the prone guitar, teases its notes before an ejaculation of lighter fluid … rose and gold flames climax … his lithe fingers, that crown huge hands, entice the flames to climb and climb the guitar's body and then the neck of the Strat, before he spins and spins it around him, slicing the air like the blades of a helicopter. Finally, the picked bones of the instrument are tossed out into a dazed audience … every man killing the things he loves …

And this iconic moment was initially captured in black and white: a pertinent metaphor for Hendrix's music moving ahead of the times. When he set his guitar alight – his Fiesta Red Strat – at Monterey, *Rolling Stone* had to colourise the snapshot from other footage of the gig after it was captured by the 17-year-old Ed Caraeff. (Hendrix would invite him to take photographs at other gigs too.)

The fragment of guitar neck that was launched into the audience should ascend and fall into a jump cut to the future, in the vein of Kubrick's *2001: A Space Odyssey.*

It's the summer of 1967, and legacies are being tested, protested, abandoned. Many have commented on the seeming paradox of igniting the instrument of both dissent and creation; the gentle offstage Hendrix with the determined seducer and annihilator of his onstage persona. But perhaps the sacrifice is not so incongruous when we consider the Watts riots and the threatening of the establishment, but we can also look wider at fire imagery at this time. Fire had been used to tame The Beatles and keep them as moptops when the bonfires were lit after Lennon's 'more popular than Jesus' remarks to Maureen Cleave of the *London Evening Standard*. However, the remarks were reprinted in the US publication *Datebook*, in which Paul McCartney described the US as 'a lousy country where anyone black is a dirty nigger!' That the country would be more offended on behalf of God than by the comments of its treatment of citizens of colour is horrifyingly revealing. Although Keith Altham suggested the flaming guitar gimmick to link in with the track 'Fire', and it had been incorporated into shows reaching back to Hendrix's tour with The Walker Brothers – debuting it at Finsbury Park – it still radicalises an act that had initially been designed to censor and censure. We can also draw parallels with the cross burnings of the Ku Klux Klan: fighting fire with fire.

Furthermore, at the beginning of 1967, the early Moon mission Apollo 1 resulted in three deaths after a fire in the cabin. The hazards had been underestimated and so the tragedy was preventable. So 1967 – a year often associated with revolutionary and experimental ideas – began with destruction and disaster. Progress, ambition, transformation, all could be blasted by fire. It seemed to be a constant image on the news throughout the turbulence and uncertainty of the 1960s. It might be said that it was the defining element; curious for the Age of Aquarius.

Conundrums abound: 'Just ask the axis (he knows everything)'. The Experience's second album of 1967 introduces an oracle that seems to answer some of the questions posed on its predecessor. In the album's central image, Hendrix personifies colours and their connoted qualities, concluding that their value is proved by their 'fight' in love. One wonders if the axis is a pun on the way The Beatles used *Revolver* to refer not only to the spinning disc itself, but its astonishing array of musical styles. Here, the axis may well be the record player rod too, sending its myriad sounds into orbit.

Hendrix's star had risen dramatically in the seven months since he'd enquired *Are You Experienced*. In that time, The Experience had toured extensively and sometimes futilely (an unwise – or canny – booking supporting The Monkees), and triumphed at the Monterey Pop Festival. Their set leapt from blues classics (as in a blazing take on B.B. King's 'Rock Me Baby') through to an obliging 'Hey Joe', a reverent 'Like A Rolling Stone', all the way to The Troggs' kitsch 'Wild Thing' (a song Hendrix had first performed with The Blue Flames), becoming playful and sensual with an orgiastic guitar solo instead of the bleating of an ocarina. Immediately after, Hendrix set his guitar alight. He'd opened his set with Howlin' Wolf's 'Killing Floor' (it refers to leaving with a friend from Mexico: a neat foreshadowing of his disavowal of 'Hey Joe'), and had deferred the slaughter to the show's ending. Hendrix's immolation of his guitar was also setting light to a back catalogue he was rapidly outgrowing. Therefore, *Axis: Bold As Love* is Janus-faced, and like its cover image, it looks to both the past and future. But, yet again, the cover was a source of contention, as Hendrix had asked for the artwork to pay tribute to his Cherokee origins. This was lost in translation, with an Indian-inspired image (as in, the country) appearing instead. However, this links back to the time recounted in Philip Norman's *Wild Thing* when Hendrix was touring with the Starliters and a group of Indian women told him he had 'the face of a Hindu god'. On the album cover, Hendrix is depicted Vishnu-like with multiple arms symbolising his virtuosity.

But disaster almost struck when the stereo master tape to side A was lost: Hendrix left them in a cab. Redding's own copy, which he'd taken home, helped, but only somewhat as the tape was ironed, with some tracks having to be remixed again from memory. Conspiracists think Hendrix might have 'forgotten' the tape on purpose because he was dissatisfied with the results.

'EXP' (Jimi Hendrix)

Teasingly, the album opens with a tremor of 'Stone Free', before unveiling its avant-garde soundscape. But just as music critic Tim Riley noted – in his book *Tell Me Why* – how The Beatles marked a new era with the out-of-time count-in of *Revolver* as opposed to the joyous 'One, two, three, four!' of the *Please Please Me* opener 'I Saw Her Standing There', Hendrix abandons 'Stone Free''s riff, to segue into a radio chat show on the dodgy topic of ETs. The track seems likely to have influenced Canadian group Klaatu's 1976 cut 'Calling Occupants Of Interplanetary Craft' – another curious link between Hendrix and The Carpenters (besides Tony Peluso's fuzzy 'Goodbye To Love' solo).

Hendrix commented on 'EXP' to *Eye*: 'We've tried to get most of the freaky tracks right into another dimension so you get that sky effect like they're coming down out of the heavens, you know.' Mitchell plays the enthusiastic host whilst Hendrix is Paul Caruso (an in-joke name-checking an old mate and fellow musician who would play harmonica on *The Cry Of Love* track 'My Friend') – an alien expert who surprises the host by boarding his spaceship: sending the track into an intergalactic sound sketch as though not just one, but a whole space fleet is launching. In fact, the rushing and hissing evoke passing through air, and initially, the cut was titled 'Symphony Of Experience'. This is Hendrix's sound-painting of the moment he first leapt from a plane. The feedback pans around the speakers as it might whirl around an axis; there's the wailing of an intergalactic ambulance siren and an impression of tectonic plates shifting, and in some ways, this piece is a rehearsal for the *Electric Ladyland* track 'And The Gods Made Love'. In fact, *Axis* can be seen as a dry run in several ways…

'Up From The Skies' (Jimi Hendrix)

…as the second track also makes evident, with its looking forward to the swooning soul of the *Electric Ladyland* title track, and by presenting a laid-back opener proper, emphasised by Mitchell's tasteful brush work. As the last track recorded for *Axis: Bold As Love*, it does seem to be pointing the way towards the more relaxed moments of the album that would follow it. The title evokes a 1950s sci-fi flick of the type Hendrix enjoyed as a kid – so much so that he was nicknamed Buster after the American film star Buster Crabbe, and later he even wore a Hussar jacket similar to Crabbe's.

Musically, this soul shuffle has elements of Curtis Mayfield (Hendrix briefly backed Mayfield in his early days), and is almost a duologue between Hendrix and his guitar, with its loquacious notes commenting after his vocal lines. However, Hendrix himself wasn't happy with the soul tag the track garnered, telling *Open City*: 'Everybody has soul. I really don't like the word in connection with The Experience. I like the words 'feeling' and 'vibration', like playing together.'

He uses the word 'vibrations' here to refer to the stirrings of memory and instinct, and to ponder the relevance of those (seemingly) new hippie slogans. Hendrix takes on the role of an alien or ancestor pleading:

> Just wanna know about the rooms behind your minds
> Do I see a vacuum there, or am I going blind?
> Or is it just the remains from vibrations and echoes long ago
> Things like 'Love the world' and 'Let your fancy flow'
> Is this true?
> Please let me talk to you
> Let me talk to you

We have an unusual positioning here à la the original 'Purple Haze' lyrics that looked up from the ceiling with the visitant being *up* from the skies and the 'stars misplaced'. There's the possibility that Hendrix might mean heaven beyond the skies and that this too has been as corrupted as its earthly mirror image. Moreover, there is 'the smell of a world that's burned', hinting at a new hell or even post-hell. Juxtaposed against the love generation's impotent mottoes, we're forced to recall that the Summer of Love saw the Newark and Detroit riots, and that interminable years of disenfranchising black citizens had been kindling these. There is a dissonance between the pensive lyrics and the bouncy melody: something that would be repeated on *Electric Ladyland*'s 'Long Hot Summer'. Potentially, Hendrix was still unsure of his role as sage or even social commentator, as the almost throwaway 'Aw shucks, if my daddy could see me now' in the fade-out implies. He later commented to Keith Altham: 'When things get too heavy, just call me helium, the lightest gas known to man.' But the mismatch between music and lyric is also powerful, as if the ideology is invading, camouflaged by a hook that would satisfy the Tin Pan Alley old grey whistle test. The vocals shift from left to centre to right, maintaining a feeling of flight, disorientation, but also indecision. Is Hendrix counting himself in or out of burning this world? Is the integration of seemingly incompatible ideas being foregrounded? The drum fills also suggest stammering or hesitancy in delivering the message. Nevertheless, the guitar's wah-wah effect increases as the track progresses, getting wetter in sound and appositely more alien. As the song decays, the bass gives a little low trill and finally breaks away from the melody, suggesting a glint of freedom. Perhaps the tune and lyrics are not so disparate after all.

The lyric phrase 'change of climate' hints at a new direction, with the album building on what Marc Bolan later called 'interstellar soul'. Hendrix's assured vocal – combined with the hummable tune that's sharpened rather than muddied by the wah-wah effect – promises that *Axis* will be stronger on melody than its predecessor, and indeed there are as many tunes as riffs here, evincing that Hendrix would go far beyond pyrotechnical gimmicks. But there is also a classic Hendrix trope still being repeated in 'Up From the Skies' – 'cages tall and cold' – although Hendrix has moved beyond the threadbare metaphor of wedlock to deadlock, now taking on a persona to explore constraints psychological and even ecological.

But if the main elements of *Are You Experienced* were fire and water, *Axis* is about air, dreaming, flying and the joy of song itself.

'Spanish Castle Magic' (Jimi Hendrix)

And then there's some solid rock in the way that the hustle and bustle of 'Crosstown Traffic' intrudes on *Electric Ladyland*'s languor. Hendrix is telling us to build castles in the air; to experience escape in the vein of The Beatles' 'There's A Place' ('Don't spend time on bad things/Just float your little mind out'). Contrarily, 'It's not in Spain/But all the same, it's a groovy name' is said to refer to a club Hendrix previously frequented: The Spanish Castle, which was demolished in 1968. However, some other writers have disputed that it inspired the song. Yet The Wailers played a legendary gig there, which Hendrix might've equated with a type of magic. Whatever, there's something especially evocative about the name; perhaps the fat assonance that is doubled by Redding's eight-string Hagstrom bass fortifying the song, and Hendrix and Redding playing in unison is a powerful foundation. The unique bass (a Swedish invention that only Redding and Hendrix owned at the time) lends a battering-ram thickness, as if pounding on the castle stones, and the eight strings increase the sustain. In the liner notes for the album's CD release, Jim Fahey insightfully remarks: 'Redding brought a guitarist's sensibilities and deftness to the bass.' Hendrix also overdubbed the bass, shadowing Redding's rumble and making the song as stolid as a castle itself. Surprisingly, only two *Axis* cuts were played live, but this was a stage favourite, attesting to the band cohesion on display. (The other track performed live – though only eight times – was the elegant 'Little Wing'.)

Indeed, 'Spanish Castle Magic' is one of the best songs in Hendrix's *oeuvre*, and one of the best from The Experience as a power trio. Mitchell's dry technique is very much in evidence with clean beats and no leakage, lending a confidence to his tone and the ability to provide a backbone to the intertwining of Hendrix and Redding's flourishes. In many ways, the gaps between Mitchell's beats are every bit as important as the fills. If we compare with Ginger Baker – especially on the Experience tribute 'Sunshine Of Your Love' – the drums constantly hiss: an anxious sibilance that doesn't allow a breath or heartbeat between. It's quite extraordinary that Mitchell was able to compete with Hendrix, and at the same time, make it noticeable when he was *not* playing.

After Kramer showed him some jazz chords, Hendrix decided to hammer these out on piano. Indeed, nearly all the instruments on this potent track are being used as percussion. A revving riff propels the song right from the opening, and the drums beat impatiently behind as we're being chased to the Spanish castle. Part of the track's unique power comes from Hendrix's use of a Mosrite Joe Maphis 12/6 Double Neck, the pickups of which are single coils, imbuing the sound with real muscle. The descending chromatic on the chorus lends a dramatic air of invocation, heightened by Hendrix's application of the Octavia, lending a fitting otherworldly ambience. In *Hear My Train A Comin': The Songs of Jimi Hendrix*, Kevin Le Gendre notes that the verse has a Native-American-style rhythm fused with the African American chorus rhythm. This might allude to Hendrix's multiracial background and the track's magic is the unifying of these.

In the 1966 Love track 'The Castle' from their second album *Da Capo,* Arthur Lee sings of going to Mexico 'on the double'. Hendrix has doubled up on the idea of a fortress here too. 'The Castle' referred to Love's Los Angeles squat – a red-bricked mansion shown on the cover of their eponymous debut album: which coincidentally includes a garage-style version of 'Hey Joe'. Perhaps Hendrix was conflating his memories of the club and of friend and rival Lee.

Hendrix met Lee in 1965 when he was backing Rosa Lee Brooks on the Lee-penned song 'My Diary'. (Or so he claimed. See *West Coast Seattle Boy* for more on this.) Despite Lee being disgruntled that Hendrix allegedly took sartorial inspiration from him, the two recorded together again. In John Einarson's biography *Forever Changes: Arthur Lee and the Book of Love*, Lee explains that he convinced Hendrix to play with him again after Hendrix was denied entry to the Speakeasy. The pair worked on 'Ezy Rider' (later to grace the posthumous *First Rays Of The New Rising Sun*), a jam called 'Loon', and 'The Everlasting First', which would find a home on Love's 1970 album *False Start*. Hendrix arranged it and, unusually, played anonymous guitar. The song opens already in flow (everlasting) and has a flavour of the B-side 'The Stars That Play With Laughing Sam's Dice', along with gospel touches. But as a collaboration between two of music's great individuals, it's disappointing. The arrangement shows a little more thought – mirroring the opening, the piece ironically stops unexpectedly, and segues into the second track 'Flying' (not The Beatles' instrumental). Lee takes up the story:

> He and I arrived together. The guy at the front door told me I could come in, but Jimi couldn't. When I asked him why, he said that Jimi had been fighting in the club on an earlier occasion and they didn't want that happening again. So I told him that Jimi was cool, the entourage that was with us was cool, and I didn't think any fighting would be going on that night. He finally agreed. I said to Jimi, 'Look, man, neither one of us is going to be around much longer, anyway, so while we're here we might as well do something together.' When I said that, whatever we were talking about or he was thinking about, just seemed to stop, and I had his full attention. He really went into some deep thought as he looked at me from across the table. He was looking into my eyes, and I knew he could only be thinking about our early deaths.

Curiously, this anecdote could be a way of explaining part of Hendrix's inspiration for 'Spanish Castle Magic' – the idea of club, a castle and an escape with a sympathetic confidante. Alas, this is too neat an explanation as their second recording session occurred in 1970.

Lee also elaborated on how Hendrix had inspired him to write 'Flying', after Lee discovered that his Finnish lover Dessa had also been close to Hendrix. Lee told John Einarson:

> Boy did we have fun at Olympic recording studio. The band and Jimi all took mescaline. Jimi came back in during the middle of it (recording 'Ride That Vibration'). He asked me, 'What did you just say in that song?' I said, 'Ride the vibration down like a six-foot grave/Don't let it get you down'. Then he said, 'I gotta go, it's getting too heavy.'

Perhaps Hendrix was reminded of his 'I Don't Live Today'.

Whatever initially inspired it, 'Spanish Castle Magic' remained an important track to Hendrix. It was re-recorded as part of The Experience's rehearsal for a Royal Albert Hall performance – stronger, controlled, skilful but devoid of the shiver of danger yet exultation in the original. That version is available on *The Jimi Hendrix Experience* box set.

On the *Axis* version, Hendrix can be heard on the fade-out, lamenting that he can't sing. Yet, the vocal is powerful and disciplined. The track is also significant in that it begins the shift to some of Hendrix's *architectural* songs – that is, tracks built broad, tall and wide, layer by layer like obelisks, which culminated in the peerless recording of 'All Along The Watchtower'.

Spin Doctors' faithful cover of 'Spanish Castle Magic' is worth a listen, with just a little of a baggy vibe and an extended screaming solo from Eric Schenkman.

'Wait Until Tomorrow' (Jimi Hendrix)

This is another song of escape, but with some twists on old themes. Hendrix wants to flee with his procrastinating lover, but is eventually a victim of 'daddy's gun' instead, in a twist on 'Hey Joe'. Musically, there's a breeziness that's undercut by the lyrics. The drums have a deeper, thicker sound than on *Are You Experienced*, mimicking the restive lover's frustration. Hendrix names his girlfriend Dolly Mae – a name he would partly reuse for 'Dolly Dagger', Dolly being a diminutive of Dorothy, and ironically meaning 'gift of God'.

The backing vocals that echo 'I think I'd better wait until tomorrow' are an imitation of the cowardly amour. Not that you'd know this from the number of humourless critics who take this as evidence of Hendrix's backing being under par – Redding's bass dances, but there's not much progression sonically from the 'Highway Chile' on-the-road tunes from earlier. This is one of few tracks that keep *Axis* grinding in a rut rather than taking flight, but its chordal riff prevents it from becoming too stolid.

'Ain't No Telling' (Jimi Hendrix)

Unfortunately, the drop in innovation and excitement is sustained with a song of compelling tempo changes but little else. The track introduces the motif of dawn – 'Well the sunrise is burning my eyes baby' – but is lyrically generic, with Hendrix wanting to escape yet another constraining relationship. The fade-in at the end is a neat twist, but this combination of jazz and soul is more successfully achieved elsewhere. Hendrix must've also realised this, as it's his shortest recorded piece. Junior Walker's 'Shotgun' is said to have inspired the track and the galloping rhythm with guitar stabs to mimic Walker's saxophone punch is evident. 'Shotgun' was produced by Berry Gordy and released on a subsidiary Motown label. The Motown link is surprising as Tony Brown's *Jimi Hendrix: Talking* quotes Hendrix as saying, 'They (Motown) put about a thousand people on tambourines, and these bells. They got a thousand horns, a thousand violins and then a singer; he overdubs his voice millions of times, and he'll sing in an echo chamber… it comes out so artificial… it's so synthetic, you know, synthetic soul.' Though the idea of building sound could also apply to Hendrix, there's more of a feel of blending tones; a rainbow soul.

Returning to 'Ain't No Telling', the reference to Cleopatra was said to have been included because Hendrix dreamed he was making love to her: probably the song's most interesting detail.

'Little Wing' (Jimi Hendrix)

The limpid 'Little Wing' is exquisite, and is the apotheosis of Hendrix's *air* songs: ephemeral, graceful, aching. The 'innocentia' (images from a mobile or perhaps a ballerina on a jewellery box) is juxtaposed with a yearning guitar that rises and dips like the flight of starlings. It's a song in watercolour.

Hendrix's mother Lucille is thought to be the inspiration for the ascending 'Little Wing', and it's interesting that a similar tone is used on The Beatles' 'Let It Be' (particularly the album version): another paean to a missed mother. Both use sky imagery to suggest distance and elevation, with McCartney's 'and when the nights are cloudy' preceded by Hendrix's 'Well she's walking through the clouds'. He is also reassured by 'When she's sad, she comes to me', and McCartney is heartened with 'And in my hour of darkness/She is standing right in front of me'. The songs share a secular spirituality; a gospel to both the earthly but elevated.

The keening yet triumphant guitar tone is heard again on 'Bold As Love', and was achieved by Kramer feeding it through a Leslie speaker. Musically, the song grew from a 1966 track that Hendrix played on – Lonnie Youngblood's 'She's A Fox': a fairly generic soul ballad. However, Hendrix builds on the riff that opens it, and we must wonder if he took inspiration from the title for another ode to women, in the less sacred – if not outright profane – 'Foxy Lady'. Wisely, Chandler advised him to make it more 'mellow'. Hendrix had also been learning how to make use of his generously proportioned hands and was able to fret the root chords with his thumb, leaving him free to improvise beautifully around the notes.

But there *is* a link to 'Foxy Lady' too – Hendrix often personified music as an unobtainable lover, a longing for the thrill of sex and musical euphoria to be united. It might also be argued that 'Little Wing' represents a fleeting feeling rather than merely a person. Hendrix spoke of the song's gestation in Shapiro and Glebbeek's *Electric Gypsy*:

> I got the idea like, when we were in Monterey and I was just looking at everything around. So I figured that I take everything I see around and put it maybe in the form of a girl maybe – something like that, you know, and call it 'Little Wing', and then it will just fly away. So I just took all these things and put them in one very small matchbox, you know, into a girl and then do it. It was very simple, but I like it though.

The song is sometimes held as an example of the Madonna/whore divide that can be found in popular music (in all art forms actually) in general, and sometimes, perhaps, in Hendrix's music, more specifically. But there is an assumption that songs of lust are somehow automatically against women. From the various aunts who raised Hendrix, including Aunt Ernestine, who'd helped him to buy his first guitar, to his friend Linda Keith gifting him a Strat, to Kathy Etchingham's constant support (possibly including the brilliant suggestion to cover 'All Along The Watchtower'), Hendrix was shaped by women and readily acknowledged their generosity. Although that's not to say he wasn't guilty of careless and even dismissive or abusive behaviour towards them as well. But 'Little Wing' is an acknowledgement of the elevation that woman helped him achieve.

The track opens with a flurry of notes before what should be a distracting drum roll, yet it lends a majesty to the phrase 'walking through the clouds': a little thunder being cleared. The drums have a rich resonance: a woodier, natural quality. The glockenspiel's counter-melody conjures a circus atmosphere similar to The Beatles' 'Being For The Benefit Of Mr. Kite!', and perhaps the 'circus mind' recalled this for Hendrix; perhaps even a sense of a flying circus with 'Little Wing' performing aerial feats and miracles, and linking to his days in the air force. There is such attention to detail in this short song, evinced in the heart-stopping note that descends like a vulnerable fledgling before the final rise and fade-out. Maybe the lack of a bridge is also significant. Is there no way to get to the soaring 'Little Wing'? No compromise between longing and actualisation, innocence and experience? The version on the fascinating *Axis Outtakes* album is compelling in its own right, even with it being devoid of vocals, but the guitar is too overdriven to suggest the lyric's delicacy of flight. Furthermore, towards the close, the bass becomes heavier: a rumble of 'If 6 Was 9', which really doesn't suit the mood. Chandler had already advised slowing the tempo, and Hendrix further reduced the ornamentation to allow the melody to shimmer. The Derek and the Dominos cover slows it even further, but is terribly earnest, overly long and much too muddy for such a lace-fine piece.

Kramer comments that in the year 3000, we'll still be listening to this song. He's not wrong.

'If 6 Was 9' (Jimi Hendrix)

Numerologically speaking, six represents domesticity, family and stability, whilst nine symbolises diversity, compassion and insight. Little wonder that Hendrix seems to be favouring its inversion. As John Lennon fetishised nine as mystical and transformative ('Revolution 9', '#9 Dream' etc.), Hendrix links it to a radical disavowal of tribalism of all kinds. He was said to have also been inspired by the I Ching, which links six to conflict and nine to gentleness. It would be convenient to reveal that Jimi Hendrix's name is 6 or 9, but is, in fact, seven: a signifier of spirituality. However, his birth name and date of birth – or his life path – total nine.

'If 6 Was 9' is preceded by an ominous rumble and then the urging to 'Yeah, sing the song, bro' (an ironic reference to brotherhood?), before Hendrix assures us that 'If the sun refuse to shine/I don't mind', and that his tribe is neither the hippie nor 'the white-collared conservative'. This tension is built in the hiss and exhale of the cymbals. Unsurprisingly, the cut was included on the soundtrack of 1969's *Easy Rider*: a film Hendrix admired. The opening of the track spins as the riders travel through developed and rural areas, showing the split between those who've dropped out, and those who compete in the rat race. Predictably, the film ends in flames.

Returning to the track, in the notes to *The Jimi Hendrix Experience* box set, Dave Marsh writes that Kramer labelled the tape as 'The Symphony of the Experience'. Certainly, the piece has distinct movements – in the first verse, the vocal and lead guitar closely follow each other in a parody of conformity, but break away in the second verse after we're told 'ain't gonna copy you'. A slab of silence joins these first sections together. After pledging allegiance to the 'freak flag', the bass runs up and down like footsteps searching for a direction. Is up down? Is six nine? This sense of urgency to nowhere is enhanced by the middle eight, where footsteps are heard (made by Graham Nash and The Walker Brothers' Gary Leeds), before the bass changes to a heavy breathing rhythm. Talking to Kevin Le Gendre, Kramer explained: 'Because Olympic recorded a lot of classical sessions, we had these different platforms. We pulled one forward to put Mitch's drums on it, and another we put microphones on top and underneath to record a foot-stomping track.'

Mitchell's drums are not as dry here resulting in a muddier sound, enhancing the thematic lack of clarity. Kramer remarked elsewhere that Mitchell's drums were both close and distantly mic'ed throughout the recording of *Axis*. Close mic'ing can lead to crisper, cleaner sounds, where distant mic'ing might enhance the room resonance. Kramer elaborated to Harry Shapiro that the bass was mic'ed with a D30 – the mic preferred by John Bonham – whilst the floor toms were amplified by a C12. This drier sound is in evidence here and contributes to the tension. The early version available on *The Jimi Hendrix Experience* box set shows how Hendrix initially used voices to shade in where he'd embroider his guitar textures. After the acceleration, the song falls back into an echo of the opening section but is disrupted by explosive drums and Hendrix's softly spoken 'I'm the one who's gonna have to die when it's time for me to die'. The music swells behind, with guitar lines like the cries of gulls, sharpened by Hendrix vamping on a recorder, a rustle of drums, a seesawing riff. The cawing sound would be used again to create a seascape in '1983… (A Merman I Should Turn to Be)'. Hendrix promises he will wear his freak flag high, and the song concludes on a victorious squawk as it's hoisted aloft. And so ends Side A.

'You Got Me Floatin'' (Jimi Hendrix)

Keeping the sense of elevation, 'You Got Me Floatin'' is an ebullient number, augmented by The Move's Roy Wood and Trevor Burton (whose follow-up to 'Flowers In The Rain' – 'Wild Tiger Woman' – was said to be a Hendrix tribute, and who accompanied Hendrix on the 1967 package tour that included Pink Floyd), and The Hollies' Graham Nash (with whom Mitchell shared a flat for a short time) on backing vocals in the chorus. Trevor Burton reminisced to *Classic Rock*:

> The Move were recording at Olympic Studios, and next door was The Jimi Hendrix Experience recording their second album. Roy and I walked in to say hello because we knew them well by then. They were doing 'You Got Me Floatin'', and Noel and Mitch weren't cutting the background vocals too good, so we asked Jimi, 'Do you want us to have a go?' and he said, 'Yeah!' I think we did it in two takes. Jimi was pleased with it. He sang his lead vocals live at the same time while we put down the background vocals.

The track begins with an echo of the otherworld sounds of 'EXP', before Hendrix explains that love is a natural high, in another of his elemental songs. The freedom theme is varied as love gives him buoyancy, but the arrangement is earthy and tight, with the verses having a lot in common with 'Fire' sonically. It's said that Redding and Mitchell's vocals were subpar, and so were augmented by the guest stars, but that they weren't adequate may not be true as the guests' backing vocals are in the vein of what the bassist and drummer had previously contributed. The backwards guitar is fun, and the rhythm guitar behind it a nice little ear treat, but the song is a tad long and would've worked better bursting like a bubble much sooner.

'Castles Made Of Sand' (Jimi Hendrix)

Here Hendrix laments the crumbling of daydreams in a series of vignettes – relationships break down, hopes are ambushed and desire forsaken, whilst 'neighbours gossip and drool': a whip-sharp portrait of suburban oppression, accentuated by an emphatic and dogmatic bass line. It fades in with a rueful little riff, and the later backwards solo resembles 'Taxman', with the cymbal crash at the end sounding like a philosophical shrug of acceptance at the nature of circumstance reversal. The original vinyl version faded out, but this revision is much more fitting. There's also a reminder of the discerning axis as the final riff spins around like the hope of the 'EXP' spaceship deserting us.

The backwards guitar that enhances a sense of futility and regression was worked out meticulously by Hendrix. In the fascinating and original take on Hendrix *Jimi Hendrix: Soundscapes* – which tracks his life and work through the buildings he frequented – Marie-Paule Macdonald comments on Hendrix's great understanding of mirror imagery and notes his 'uncanny reverse sequential memory'. He was able to hear the notes backwards in his head, and play not just with random psychedelic abandon but with precision, as evident on this track.

Lyrically a little thick in places, the thickets of words tripping up the reflective melody, it nevertheless does lend a sense of something tumbling, falling, being overcome. The verse about the Indian brave and the surprise attack that kills him in his sleep foreshadows the shocking death of George in *Easy Rider*: the ultimate comment on crumbling castles. Furthermore, the final verse – which is often interpreted as a chink of optimism – is rather more ambiguous – the mute, disabled woman who spots this 'golden-winged ship' seems to be forsaken by it as it passes her by, yet its apparition gives her voice, then the title refrain is repeated again, increasing the ambiguity.

However, Leon Hendrix explained that Hendrix called the track 'our family song'; something of a totem, with each section symbolising a family member – the Indian brave being Leon and the final verse an allusion to their mother's poor health. Leon told Philip Norman that he and his brother last saw Lucille lying in a bed in a hospital corridor. She was moved to a wheelchair for this visit and looked like a ghost to her two sons. Perhaps Hendrix is allowing this final but not defining image of his mother to ebb away. Furthermore, Hendrix had four siblings – Joseph, Kathy, Al junior and Pamela – who were born with disabilities and required special care; the mothership may literally be leaving them behind.

Some biographers have suggested that the guitar became an object of comfort for Hendrix after his mother's death, and his love and affection were transferred to it. (Incidentally, B.B. King's guitar was called Lucille.) This isn't entirely baseless, but isn't entirely accurate either, as Hendrix had been playing an acoustic guitar assiduously already. He was so desirous of having a guitar that a child psychologist and a schoolteacher had suggested that being without the instrument was causing him serious psychological anguish. Sadly, Hendrix didn't acquire a guitar at this time, with Al dismissing his need as a luxury he couldn't afford. However, within weeks of Lucille's death, Hendrix was bought his first electric guitar: a Supro Ozark. Some critics have challenged his virtuosity, on the grounds that he rarely played an acoustic, and so potentially was hiding behind electrical effects and gimmickry. This is unfair because his medium was essentially rock – amplified music – and it's like saying a playwright is only a playwright because they can't write essays; they're different mediums. But perhaps Hendrix associated the electric sound with life after Lucille – half bereft primal scream and half rebel yell. Furthermore, Leon revealed that Hendrix was always softly spoken: 'It came from being told to shut up as a kid.' The guitar amplified his ideas, his feelings, his voice. It gave them the exclamation marks that he couldn't quite reach when conversing.

'She's So Fine' (Noel Redding)

With hints of The Who and The Kinks, this is a bouncy track from Redding, enhanced by a scribbled guitar solo. Often derided as inessential, it effectively changes the tone of the album. Perhaps if it wasn't by The Experience and was a track on a *Nuggets* compilation, it might be more kindly and honestly received, and the same can be said for 'Little Miss Strange'. Lyrically, it's obscure and a little bizarre: 'Her hair glistens like robins on a deck/Branches attack me from her neck'. Redding seems to be going for the 'She's Not There'/'Strange Brew' type of muse, but not so successfully. Musically, the track has shades of The Who's 'Happy Jack', and Mitchell channels Keith Moon in a fun few minutes.

The early cut on *Axis Outtakes* displays Redding's underconfident and rather gauche vocal delivery. Thankfully, it's much improved on the final version.

'One Rainy Wish' (Jimi Hendrix)

This plaintive song recounts meeting a peaceful lover in a prismatic idyll. Hendrix opens it with some lyrical colour imagery: 'Golden rose, the colour of the dream I had/Not too long ago/Misty blue and the lilac too/Never to grow old'. Sometimes the lyrics are transcribed as 'gold and rose', and it's not clear from his vocal what he intended. Incidentally, the Golden Rose is a sacred object in Roman Catholicism and is blessed on Rose Sunday – a day of hope during Lent – and rose-coloured cloths replace the penitential purple. It might seem unlikely that Hendrix would explicitly reference Catholic iconography, but it's interesting that colour imagery by itself is a lexicon for Hendrix. If we move from the experience of 'Purple Haze', is it that we're moving to the innocence of misty blue and lilac too? Hendrix did speak of music in religious terms, and described his later direction (and named a jam) as the 'electric church'. In the language of liturgical colours, misty blue signifies purity and the Virgin Mary, and perhaps Hendrix is evoking his mother: another curious link to 'Let It Be''s mother Mary.

Inspired by dreaming of rainbows, 'One Rainy Wish' employs 3/4 time in the verse, to embellish its wistful mood, but has a shift to a more prosaic 4/4 to signify the intrusion of reality as he knows his heart is gone forever.

Queen guitarist Brian May's cover from his 1998 *Another World* album (tellingly dedicated to his mother) is partly tender and partly ecstatic, with an orchestral arrangement by Michael Kamen.

'Little Miss Lover' (Jimi Hendrix)

This heavy rocker brings us back down to earth, with Hendrix wondering, 'Excuse me while I see if the gypsy in me is right'. Instead of kissing the sky, the gypsy in him is now wondering if 'Little Miss Lover' would 'like to tag along' on his wanderings. There's an almost wolf-whistling trilling in the fade-out; indeed, the early version on *Axis Outtakes* opens with a wolf whistle and has a more relaxed atmosphere, making it almost preferable to the album cut. Furthermore, the version on *The Jimi Hendrix Experience* box set finds him still working out how to use phasing to its most powerful effect, but has a triumphant air about it, and the track was mooted as a single to follow 'The Wind Cries Mary'. As an album cut, it changes the tone from reverent to assertive, but would've made a rather one-dimensional single. Nevertheless, it's an exciting performance overall.

'Bold As Love' (Jimi Hendrix)

There is a technicolor and pyrotechnic brilliance to the finale's two orbiting solos, spinning like catherine wheels. In a 1967 interview with Meatball Fulton, Hendrix recounted a time he was hospitalised with pneumonia. A nurse lifted him to gaze through the window at a firework display: 'I was looking, and the sky was just whew-whew-whew!' In some ways, it was as if he'd been chasing this fever dream in his songs ever since. This track captures it better than any, with its false ending, suspenseful drum solo and then the explosion of notes, trills and bends. Kramer's inspired suggestion to add phasing to the guitar enhances the euphoria, coming in waves or rotations, evoking a feeling of circularity. Author Keith Shadwick has less time for this track, believing it to be too much of an earnest attempt for a big finish: 'over-ripe, faintly ridiculous'. But much of great rock music *is*. Its grandiloquence, its howling triumph, is exactly why it's one of the greatest guitar moments ever. Perhaps it is more a lap of honour than anything else, but it's the victorious *YES!* that the ending of *Are You Experienced* lacks.

The song explains that the axis is an oracle that can unify the myriad emotions and uncertainties of life, with Hendrix personifying these as royalty, armies and ingénues symbolised by colours, e.g. 'Anger, he smiles/Towering in shiny metallic purple armour/Queen Jealousy, envy waits behind him/Her fiery green gown sneers at the grassy ground'. Its use of colour imagery seems to be echoed on Aphrodite's Child's 'The Four Horsemen' from their 1972 album *666,* which was also inspired by the Book of Revelation. The axis itself seems to be a kind of revelation or modus for epiphany. The guitar work is similarly kaleidoscopic, with bright licks and counter-riffs that shadow, whilst the outro makes thrilling use of tremolo, keeping us whirring about the axis. Harry

Shapiro linked 'Bold As Love' to *Book of the Hopi*, which discusses how life was created, describing a shared axis, and a backbone, along which vibrations echo the sounds of life. Interestingly, Hendrix is waiting to give his life 'to a rainbow like you', that is, an incomplete arc.

An earlier version (available on *Axis Outtakes*) shows a rare vocal style from Hendrix – lighter and higher; he seems to be less self-conscious and working out his phrasing. This cut also enhances how on the fade-out solo, he was able to create a zither-like effect, which becomes a little buried once the dazzling solo shines above it. This is testament to how Hendrix layered sounds, or bent them to create new hues like an artist and his palette, and it contests those who criticise him for the supposed chaos of some of his compositions. The *Axis Outtakes* collection also attempts to right the misunderstanding that resulted in the cover showing Hendrix as an Indian rather than a Native American, and represents him with a multicoloured war bonnet.

Axis: Bold as Love is lively, with a joy often found on a band's debut work. But there's an urgency and a rush to move on, emphasised by how the tracks barely have gaps between them. And Hendrix's vocals were getting stronger, partly due to the guitar down-tuning, so allowing him freedom in the topic as well as the songwriting style. Here, he's becoming a frontman in all senses of the word.

Musician Rick Springfield – who covered 'Red House' and 'Fire' – told *Classic Rock*:

> *Axis: Bold As Love* is where Jimi demonstrated what you could do if you turned the guitar down and used tone. He turned the world on to Strats, and showed what a melodic solo truly was. Hendrix changed music, and guitar-playing in particular, forever. Not bad for the first two albums. I still don't know where those first two albums came from. They were magic. And he had the authenticity to make phrases like 'comin' to gitcha' sound so real, you never questioned that he was posturing or faking it.

But Hendrix *did* feel he was faking it, and wanted to break out of the mould for his next work. He'd make it a double.

Electric Ladyland (1968)

I pick up all the pieces and make an island…

Personnel:
Jimi Hendrix: Guitar, vocals, piano, kazoo, bass, electric harpsichord
Mitch Mitchell: Drums, backing vocals, lead vocals
Noel Redding: Bass, acoustic guitar, backing vocals, lead vocals
Dave Mason: 12-string guitar, backing vocals
Steve Winwood: Hammond organ ('Voodoo Chile')
Chris Wood: Flute ('1983… (A Merman I Should Turn To Be'))
Mike Finnigan: Organ ('Rainy Day, Dream Away', 'Still Raining, Still Dreaming')
Al Kooper: Piano ('Long Hot Summer Night')
Jack Casady: Bass ('Voodoo Chile')
Buddy Miles: Drums ('Rainy Day, Dream Away', 'Still Raining, Still Dreaming')
Larry Faucette: Congas ('Rainy Day, Dream Away', 'Still Raining, Still Dreaming')
Freddie Smith: Tenor saxophone ('Rainy Day, Dream Away', 'Still Raining, Still Dreaming')
Brian Jones: Percussion
Recorded at Olympic Studios; Record Plant; Mayfair Studios
Producer: Jimi Hendrix
Engineers: Eddie Kramer, Gary Kellgren
The Sweet Inspirations: Backing vocals ('Burning Of The Midnight Lamp')
Chart placings: UK: 6, US: 1

The axis had predicted a return 'to the smell of a world that has burnt'. After the flames had been doused at Monterey and The Experience's second album had been declared by *Rolling Stone*'s Jim Miller as 'the finest voodoo album' – an insightful and prescient labelling – it was already apparent that Hendrix's sound was developing beyond blues rock. The voodoo religion blends African and Catholic beliefs, and Hendrix was said to have been energised by Miller's epithet, and considered his next works as 'electric church' music, consolidating his sound as an artefact of – and simultaneously a focus of a type of – worship; not in the sense of shallow acclaim, but as a concretion of experience, and increasingly the experiences of the disenfranchised.

The innocence (or experience, depending on whose side you're on) of the Summer of Love, was turning to fear and anxiety. The same month The Experience's third and final album was released, also suffered the obscene murder of Martin Luther King: dreams already seemed to be ashes. Nevertheless, Hendrix responded creatively to not only this appalling act, but to a deeply disturbing coda – Hendrix had seen revellers in a Virginia bar 'celebrating' the assassination. In his Newark set the next night, he played a profoundly moving jam in praise of King, while many of the audience wept. A later instrumental 'MLK' found its way onto bootlegs; 'MLK' standing for Martin

Luther King. It's a piece that echoes 'Angel' and 'May This Be Love' in its tender strength. Hendrix also later donated $5,000 to the King memorial fund.

However, 1968 began inauspiciously with Hendrix facing police charges over his destruction of a hotel room in Sweden, inspiring the track 'My Friend'. His live triumphs were beginning to pall, with a seemingly endless tour that had the band exhausted from zigzagging across America, taking him further from Record Plant and Mayfair: the New York studios where much of the double album *Electric Ladyland* would be born. Nevertheless, despite Hendrix's frustration with constant gigging and the requirement to perform, he often filled the studio with a posse of fans. Perversely, that which he was trying to escape, he encouraged, and recording sessions were sometimes sprawling and unfocused, as he was responding to his live audience more than to the needs of the recorded material. Notwithstanding, innovation and perfection was attained, but at a cost. Chandler quit during the recording because of the endless takes: a far cry from the quicksilver *Are You Experienced* sessions. He remarked on the bonus DVD with the debut album reissue that recording songs rapidly made them more 'current'. As the first album was reflecting contemporary sound as much as it was innovating, this seems a fair comment. But *Electric Ladyland* was developing beyond this, and its originality was always going to reflect Hendrix's 'current' vision, however long that might take. But some of Chandler's production was used, despite him not being credited.

Chandler wasn't the only one moving on. The days of The Experience's power trio were also numbered, as other (credited) musicians augmented their sound on the album, and Redding felt excluded. He told Chris Welch that there were times he'd nap in the studio, waiting for his cue, as Hendrix laid down track after track. But *Electric Ladyland* is the true masterpiece in Hendrix's *oeuvre*, and was entirely worth these 'sacrifices'.

In what was becoming a bizarre tradition, the cover work once again irked Hendrix. This time the gatefold sleeve included a spread of naked women photographed by David Montgomery. Hendrix did not disagree on the grounds of decency (indeed, the band can be found posing with two topless women for some earlier publicity shots), but felt the photography was poor and the concept wasn't indicative of the album as a whole. Predictably, the album was banned from some shops, with others using brown paper to clothe it. Even though Hendrix felt it was tacky and poorly executed, it perhaps influenced the cover of John Lennon and Yoko Ono's 1968 album *Unfinished Music No. 1: Two Virgins*: the nude couple *also* being obscured by a brown paper bag. Yet, according to Kathy Etchingham, Hendrix purchased *Two Virgins* because of his curiosity. Incidentally, Lennon and Ono had posed for the photograph at Hendrix and Etchingham's previous address, Montagu Square. Nevertheless, for his own work, Hendrix had preferred some shots by Linda Eastman (soon to be McCartney) of The Experience posing with the Alice in Wonderland sculpture in Central Park. The relaxed images and the association of a parallel world are certainly a better fit, the album being a kind of electric wonderland.

But there's also a sense of going through the looking glass too. It's illuminating to take a closer look at the 'Letter To A Room Full of Mirrors' that Hendrix wanted to be part of the album artwork. Moreover, the image was important enough to be remade for a *Rising Sun* track too. The letter is in the style of author Jack Kerouac: a beatific stream of consciousness, blended with the rancour of 'Like A Rolling Stone'. It could be that Hendrix's letter is to himself, if we extrapolate from the song too: 'I used to live in a room full of mirrors/All I could see was me'. But the target does seem wider – perhaps his critics characterised by 'the slow-motion speeded up sound that sometimes cut so deep, that sound was from those chellophane (sic) typewriters'. It seems like nonsense, but the phrase 'slowed down' implies a lack of insight because of the speed of the jobbing hack, and the 'chellophane' has a fat, artless echo like the gossipy typewriter itself. It continues, relentlessly:

> ...the sky cracked wide open and split many of his Brothers and Sisters heads all over the world apart at the approximately same... "That's law and order", said the Border Guard as his hard head weighted something like wet bread – which to explain through brain rain as that's...well...Bro, is this here country all what much ahead?

The allusion to nationalism is incisive, with the wet bread image startling, and the 'static' in the air that Hendrix would later comment on here, a brain rain. The 'chellophane' becomes the threatening telephone (a trope that will reappear in 'Long Hot Summer Night'.) But what is the letter about? Perhaps it recounts a spiritual and physical journey; an epiphany on the nature of freedom. Whatever, it introduces the experience of listening to this album, perfectly, with Hendrix meeting Terra Mama – or Mother Earth – finding the Ladyland.

Electric Ladyland is a towering work and the true masterpiece in The Experience's canon. Admittedly, some of the production isn't as crisp as on the previous two albums, and it demands much from the listener in terms of concentration, even stamina. But there's a feeling of alchemy about it. Nine months in the making, *Electric Ladyland* continues to birth innovations on each listen.

'...And The Gods Made Love' (Jimi Hendrix)

Opening the album with a big bang in more ways than one, this is a storm of noise and turbulence with panning drum effects. It stands amongst Hendrix's creation-myth songs, but now it's entirely conveyed through sound. Hendrix had revealed that he wanted to write 'mythology stories' through his music, and this track is an aural genesis. The storm gathers pace, swirling and twirling, building to the rustling of the climax before falling away in deep breaths. It's a curiously wintry sound, linking it to Hendrix's airy elemental songs like 'Little Wing'. This might seem a curious comparison, but the sense of rise and fall and ethereal elevation is evident in both. Previously, Hendrix described to *NME* what it was like to leap from a plane with only the promise of the parachute: 'It's the most alone feeling in the world. Then you feel that tug on your collar, and there's that big beautiful white mushroom above you, and the air's going shhhhhhh past your eyes.'

This seems to be the closest he got to recreating that sound and atmosphere. Whilst it divided fans, it's an arresting opening, a feeling of birth. Moreover, part of the sound comes from a slowed-down recording of Hendrix saying, 'Okay, one more time,' hinting at the last and definitive word of The Experience. Tellingly, the piece had been previously monikered 'At Last The Beginning'.

'Have You Ever Been (To Electric Ladyland)' (Jimi Hendrix)

After the Sturm und Drang of the opener, this soul ballad is anticlimactic. Whilst the vocals and arrangement are strong, it's *lyrically* more pertinent to the feel of the album than sonically. 'Electric ladies' was Hendrix's term for groupies, but it could also be reasoned that the real electric lady was his Fender. The track is joined to the previous one by that familiar knock-knock sound that keeps haunting Hendrix: the train track's rattle first heard on *Are You Experienced.*

The guitar lines are dreamy, and the track's brevity prevents it from becoming too torpid. The solo is gorgeous, but the 'make love, make love, make love' refrain takes it close to Floaters territory (American 1970s R&B group), and at times it skirts close to parody, which could be intentional. Yet it does show Hendrix more in control of the timbre of his voice. Whilst on a package tour with Engelbert Humperdinck, it's said that Hendrix would watch him, to steal singing tips (and his record collection contained at least two Bing Crosby albums).

The track is also notable for having Hendrix on the bass, making this a two-piece performance, as Redding doesn't play anything: a sign of things to come.

'Crosstown Traffic' (Jimi Hendrix)

The attack of this song comes like a car accelerating, then rushing past – the sound given speed by its panning across the speakers, stridently impatient yet vivifying New York taxi horns that are really kazoos. This is one of Hendrix's best-loved and well-known songs, but is curious in that there's no solo (Living Colour's joyful cover adds one), and the hook doesn't really come from the guitar as much as the kazoos and the backing vocals (which include Traffic's Dave Mason). Coincidentally, New York saw the first mass production of the kazoo, though its invention has been traced back to Africa. In fact, Hendrix doesn't use a genuine kazoo, but a comb and paper improvisation. The kazoo's distinctive sound can be found on Frank Zappa's *Freak Out!*, *Sgt. Pepper*'s 'Lovely Rita', and on 'Corporal Clegg' by Pink Floyd, who took the surname from Thaddeus von Clegg, the kazoo's craftsman. 'Lovely Rita' may have been echoing in Hendrix's mind, not only for it being a song about traffic control but because of its honky-tonk-like piano – an aspect Hendrix added to 'Crosstown Traffic', most obvious in the intro and fade-out. It's also one of his most straightforward rock 'n' roll tracks – certainly made his own by the syncopations – and it may also have awakened memories of Little Richard, even though Kramer has said the piano was his idea.

But the inspiration might lie elsewhere too. In *Jimi Hendrix: The Man, The Magic, the Truth*, Chris Stamp told Sharon Lawrence about the time he spent with Hendrix in his London flat:

> Everyone's talking. The music is playing. There's traffic noise from Edgware Road. Everything is noisy. Loud! As I'm sitting there, every minute, Jimi looks up and says something about a sound. After ten minutes, I start to realise this guy is hearing sounds like no one else hears them. He was extracting things from the air in this great big pitcher of sound.

'Crosstown Traffic' is evidence of this; of taking the urban mood and getting it onto vinyl. The metaphor of Hendrix having a 'great big pitcher of sound' is gorgeous, with his pouring these out through the strings of his guitar: a cornucopia of sound. But we can also hear *picture* of sound here, too, with Hendrix drawing a city in parps, squalls and squawks. There might even be some kind of pun with Traffic's Dave Mason on backing vocals. Furthermore, the surprising poignancy of the 'blue' traffic lights from 'The Wind Cries Mary' are subverted with 'But ah, darling, can't you see my signals turn from green to red/And with you I can see a traffic jam straight up ahead'. This is Hendrix speeding away from his musical past.

On the surface, the extended metaphor of trying to get through traffic is employed to demonstrate frustration in communicating with his lover. The conceit was previously used on Soul Survivors' 'Expressway To Your Heart' ('I've been trying to get to you a long time!'): an American top-five hit in 1967. Furthermore, Amen Corner covered it on their 1968 debut album *Round Amen Corner*. Hendrix had jammed with them at the Speakeasy, playing the *Sgt. Pepper* title track, and later gigged around the UK with the group on a package tour that also included Pink Floyd and The Move, and Amen Corner's set may well have reminded Hendrix of 'Expressway To Your Heart'. Andy Fairweather Low – Amen Corner's vocalist and later guitarist for Bill Wyman's Rhythm Kings – sang backing vocals on a re-recording of 'Stone Free' with Hendrix in 1969 too.

But another spark for 'Crosstown Traffic' is more worrying: Hendrix told *International Times'* Jane Mendelsohn: 'People, they don't give me any inspiration except bad inspiration, to write songs like 'Crosstown Traffic' 'cause that's the way they put themselves in front of me, the way they present themselves.'

Despite Billboard predicting that it would be a big hit on the heels of 'All Along The Watchtower', 'Crosstown Traffic' merely dented the US top 50 and UK top 40, backed with another travelling song: 'Gypsy Eyes'.

'Voodoo Chile' (Jimi Hendrix)

This is a superb jam that reveals more with each listen. Hendrix explained his definition of jamming to *Eye* magazine: 'And half the people don't know how to jam nowadays. They don't play together... they don't really think about the other person. That's what jamming is about: it's playing with everybody.'

This song is the apotheosis of this.

Chandler remarked that by the time this album was being recorded, Hendrix had moved away from arriving with completed songs. Kramer added that, nevertheless, Hendrix had 'visions' about the sounds he was trying to achieve. Whilst he might not have been armed with chord sequences and lyrics, he had moods he wished to recreate. Part of the vision (or rather sound) for this cut is the overdubbed audience murmur, lending it a smoky blues club atmosphere. There's a real shift in Hendrix's sound here, as The Experience is heightened by Traffic's Steve Winwood on organ and Jefferson Airplane's Jack Casady on palpitating bass.

Hendrix's half-mournful/half-prideful voice confesses, 'I'm a voodoo chile/ Lord I'm a voodoo chile', before the band slink in. As he recounts his ominous birth, the organ swells, thickening right at the moment he begins to invoke imagery of flight. The organ then tethers the sound whilst Hendrix's first solo trills. It's the sound of a gathering mist, of the destiny of midnight clouds, of a blood moon rusting the landscape.

The animal imagery that stalks the lyric is interesting too. Eagles and lions hunt – delineating the antihero as brave but predatory; savage; fierce. Steve Winwood's staccato organ is like the lion – low, growling, pouncing – and the guitar is in the air element as a night bird. It's as if the guitar and organ are two halves of a psyche, with the frenzied organ dominating until the close when the guitar claws it down in a howling explosion of orgiastic triumph.

The lyrics take us on a journey from the fiery opening of the red moon to the airy hummingbird, the predatory mountains, the 'liquid gardens' and 'new red sand'. The song's landscape may have been inspired by Hendrix's ambivalence towards his home town: 'pretty Seattle'. He continued in Michael Lydon's *Flashbacks: Eyewitness Accounts of the Rock Revolution*: '...all that water and mountains. I couldn't live there, but it was beautiful'. The various religions that make up voodoo are not homogenous, but share certain principles, especially regarding the worship of ancestors and the turning of everyday objects into sacred items. Conventions of the blues are teamed with totemic animal imagery, including the American hummingbird, which creates its sound through the flapping of its wings, making them an apposite symbol of Hendrix's longing to recreate the ambience and experiences of his parachute jumps. The voodoo chile has control of the elements, whereas the highway chile merely controlled the miles – and moving from reporting in the third person, Hendrix is now singing in the first person.

The line 'My arrows are made of desire' alludes to Blake's 'Jerusalem', which describes the defending of a utopia, although Hendrix's arrows have a sharper, phallic quality, but Blake also continues with air and fire imagery, using experience to defend and protect innocence. Additionally, not only is Hendrix citing from various cultural sources, but Mitchell and Winwood's contributions are also diffuse, evoking an eastern tone; traditional church music being evoked too. The deservedly ubiquitous 'A Whiter Shade Of Pale' used organ to imbue a quasi-religious solemnity, but Hendrix's employment is no longer reverent, but somehow excitingly profane in this context, whilst Mitchell's jazz-influenced drum solo is the sound of church spires cracking and falling. The guitar riffs in unison with Hendrix's vocal, keeps the song in the blues tradition, but it's also looking forward in the symbolist work of the solo, drums and organ. Kramer felt this line-up was Hendrix's ideal band, and this track is certainly testimony to a fantastic chemistry.

On Marc Bolan's first electric album with Tyrannosaurus Rex – *A Beard of Stars* – he sings of the 'Elemental Child': a song that recounts, 'Torch girl of the marshes/Her kiss is a whip of the moon…' The tracks play out with a frenzied jam, owing much to 'Voodoo Chile' in imagery and tone. Bolan's producer Tony Visconti recalls Bolan expressing a desire to play like Hendrix. It seems likely that The Experience were an influence on Bolan plugging in again and the shift towards T. Rex. Furthermore, the second T. Rex album *Electric Warrior* seems to take inspiration from The Experience's final album title. Indeed, Hendrix's influence on glam rock seems under-explored. As a flamboyant performer whose clothes and hairstyle could be seen as a move towards androgyny, and with Hendrix's revivifying of 1950s rock 'n' roll licks, his space lyrics and his sexual simulations with the guitar (to be taken further by David Bowie fellating Mick Ronson's Les Paul), he's something of a glam blueprint. Hendrix's Hopi imagery and fuzz tone informed Norman Greenbaum's proto-glam 'Spirit In The Sky', which fed back into the fuzz and fey of T. Rex's 'Ride A White Swan'. Indeed, Greenbaum told *Rolling Stone*: 'I had come across a greeting card that said 'Spirit in the Sky'. And it was American Indians sitting in front of a tepee, with the fire going, and being spiritual towards what they had deemed God, which was a spirit in the sky. I think it was the Hopi. So I went, 'That's kind of interesting.'

'Little Miss Strange' (Noel Redding)

Although it's something of a palate cleanser after the previous track's dense flavours, 'Little Miss Strange' nevertheless has many compelling moments. Whilst waiting for an increasingly tardy Hendrix, Redding decided to use his time wisely and recorded this song. When Hendrix eventually heard it, he was impressed enough to add some of his most concise and sprightly guitar work. In some ways, the track demonstrates the guitarist's 'personalities' – that is, there's the first tight rock 'n' roll solo that he might've played whilst backing Little Richard that segues into a bluesier rock vibe à la Cream, before finally squawking out with liberal use of psychedelic wah-wah: the guitar's evolution, if you will. Hendrix's use of plucking and damping is effective and keeps the attention, whilst the song itself is a respectable attempt at power pop with a noticeably English sound. Redding's contributions (admittedly, not many) have been unfairly assessed. It's to be remembered that Hendrix was a fan of the parochial – and at times lovely – songs of Scottish pop band Marmalade, and respected well-crafted pop as much as blues or rock. The change in tempo at the end is a little treat too, with an almost Celtic feel. Whilst the lyrics:

> Little miss strange came out of the darkness
> Walked across my head
> And stood beneath the light
> I told her about the dream I had the other night

This shows the 1960s tradition of songs about uncanny women, like Redding's 'She's So Fine', and continues the 1960s obsession with fever dreams – as apparent in The Electric Prunes' 'I Had Too Much To Dream Last Night', The Zombies' 'Hung Up On A Dream', and of course the dream imagery Hendrix himself used.

'Long Hot Summer Night' (Jimi Hendrix)

This song's title was a phrase the media had previously used to describe the race riots that thundered across America, especially in the summer of 1967. Whilst this can't be dismissed, the song seems an almost frivolous tale of sexual longing. But alongside this are images of chaos, with 'everybody on fire' and 'the telephone keeps on screaming'! The guitar line after this exclamation is a superb recreation of anguish, and there's the first mention of a baby coming to rescue Hendrix, that would reappear on the more reverent 'Angel'.

The arrangement has a suitably torrid quality, with Hendrix playing bass and Al Kooper providing a (low-mixed) piano, lending an undercurrent of sound like a heat haze surrounding it. Hendrix rated Kooper's work with Dylan, and gifted him a guitar. Sadly, Kooper eventually sold it, his homes repeatedly broken into as unscrupulous thieves coveted the prized relic. Kooper's piano is most audible after the line 'But the silliest move melted all those inside', as it announces 'everyone's on fire'. The song might also be alluding to Hendrix's friction with his bandmates: in particular, Redding. Kooper told *Classic Rock*:

> Working on *Electric Ladyland*, I didn't see any evidence that he'd fallen out with Noel Redding. I was only there for a three-hour session. We recorded 'Long Hot Summer Night' from scratch. The song had never been done before. I got paid union scale. I played and he said, 'Thanks, man, catch you later on.' In the room, it was his band and me. It was no stretch at all as a musician. Noel did play bass when I was in the room. Maybe that was replaced afterwards by Hendrix. Jimi sang the backing vocal tracks.

James Marshall Hendrix igniting the world with his Fender Strat and Marshall stack.

Above: The Jimi Hendrix Experience. Producer Chas Chandler said, 'That's what made the money: them three.' (*Polydor*)

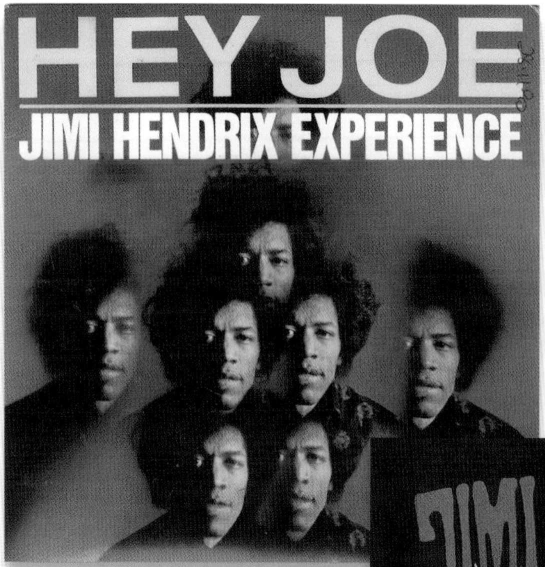

Left: The cover for the debut UK single in December, 1966. Despite there being approximately 1800 cover versions, this one remains definitive. (*Polydor*)

Right: Thrilling and unsettling use of the Hendrix chord, E7#9, characterised the Experience's second single, March 1967. (*Polydor*)

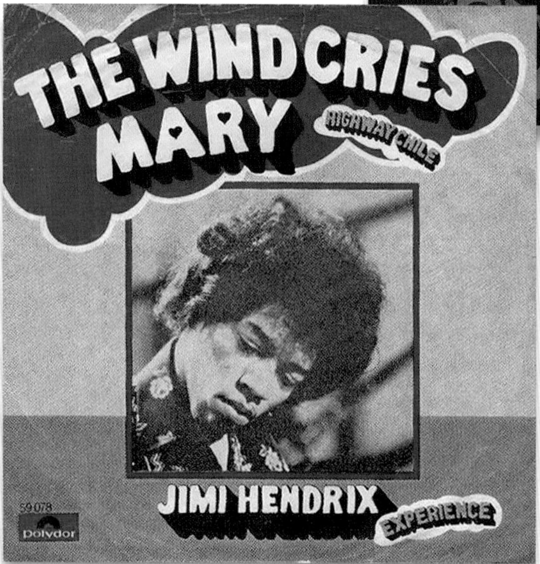

Left: The third UK single, May 1967, referenced colour for more sober effect: 'The traffic lights turn blue tomorrow.' (*Polydor*)

Right: Mitch Mitchell and Noel Redding finally get a look-in on their debut album's cover from May 1967. (*Bruce Fleming / Polydor*)

Left: Hendrix's hand-drawn sketches for the cover design more closely matched this image. (*Karl Ferris / Polydor*)

Right: Infrared technique illustrated well the album's psychedelic experimentation on the US cover of their debut. (*Reprise*)

Left: Performing 'Hey Joe' for TV show Beat Club in March 1967. 'Purple Haze' followed.

Right: Drummer Mitchell Mitchell was described as a player of 'riffs' by Queen's Roger Taylor.

Left: *Ultimate Guitar* declared Noel Redding as one of the most under-rated bassists, whose technique was 'perfect' for Hendrix.

Right: The Monterey Festival in June 1968 saw Hendrix perform a searing version of The Trogg's 'Wild Thing'.

Left: Hendrix invited Redding into the band for two reasons: his blues techniques and his magnificent hair!

Right: At the climax of 'Wild Thing', Hendrix sets fire to his guitar, outdoing The Who's 'auto-destructive art'.

Left: *Axis Bold as Love*. Released in December 1967, Hendrix wanted to acknowledge his Native American roots. (*Polydor*)

Right: …however, a miscommunication resulted in Hendrix being recast as a Hindu God in this design by David King. (*Polydor*)

Right: Hendrix's magnum opus *Electric Ladyland* from October 1968, was almost overshadowed by David Montgomery's controversial UK cover photography. (*Polydor*)

Left: The US plumped for a Karl Ferris image again – this time Hendrix was, tellingly, alone. (*Reprise*)

Above: The newly formed Gypsy Sun and Rainbows shredding the Star-Spangled Banner at Woodstock in August 1969.

Below: Hendrix performing in Maui, Hawaii in July 1970, with Isabella, his white Strat.

Above: Mitch Mitchell returned to the drums and Billy Cox had stayed with Hendrix on bass from the previous line up, Band of Gypsys.

Below: The Live in Maui album is a powerful collection including both past cuts from The Experience and future classics.

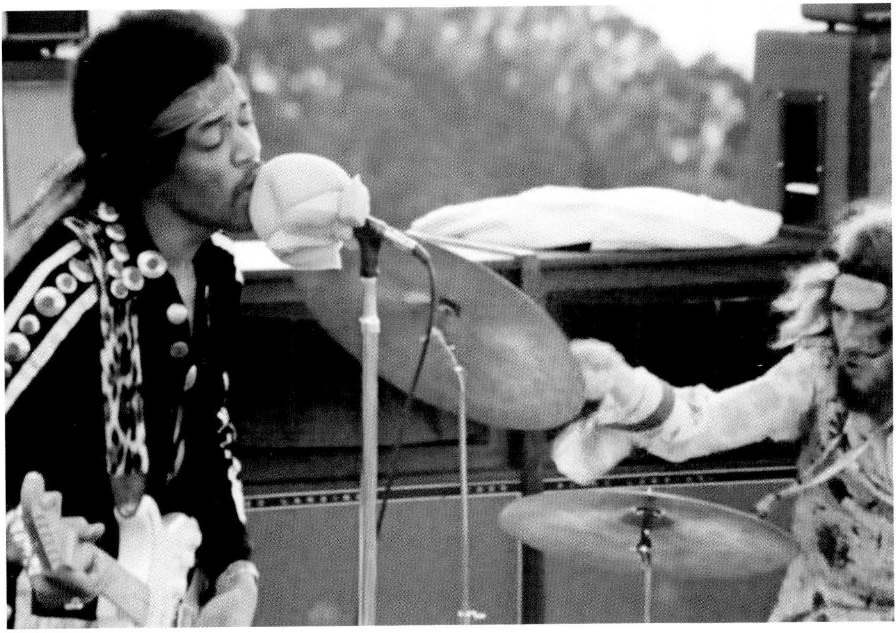

Left: 1970 began with Hendrix recording this live set in the Fillmore East. He opened with 'Auld Lang Syne'. (*Capitol*)

Right: Band of Gypsys found Hendrix sharing the frontman's limelight with drummer Buddy Miles, who sang two of the tracks.

Right: This box set from 2000 showed the Hendrix vaults still had much to offer - from the alternate 'Purple Haze' to unreleased cuts like 'Country Blues'. (*MCA*)

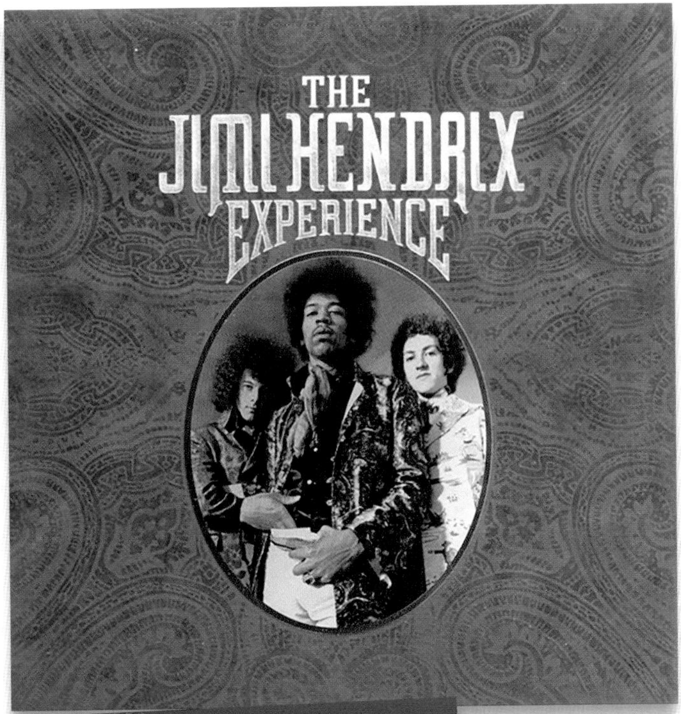

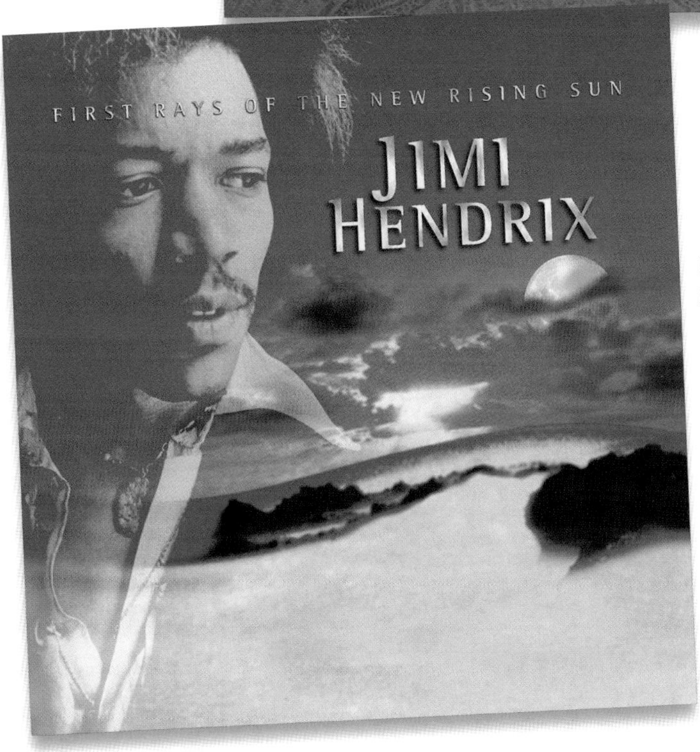

Left: The best posthumous Hendrix release, this compilation from April 1997 is evidence of how much more he could have achieved. (*MCA*)

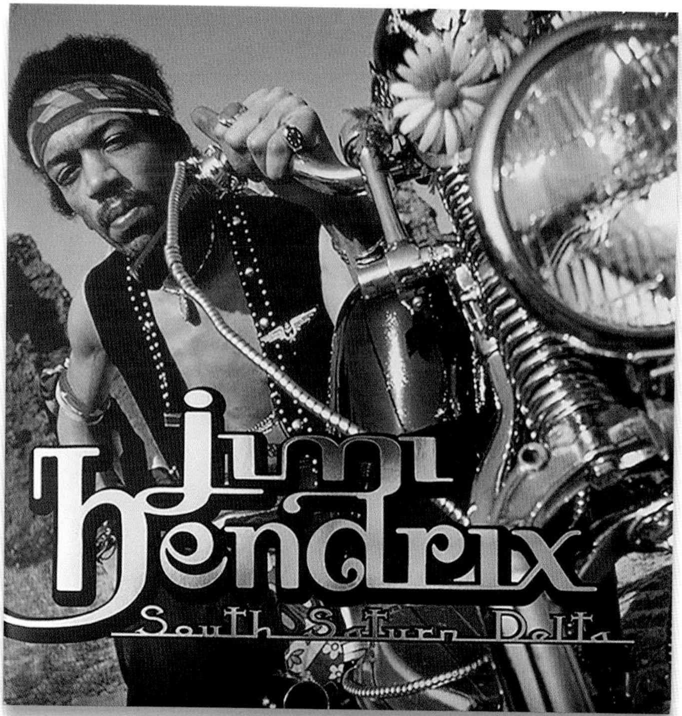

Left: Another Bob Dylan cover, 'Drifter's Escape', is one of the unreleased tracks on this collection from October 1997. (*MCA*)

Right: Appearing in March 2010, Hendrix finally got his wish – a Linda McCartney photograph for his album cover art. (*Legacy*)

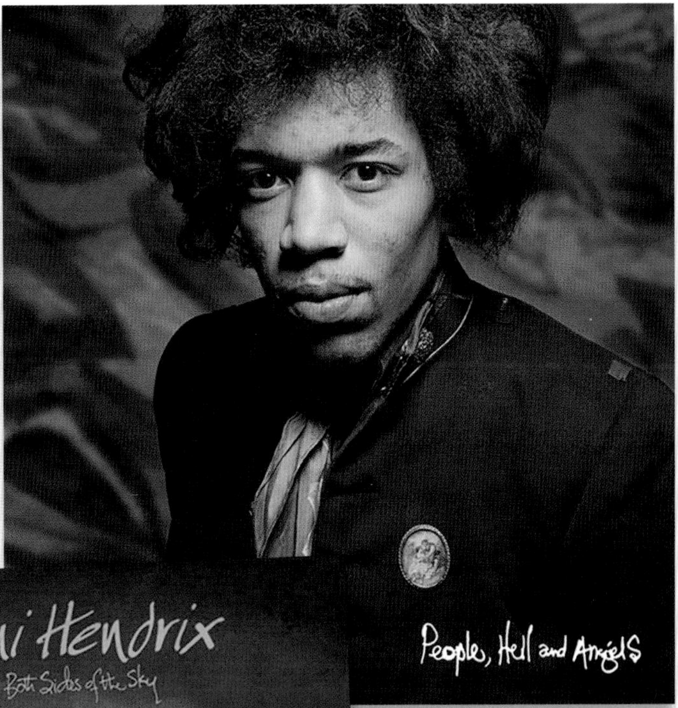

Right: March 2013 saw Hendrix hitting number two on the US *Billboard* chart. (*Legacy*)

Left: This compilation from March 2018 includes collaborations with Stephen Stills and Johnny Winter. (*Legacy*)

Left: Here Hendrix is a one-man power trio for the cover of the only compilation released in his lifetime, April 1968. (*Polydor*)

Right: David Montgomery's image was first used inside *Electric Ladyland's* cover: a petrol fire created the effect behind Hendrix.

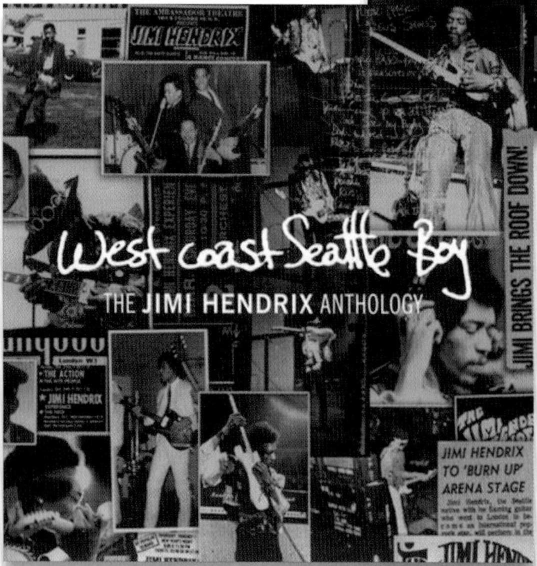

Left: An excellent overview from 2010, this includes a documentary by Bob Smeaton, who also worked on The Beatles' *Anthology*. (*Legacy*)

Right: This 1997 release has performances from *Top Gear*, *Saturday Club* and *Happening for Lulu* amongst others. (MCA)

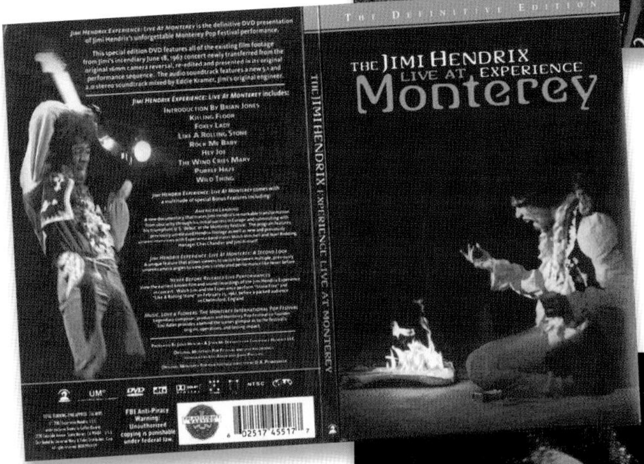

Left: The coincidentally named Jim Marshall captured this image of Hendrix igniting his guitar. He'd suffered hand burns on previous attempts.

Right: This round up of live recordings from the UK and US includes a rare version of Johnny B. Goode. (*Polydor*)

Left: Archivist John McDermott derided this counter-culture film as 'an embarrassing failure.' Hendrix is the best thing about it. (*Reprise*)

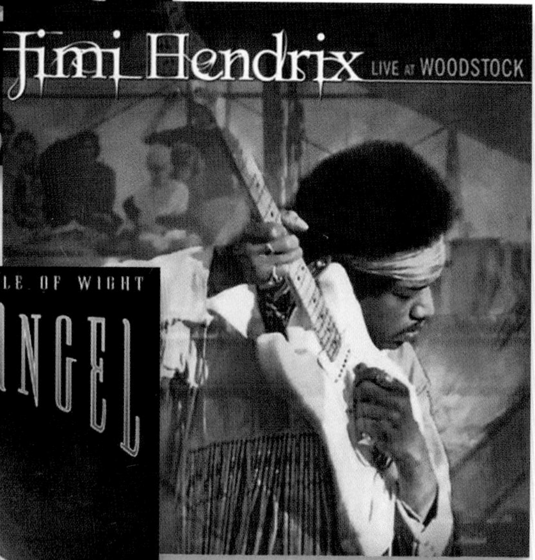

Above: *Hendrix at Woodstock*, where his controversial 'Star Spangled Banner' also powerfully referenced military funeral hymns. (*Universal*)

Left: Like many artists that appeared at the Isle Of Wight festival, Hendrix's appearance at the famous 1970 event was filmed for posterity. (*Sony*)

Kooper also recalled how they'd come to be acquainted:

> I met Jimi at a soundcheck at the Monterey Pop Festival, where I was the stage manager. We spoke in the wings and he invited me to play with him that night on 'Like A Rolling Stone', but I had to turn him down because I was working, and (promoter) Lou Adler would have got very mad at me if I'd ducked out. You don't want to fuck with Lou Adler. Every inch of me wanted to do it.

'Long Hot Summer Night' talks about two characters: Little Annie and Roman the Candle. John Waters' short 1966 film *Roman Candles* – featuring bizarre collages including drag artists dressed as nuns – seems to link to these implied sexual gymnastics. Furthermore, the drag queen Divine plays hide-and-seek in the film, just as Roman the Candle does, making this song a weird but effective and surrealistic blend of politics, sexuality and voyeurism, with even the telephone seeming to have a phallic potency: 'Blew its horn across the room and scared Little Annie…'. The reference to 'sugar walls' and 'candy canes' might have inspired Prince's similarly steamy and suggestive 'Sugar Walls' – recorded by Sheena Easton in 1984, and which found its way onto the notorious Filthy Fifteen list.

The early version of 'Long Hot Summer Night' to be found on *West Coast Seattle Boy* is slower and softer, with a sleepy vocal, showing that Hendrix first heard it as a soul number in a similar vein to 'Have You Ever Been (To Electric Ladyland)'. Perhaps realising that this might seem derivative, he sped it up. Its recalling of 'Wild Thing' is less evident in the album version too.

'Come on (Let the Good Times Roll)' (Earl King)

A rip-roaring cover of the Earl King song, but nevertheless, it seems superfluous on *Electric Ladyland.* Mitchell felt it was to pad the album out, and indeed it was a late addition that does seem to stall the meticulous building of the album's atmosphere. Perhaps this was Hendrix looking back over his shoulder, acknowledging the roots of these brave new sounds, or it might've been a little talismanic as he made a sonic leap. However, towards the close, Redding's bass really kicks up its heels, and it directs us to the more futuristic blues of 'Gypsy Eyes'.

'Gypsy Eyes' (Jimi Hendrix)

Opening with a drum rhythm that builds anticipation before Hendrix's guitar blindingly lasers in, 'Gypsy Eyes' is a skilful blend of the static and dynamic. The scratchy guitar fills after the first chorus and the slight increase in tempo imply a delicious and infectious impatience, with the best parts of 'Stone Free' and '51st Anniversary' coming together.

The lyrics refer to a curious incident whereby strange men had contacted Hendrix, claiming to be his real father: 'Two strange men fighting to the death for me'. Although, in some ways, this could also allude to a tussle between the contractual obligations of Chalpin and Jeffery. The song continues:

Well I walked right on up to your rebel roadside
The one that rambles on for a million miles
Yes, I walked down this road searching for your love

Now the nomad is looking for a place to drop anchor; 'hypnotised', ironically, by gypsy eyes. The relentless backing has a hypnotic feel that complements this well. The shifts to double- time meant that this was a difficult track to record, requiring multiple takes, so much so that Chandler quit. In the notes for *The Jimi Hendrix Experience* box set, Kramer explained: 'Jimi really was taken with the concept of sound moving in front and behind you rather than simply at you.' Hence the multiple takes to sculpt a three-dimensional sound. Hendrix's guitar vibrates, rolls and leaps around the track, even managing to sound like a laser or death ray at times. Indeed, the guitar tone sounds as if it's *illuminated*, perhaps mimicking searchlights striking gypsy eyes. Kramer's comment is a fascinating insight, and builds on the 3D idea that Hendrix tried to use to revitalise 'Hey Joe'. In some ways, 'Gypsy Eyes' is the track that captures much of where Hendrix's music would grow to in the future, with flashes of 'Freedom' in its embroidered textures.

Later on, Band of Gypsys bassist Billy Cox told John McDermott: 'We weren't playing by notes. We were playing by patterns. We were always trying to hook these patterns together to make songs.' This is the technique Hendrix is using here, though losing Chandler and possibly Redding in the process, and is why he'd be ready to form a new band after *Electric Ladyland*.

'Burning Of The Midnight Lamp' (Jimi Hendrix)

The album's oldest track – the compellingly baroque 'Burning Of The Midnight Lamp' – had been recorded in 1967 and released as a summer single in the UK, backed with 'The Stars That Play With Laughing Sam's Dice'. For the first time since 'Hey Joe', Hendrix decided to use female backing vocals, supplied here by The Sweet Inspirations: including mother of Whitney, Cissy Houston. Certainly, their sweet but powerful embellishments are much more effective than on 'Hey Joe', lending an elegance and gravitas.

The track is also notable for its debuting of Hendrix's wah-wah guitar effect – a sound he admired on Cream's 'Tales Of Brave Ulysses' – but is more defined by the harpsichord that Hendrix plays. Harpsichord can be heard on The Beatles' 'Fixing A Hole' from *Sgt. Pepper*, but Hendrix's record collection also contained an album of Bach compositions arranged for the instrument. Furthermore, The Bonzo Dog Doo-Dah Band would make similarly unexpected use of the instrument on their wonderful 'Music For The Head Ballet' from their debut album *Gorilla* in the autumn of 1967. The harpsichord predates the piano, and operates by plucking rather than hitting, making its more immediate attack a complementary sound to the guitar. Hendrix was said to be delighted when he first played the riff on it, as – so rarely for him – it matched the sound in his head. There's a tenderness to the riff; a contained gentle warmth like a candle flame, and a simultaneous melancholy haunts it. In contrast, the guitar is a wetter sound to threaten the midnight lamp, and the combination of the harpsichord with the wah-wah guitar increases the feeling of transition at the heart of the piece as symbolised by the midnight setting. Shapiro quotes Hendrix on the song's gestation: 'There are some very personal things in there. But I think everyone can understand the feeling when you're travelling that no matter what your address, there is no place you can call home. The feeling of a man in a little old house in the middle of a desert where he is burning the midnight lamp...'

There are further striking images in the song, including 'Now the smiling portrait of you is still hanging on my frowning wall'. Here there is a clever transference of his feelings to the house – a kind of pathetic fallacy that would be continued in the imagery of 'Long Hot Summer Night'. 'Burning Of The Midnight Lamp' isn't often cited as one of Hendrix's (few) love songs, but it really functions as one, with the midnight lamp being a metaphor for a memory of a lost love, though not necessarily love of a person, i.e. 'I continue to burn the midnight lamp'. Often Hendrix's best love songs are odes to music itself, and the midnight lamp might really be a metaphor for the effects of his past and the afterglow of the blues as he moves into increasingly more complex music: 'The morning is dead/And the day is too'.

Indeed, there is something nocturnal about the sound of *Electric Ladyland*: the Dionysian flip to the Apollonian *Axis: Bold as Love*. To return to Hendrix's fascination with innocence and experience, there's the confessional line, 'Soon enough, time will tell about the circus and the wishing well'. That is, his innocentia will be reconfigured by experience. It's a track that reveals more with each listen, and Hendrix remained understandably proud of it. Even his live versions have a rare reverence not extended to the rest of his work. In the stage performances, his guitar stands in for the harpsichord, lending a foggier sound that doesn't evoke the little house in the desert, but shows the song works well beyond this idiosyncratic tone, having a deep poignancy.

Hendrix did admit to being unhappy with the production, and wondered if it could be re-recorded. The clarity heard on his earlier singles certainly isn't as acute, but the hazier sound imbues an apposite glow. But Hendrix's affection is clear by his including it on an album released a full year later. In fact, 'Voodoo Chile' shares a twilight atmosphere with it, making it clear that the home of 'Burning Of The Midnight Lamp' really is The Experience's third album, despite it being recorded earlier.

Unjustly, the single merely dented the top 20, stalling at 18. Reviewing it for *Melody Maker*, Bruce Johnson was lukewarm but did admire the song's 'Wagnerian climax' with The Sweet Inspirations keening like Valkyries. The song is much less bombastic than this implies, having more in common with the elegance of an elegy. Rotary Connection – a psych soul band that included vocalist Minnie Riperton – make this apparent in their cover version on their 1969 album *Songs*.

'Rainy Day, Dream Away' (Jimi Hendrix)

A laconic, smooth piece of jazz-funk, this presents a change of weather after the earnest 'Burning Of The Midnight Lamp'. Indeed, this might be the sound of a voodoo chile who was born when the moon turned a sunflower yellow with its carefree shuffle and the chuckle in Hendrix's voice. Freddie Smith plays the saxophone, illustrating how complementary it is to Hendrix's sinuous guitar. The piece has the carefully informal atmosphere of Traffic's *Mr. Fantasy,* and Hendrix himself had occasionally played their (almost) title track live.

'Rainy Day, Dream Away' sways on until Hendrix's acquiescent guitar begins to squawk like a bird seeking freedom, and then temporarily fades away… a seagull passing overhead…

'1983… (A Merman I Should Turn to Be)' (Jimi Hendrix)

… leading us to the beautiful seascape that is '1983'.

At each corner of the earth is a cord fixing the planet to the sky. What will happen when the cords fray? Cherokee myth warns that the earth will plunge into the ocean, and all life will be lost. Hendrix seems thrilled by the idea of a subaquatic lifestyle, and this legend haunts many of his lyrics. The nature of the *transitional* is explored on other Hendrix tracks, but this is the most realised fruition of his ideas on this theme, perhaps only rivalled by 'Burning Of The Midnight Lamp', as the music rises as much to the challenge as the lyrics do. Hendrix elucidated on his employment of fantastical imagery, to Jane Mendelsohn in *International Times:*

> A lot of songs are fantasy type songs, so that people think you don't know what you are talking about at all, but it all depends on what the track before and after might have been. Like you might tell them something kinda hard, but you don't want to be a completely hard character in their minds and be known for all that, 'cause there's other sides of you, and sometimes they leak on to record too… that's where the fantasy songs come in. Like for instance, '1983' – that's something to keep your mind off what's happening today, but not necessarily completely hiding away from it like some people might do, with certain drugs and so forth…

Whilst the track is an aquatic fantasia, there is an implied dystopia that the song's characters are leaving behind, lifting it from the purely whimsical.

It's worth breaking down Hendrix's statement further. He seems to be revealing not only his method of reaching an audience, but his conflict too: that between the outrageous showman and the responsive virtuoso. There's also some impatience with the rock media's caricature of him: 'there's other sides' evinced by his moving to the double album format. But there's also an unease with being a spokesman. When Elvis Presley was asked his views on Vietnam in a 1972 Madison Square Garden interview, he remarked: 'Honey, I'd just sooner keep my own personal views about that to myself, 'cause I'm just an entertainer and I'd rather not say.' There is a canniness to this, in that Presley (and probably his manager Colonel Tom Parker) didn't want to deter listeners by declaring political allegiances because allegiances can also limit how an artist's work is received. That is, being a hard character can impact on the music, not just on it as a form of escapism, but can cloud the listener's experience, obscuring the innocence of song itself. Hendrix oscillated between anti-establishment fervour and, at times, deeply conservative comments; sealing either in print or music could potentially *classify* his work. Nevertheless, there are allegiances hinted at in his lyrics, and even in the music itself.

Arrestingly, '1983' opens with: 'Hurray I awake from yesterday/Alive but the war is here to stay', before painting a picture of an apocalyptic world (it's illuminating that Hendrix should choose the year before Orwell's hell) that the speaker and his love Catherina need to escape. Catherina evokes Kathy Etchingham, who explained in her autobiography *Through Gypsy Eyes* that she had no intention of following him to the bottom of the sea (!), and the name Catherina itself signifies purity, showing Hendrix was looking back nostalgically and regretfully as the earth is now a 'fighting nest'. Again, there is a keen image of domestic disharmony here. The song has also been thought to be partly a paean to Catharina Koch, whom Hendrix met when she was a chambermaid in a Gothenburg hotel, and whom he later mentioned in several interviews as being his girlfriend. However, the track is not a straightforward love song. The need for this submarine bolthole is much less about a pleasant diversion à la 'Octopus's Garden', and more about the need for colonisation of other worlds in the shadow of the bomb: 'Giant pencil and lipstick-tube-shaped things/ Continue to rain and cause screamin' pain'.

The idea of a civilisation below us might have germinated when Hendrix was a boy and exploring Seattle. When the city was built, it was at sea level and endured terrible flooding. The city was rebuilt but, thrillingly, left a hidden ghost town beneath. In Leon Hendrix's *Jimi Hendrix: A Brother's Story,* he recounts a time when they explored it: 'slipped through a portal into a forgotten world. There was an old, boarded-up barbershop, a general store and a hotel above, the city had built glass blocks into the new sidewalks - sun streamed through and illuminated our way.'

Not only did Hendrix experience unique aerial views of the world as a parachutist, but he'd looked up from a subterranean land too. His desire to not have music purely 'coming at' the listener, could partly stem from these unusual perspectives on the landscape.

The song guides us through the elements, with a sound collage that whistles, tinkles and whispers in the way Led Zeppelin would employ for the middle of

'Whole Lotta Love', before finally settling on water as the one element that will save us: linking us back to Catherina's purity. The track also shows Hendrix playing in a style similar to Fleetwood Mac's Peter Green, with crystal notes that Green would later use on another piece with a loose oceanic connection: 'Albatross'. It's simply one of Hendrix's most beautiful tones. As with 'Voodoo Chile', other musicians augment the band, including Traffic's Chris Wood on the avian-sounding flute, but 'Voodoo Chile's' elements were earth and fire. The album's second overture now balances this with its symbolism of air and water.

Rolling Stone's Tony Glover was disheartened by the track, lamenting: 'Hendrix structures a beautiful undersea mood, only to destroy it with some heavy-handed guitar. My first reaction was, "Why did he have to do that?" Then I thought that he created a beautiful thing but lost faith (in) it, and so destroyed it before anybody else could: in several ways, a bummer.'

Certainly, the undersea mood is tangible, but the guitar always seems controlled, with judicious embellishments provided by the percussion instrument the flexatone. This gives the impression of a bell, but here the bell tolls for a beginning, whilst the bell effects of 'Are You Experienced' implied an ending.

'Moon Turn The Tides… Gently, Gently Away' (Jimi Hendrix)

The seagull caws, flying out to dry land and the sound of wind through sand… It's a gasp of fresh air from a window before the storm continues and we must hurry inside.

'Still Raining, Still Dreaming' (Jimi Hendrix)

And that squawking bird again, portending the return of the rain here. Hendrix had recorded 'Rainy Day, Dream Away' as one piece, but felt it wasn't as evocative in its longer state. It would've unbalanced the album by having this and '1983' in the second half too. Here the guitar and Mike Finnigan's organ duet more together than in the first half, now resigned to the rhythm of the downpour. The organ builds and blurs like sheet rain on a window. Hendrix's guitar has previously blazed, stormed and thundered on this album, and now it's a deluge of sound. The track has a running, liquid timbre with drums splashing behind it.

Hendrix's music often works in two halves, or diptychs, as this track makes evident. It's as if there are movements to each of his songs, but he shrewdly splits them up, as in 'Little Wing' and 'Angel'; most obviously 'Voodoo Chile' and 'Voodoo Childe (Slight Return)', but also 'The Star-Spangled Banner' with 'Machine Gun': which would've been one of the most powerful A- and B-side singles if they'd been combined. In some ways, Hendrix didn't write songs as such, but movements, and what can seem repetitive in the early days, becomes one of his strengths later on: developing a theme across a number of songs.

'House Burning Down' (Jimi Hendrix)

When asked about the Los Angeles Watts riots, Hendrix told *Open City*: 'I don't like to see houses burning down… Maybe I'll have more to say later when I get more political.' Hendrix was never apolitical. Simply by being a mixed-race band, The Experience were making a social comment. But while Hendrix's political musings had been more oblique in the past, now they were becoming direct and provocative:

> Well I asked my friend where is that black smoke comin' from
> He just coughed and changed the subject and said, 'Oh I think it might snow some'

This continues with the apocalyptic (and also hints at 'All Along The Watchtower' imagery):

> Sisters and brothers, daddies, mothers standin' 'round cryin'
> When I reached the scene the flames were makin' a ghostly whine
> So I stood on my horse's back
> An' I screamed without a crack
> I say, 'Oh baby why'd you burn your brother's house down?'

Hendrix has moved from asking the vague 'Are you experienced?' to challenging protest and its causes. Being experienced is no longer about sex or drugs, but understanding the paradoxes of destruction for creation's sake and creative acts that lead to destruction. The red house over yonder is glowing with flame, and still, there's apathy. The snow imagery could allude to white power, yet Hendrix's views on race were not straightforward. In an interview with *Top of the Pops*' Tony Newmark, Hendrix developed Mark Twain's comments by giving his views on America: 'The dollar is their god. There is no such thing as a colour problem. It is a weapon for the negative forces who are trying to destroy the country. They are striving for dead, useless things, like sending guys around the moon.'

This reminds us of Hendrix's use of fire imagery in the wake of the combusting shuttle, but it also illustrates an exasperation with reducing America's social problems to race alone.

Nevertheless, questions of race were dividing the nation, with The Supremes' Mary Wilson commenting in *1967 – A Complete Rock Music History of the Summer of Love*: 'We were a black America. But we were still black first.' This captures Hendrix's ambivalence as ex-military – on the one hand, a patriot; on the other, seen as an inferior. As the first album that Hendrix recorded outside of London, it's to be expected that something of the combustible tension of the *long hot summer* would pervade the atmosphere of *Electric Ladyland*. In his autobiography, Noel Redding opined: 'In my experience, Jimi had blackness thrust upon him in certain respects - he was no keener on letting black people use him than he was willing to be exploited by white people.' Others felt that even if Hendrix was ambivalent politically, his race certainly informed his art. Mike Bloomfield – guitarist with The Paul Butterfield Blues Band and The

Electric Flag – observed to *Guitar Player*: 'Jimi was the blackest guitarist I ever heard. His music was deeply rooted in the blues, the oldest musical forms, like field hollers and gospel melodies.' Hendrix didn't have the blues 'thrust' upon him, but sought to preserve them whilst adapting and innovating. As many have pointed out, whether he chose to address race directly or obliquely, being in a multiracial band that combined music of black origin with elements of white music, couldn't be anything other than a political statement. It was much less what Hendrix *said*, and much more what he *did*. Despite many welcoming him in London, he also experienced hatred there. Brian Auger told *Classic Rock*:

> There was one night at Blaise's (September 1966). We'd just finished our set and Jimi had sat in, and he was leaving the club. The club was in a basement, so there was a big flight of stairs down, and then his girlfriend ran in saying, 'Brian, you've got to help Jimi! There's these guys who are threatening him!' This was a very strange thing to happen in London at that time, because it didn't matter what colour you were, man. So I told my roadie and a couple of guys from the band, and we all went, a crowd of us, to the bottom of the stairs and looked up, and there were these four huge South African guys – they looked like rugby players, all white guys – and they were shouting to Jimi, 'Come up here, kaffir!' We basically told them to fuck off, and fortunately for us, they actually did. A cab drew up and they decided they'd leave. I'd never seen anything like that in London.

But Hendrix had certainly experienced its like before, and 'House Burning Down' is the anguished sound of frustration at ingrained prejudice.

The track opens with an almost sobbing riff, before the verse's tango rhythm implies a blithe continuation in the face of coming chaos, but also the cliché of two-to-tango: a hint of the complexities in the societal conflicts. It then shifts into the gallop of the chorus, the consensus being disrupted by the hellfire-red sky, the situation getting beyond anyone's control. Hendrix told *Guitar Player*:

> All of my songs happen on the spur of the moment. On some records, you hear all this clash and bang and fanciness. But all we're doing is laying down the guitar tracks, and then we echo here and there. We're not adding false electronic things. We use the same thing anyone else would, but we use it with imagination and common sense. Like in 'House Burning Down', we made the guitar sound like it was on fire. It's constantly changing dimensions, and up on top, that lead guitar is cutting through everything.

The idea of 'changing dimensions' is the crux of Hendrix's unique style, and evokes his idea of 3D music. Furthermore, the fade-out looks forward to the thick turmoil of 'All Along The Watchtower', swooping and soaring above the flames, and also foreshadowing the assault and battery of 'The Star-Spangled Banner': songs that 'change the dimensions' of other people's music too.

'All Along The Watchtower' (Bob Dylan)

Are all covers ultimately acts of iconoclasm? Hendrix had already taken the traditional 'The Star-Spangled Banner' and deconstructed it; in some views, even vandalised it. He'd do the same again, taking a sepia Dylan track and transforming it into a vorticist masterpiece: a 2D blueprint of a song becoming 3D. It might very well be the greatest cover version ever.

Hendrix had contributed to other sub-genres of 1960s music before, e.g. childhood images to evoke the 'doll house darkness' (to steal from Pink Floyd's 'Matilda Mother') after his use of innocentia, but he definitely created the sub-genre of apocalyptic rock. And it began here to be continued by The Rolling Stones' declamatory 'Gimme Shelter'. Of course, there had been lyrics of Armageddon previously, with Barry McGuire's 'Eve Of Destruction' and Zager and Evans' 'In The Year 2525', but their music is comparatively lily-livered. 'All Along The Watchtower' would be as compelling if stripped of its lyrics. Indeed, this is the cover that 'Hey Joe' promised right at the beginning of Hendrix's career proper. This track finds Hendrix able to take any classic and recast it; remodel it with a genius like a Dadaist ready-made. And speaking of ready-mades, he even used a cigarette lighter to achieve the woozy slide effects after the first startlingly lucid solo.

There are a number of links to Armageddon-like thinking, with some critics – including Clinton Heylin and Andy Gill – remarking on the parallels between Dylan's imagery and that in the Book of Isaiah: one of the gospels mostly concerned with judgement and salvation. The following is said to describe an indulgent feast of Belshazzar before the fall of Babylon:

> Prepare the table, appoint the watch; eat, drink: arise, ye princes, anoint the shield. For thus hath the Lord said unto me: Go, set a watchman, let him declare what he seeth. And he saw chariots, horsemen by pairs, a chariot with asses, a chariot with camels; and he hearkened diligently with much heed. And he cried as a lion, Lord, I stand continually upon the watchtower in the daytime, and I am set in my ward whole nights. – And behold, there cometh a chariot of men; horsemen by pairs. And he answered and said, Babylon is fallen, is fallen; and all the graven images of her gods he hath broken unto the ground.

Whilst Dylan might've been shrewdly commenting on the need for vigilance on the dawn of this brave new world, or warning rock royalty of the need to remain humble, others have taken exception and see the lyrics as little more than elevated nonsense, with folk singer Dave Van Ronk opining that even the title is illogical, as watchtowers don't lead anywhere, so the 'along' part is nonsensical. Yet the Jehovah's Witness magazine is named *Watchtower* – a metaphor for God's omnipotence, and by extension, watchtowers must lead to everywhere. Hendrix's interpretation is an omnipotent force, swooping, surging, rising, falling. This is what the all-seeing sounds like. Moreover,

Harper Lee's supposed sequel (but in all probability a first draft) to *To Kill a Mockingbird* is titled *Go Set a Watchman* (an observation Philip Norman also makes in the introduction to *Wild Thing: The Short, Spellbinding Life of Jimi Hendrix*): a comment on the *Mockingbird* character Atticus Finch as the *conscience* of Maycomb. The lulls and explosion of Hendrix's interpretation, certainly imply a conflict between the aware and the ignorant, the guilty and the innocent; we might even say the experienced and the innocent. We can also ask, do watchtowers limit our understanding? Is Dylan suggesting that we think we move around in our perspective, but are in fact static? The 'along the watchtower' may even be more vertical than horizontal: something that springs alive in the music of Hendrix. In fact, Hendrix's music coheres the lyrics by delineating depth and direction. Perhaps Dylan was getting away with quasi-biblical tosh, but Hendrix wasn't. In *Crosstown Traffic*, Charles Shaar Murray notes that much pop music analysis has focused on lyrics at the expense of music, and so some musicians of colour have been disadvantaged by this as their musical lexicon remains under-explored. Here, Dylan's lyrics (which sometimes seem to be treated more seriously than they deserve) are almost irrelevant once Hendrix infers and then implies them through sound.

But what led to such a revolutionary reworking of Bob Dylan's minimalist track from *John Wesley Harding*? Writing to his father after his first experiences of parachuting, Hendrix described:

> When I got to the top, the jump master snapped these two straps on to my harness, and slapped me on the butt and said, 'Go, Go, Go.' I hesitated for a split second, and the next thing I knew, I was falling. All of a sudden, all the slack was taken up on the line, I was snapped like a bullwhip, and started bouncing down the cable.

This may be what the title – let alone the rest of the lyrics – meant to Hendrix. The cover takes us through a feeling of being pushed out into space – the rush of wind, plummeting, slowing, being caught and buffeted away again. It's a vertical song, pulling its listener up and down the cable that Hendrix wrote to Al about.

Electric Ladyland saw the move from 4-track to 12-track, and then for 'All Along The Watchtower', 16-track, and it benefits enormously. Whilst Hendrix felt that four tracks was adequate for most recordings, this album – a move from just guitar, bass and drums – needed more, and he explained to *Beat Instrumental* that the album required further tracks to support his 'expression music'. This track has several overdubs and includes Dave Mason on 12-string – unusual for a Hendrix recording in that much of its drive and atmosphere comes from an acoustic instrument. Brian Jones added some stoned piano that didn't make the final mix, but he can be heard on vibraslap during the intro. Curiously, Kathy Etchingham recalls that Jones brought a sitar to the session. (This could shed light on another Jones/Hendrix collaboration – 'Little

One' from *West Coast Seattle Boy* opens with a sunrise of sitar, rumoured to be played by either Dave Mason or Brian Jones. However, some sources say the track was once called 'Jam With Brian Jones', so that might be a clue!) Thankfully, the sitar can't be heard on the final take either. The vibraslap is based on the African jawbone, making this slice of Americana much broader in its arid atmosphere. Hendrix also took over bass duties after a falling out with Redding, but it's likely too that he'd worked out the backing as meticulously as he had his guitar parts. Hendrix played the solo on a Flying V, and worked it out in great detail beforehand. Mitchell praised Hendrix's 'Motown style' (though Hendrix himself was not a Motown fan), and elaborated that Hendrix's bass licks made his drumming on this track much more disciplined. Certainly, Mitchell carefully augments, resisting the temptation to lead the track into the maelstrom too soon.

The track opens with one of the most famous intros ever: a dry-thundery sound strangely recalling the rhythm of 'Louie Louie'. Whilst it borrows from folk, country, rock and blues, it also has an element of garage, gifting a shiver of primal excitement beneath the precise and sophisticated sound layering. The intro establishes a cinematic feel too: this is the wide shot of the blasted heath. The guitar line that follows is a tracking shot, foreshadowing the joker and the thief, before the guitar sinks low in the verses, twisting behind like the shadow of a high-flying bird's wing. The first wary, vigilant solo lifts us, and keeps us aerially speeding through this landscape ('No reason to get excited'); the second twists like a sidewinder almost outrunning us, and then the slide takes us into slow motion as we've paused to look closer and we're now staring right down the watchtower. The wah-wah responds, circling around, rotating us around and around the watchtower. The sound never comes at us, but always around. Finally, the guitar is transformed into a wailing wind; the piercing outro of 'Purple Haze' being echoed, and there's every reason to get excited… the whole tower might fall. It's simultaneously and ingeniously a paean to creation and destruction; its innocence and experience crashing together, and therefore, it's one of the most authentically 1960s songs in Hendrix's oeuvre. It's an expression of the sublime as defined by the philosopher and statesman Edmund Burke: 'Whatever is in any sort terrible or is conversant about terrible objects or operates in a manner analogous to terror, is a source of the sublime' and the imagination is awed by it. Wordsworth felt the sublime was more the removal of 'the burden of mystery'. The removal of innocence? The ellipses of Dylan's version have certainly been removed by Hendrix's unequivocal and astonishing soundscape.

This wasn't lost on Dylan, who praised the interpretation, noting to the *Fort Lauderdale Sun Sentinel* in 1995: 'He had such talent, he could find things inside a song and vigorously develop them. He found things that other people wouldn't think of finding in there. He probably improved upon it by the spaces he was using.'

As Dylan was reacting to the present musical scene of psychedelia and studio alchemy with the retrospective *John Wesley Harding*, Hendrix reacted to this by hauling Dylan's song into the future. Nevertheless, Dylan and Hendrix share a sympathy, because they both looked back to their musical legacy to build their sound, with Dylan using Woody Guthrie as a template, and Hendrix wanting to not only develop his own sound, but recreate the blues of Howlin' Wolf and Elmore James, and claim his heritage in a way that the white British players of the blues boom couldn't. Dylan and Hendrix were both adept at keeping the sounds of the past alive whilst developing their own. But on 'All Along The Watchtower', Hendrix triumphs over Dylan spectacularly. It still sounds just ahead of the age.

The Simpsons use 'All Along The Watchtower' as its soundtrack to a 1960s montage in the episode with Homer's radical mother, with newsreader Kent Brockman summing up the era as 'a shrill, pointless decade!'. Through his Dylan cover, Hendrix made not only the 1960s but the end of the world sound shrill, orgiastic, desirable, justified and meaningful.

When The Jimi Hendrix Experience were inducted into the Rock & Roll Hall of Fame in 1997, Neil Young played 'All Along The Watchtower'. Wise move.

'Voodoo Chile (Slight Return)' (Jimi Hendrix)

'Well, I stand up next to a mountain/and I chop it down with the edge of my hand'. Hendrix's music had been mountainous; markers on the musical landscape, but again, he was threatening to destroy what he was creating. The Experience itself would soon be chopped down.

If 'Voodoo Chile' is the sound of midnight, then this is the dawn. It's an audacious way of realising what Hendrix heard in his head – the same song reconfigured; covering his own material in a way. The Beatles had toyed with this on the 'Sgt. Pepper' reprise, but how might it have been if Lennon had kept the different versions of 'Strawberry Fields Forever'? The Beatles did try this out with 'Revolution', slowing the rocker down to a bluesier tone for 'Revolution 1', and a sound collage in 'Revolution 9', but *The White Album* was released a month after *Electric Ladyland*, although the single had been released in the summer. Hendrix was said to have thought that *The White Album* was a backwards step for the group, because it looked too much to the 1950s for its source. Nevertheless, The Rolling Stones might've taken inspiration from Hendrix or The Beatles, too (The Stones reworked 'Honky Tonk Women' into 'Country Honk'), because whilst the studio was leading to perfected pieces, it also presented the problem of what was going to be definitive. For Hendrix, the studio was now functioning as the stage – catching the innovations, the moods, different attitudes, and Hendrix was one of only a few artists who really began to see his songs as partially finished; as chapters rather than vignettes.

The LP becoming *the album*, also helped artists to think beyond the one artefact of their single. Indeed, this track works like another favourite Hendrix technique: the dyad. This technique – playing two notes to imply a chord – creates a yearning, unfinished quality, as evident in 'The Wind Cries Mary' and 'Little Wing', and was part of Hendrix's guitar lexicon leading to him thinking of songs in pairs too. But this was also evident in his formative years when playing on the Isley Brothers' bipartite 'Testify' and Ray Sharpe's 'Help Me (Get The Feeling) (Part One and Two)'.

Unlike 'Voodoo Chile', this continuation features Redding, and ABC were recording the group for a shelved documentary as they rehearsed and then laid the track down. Opening with a scratched flicker before its primal riff fattens, the track is made fleshy by the corporeal wah-wah crashing into a 3D sound before the notes are howling about the listener's head. It's like being up high and having the most enervating cyclone whip around you. We're not in New York anymore… we've landed in *Electric Ladyland*. The backing by Redding and Mitchell is comparatively restrained, and allows Hendrix to take his lap of honour here at the close of the album. This is the promised sound of that utopia; the whole landscape galvanised, crackling with a fire-red energy, a triumphant maelstrom. Then Hendrix takes it down, trilling the notes, strumming a little before the tumult swirls again, warping and finally threshing. It is a masterclass in the techniques that electric guitarists can conquer, and the imagery of the eagle's wing and the lion's roar begun in 'Voodoo Chile' come together as the voodoo child's destiny. Hendrix sometimes billed the epic as the Black Panther's national anthem, or as an alternative American anthem. It should be.

Eddie Kramer recounted its recording to *Guitar Center*:

> Everyone talks at length about the bold new sounds Jimi created on *Electric Ladyland,* but you also captured some incredible straightforward guitar tones and performances from him, like on 'Voodoo Chile'. I remember that Jimi played a white Fender Stratocaster on that song. Surprisingly, the amp he used on that song was not a Marshall stack. It was actually a Fender Showman top with a huge cabinet with eight 10-inch speakers in it. You can hear it rumbling around on the floor of the Record Plant when you listen to the beginning of the song. He's standing right in front of the amp and singing into the microphone, which was a Beyer M160: a ribbon mic that I always used on him.

Incredibly, Hendrix was disappointed by the final product, confessing to *Hullabaloo*:

> So some of the mix came out muddy – not exactly muddy, but with too much bass. We mixed it and produced it and all that mess, but when it came time for them to press it, quite naturally, they screwed it up, because they didn't know what we wanted. There's 3D sound being used on there that you can't even appreciate because they didn't know how to cut it properly. They thought it was out of phase.

Unsurprisingly for a titanic rock classic, 'Voodoo Chile' has been performed by several other artists, including Gary Moore, The Gil Evans Orchestra, Red Hot Chili Peppers, and Buddy Guy even teamed it up insightfully with 'Sunshine Of Your Love'. However, once again, the most interesting *cover*, or at least response, is Miles Davis' 'Miles Runs The Voodoo Down' (from *Bitches Brew* in spring 1970), which blends the assured defiance of 'Voodoo Chile' with the attack of 'Voodoo Chile (Slight Return)' – John McLaughlin's guitar sparks, and the piano of Chick Corea and Joe Zawinul is rivetingly frenetic.

More recently and surprisingly, 'Voodoo Chile (Slight Return)' was used as part of the soundtrack to Pauline Harris' Radio 3 production of John Webster's Jacobean revenge tragedy *The Duchess of Malfi.* It certainly enhanced the play's crackling intensity.

Band of Gypsys (1970)

I said find yourself first and then find your talent

Personnel:
Jimi Hendrix: Guitar, vocals
Buddy Miles: Drums, vocals
Billy Cox: Bass, vocals
Recorded live at Fillmore East
Producer: Jimi Hendrix
Engineers: Wally Heider, Eddie Kramer
Chart placings: UK: 6, US: 5

...and finally, that Ed Chalpin contractual obligation...

Hendrix sometimes introduced older tracks to his audience as 'oldies but baddies', or even as 'SOS': same old shit. His back catalogue was becoming a bore, and he was ready to stride ahead, but Capitol required another album. Recorded on New Year's Day at New York's Fillmore East, *Band of Gypsys* is the only live Hendrix album to be released in his lifetime. It was much less a document of his newly emerging sound, and more an appeasement to the record company, decided upon because of the speed with which it could be distributed. Nevertheless, it does capture Hendrix at a turning point. Already jaded, even at the start of a new year – *nay*, a new decade – Hendrix dutifully wishes the crowd a happy new year, before remarking, 'I hope we'll have a million or two million more of them... if we can get over this summer...' Hendrix barely did, dying in the early autumn.

Predictably, the album covers were a bone of contention. America plumped for the uninspired but acceptable live shot of Hendrix, whilst Track Record created a tableau using puppets of Hendrix, Bob Dylan, Brian Jones and John Peel. The associations are not immediately obvious. Admittedly, Hendrix had reworked Dylan compositions and played with Jones and performed for Peel's radio show, but it's a knackered riffing on the ensemble idea of *Pepper*, with an unkind and downright thick swipe at Hendrix as a mannequin; albeit a cruelly insightful comment on the reasons for the album. Nevertheless, as bland as some of the tracks are, an album packing 'Machine Gun' deserved much better.

Whilst this album should've seen a move towards newbies and goodies, it's more a sidestep, giving a glimpse of Hendrix as a session man. At times there's cool, clean playing with reliable support from army pal Billy Cox on bass and Buddy Miles on drums; at others, the music has an odd anonymity about it. Many of these tracks developed from studio jams and don't yet seem fully realised, but many would be protean forms that Hendrix retuned to (often more successfully) later on. Billy Cox had already played with Hendrix – at Woodstock in Gypsy Sun and Rainbows – and had also worked with Slim Harpo and Etta James; Buddy Miles founded The Electric Flag and had worked with Wilson Pickett. Christened George as a baby, Buddy's grandmother nicknamed him after jazz drummer Buddy Rich. Buddy Miles met Hendrix when in a backing band in Canada, coming together again at a Stephen Stills jam.

As a set, *Band of Gypsys* is Hendrix looking back to crisp and efficient R&B cuts, but there are rumours of where he wanted to venture in the controlled mayhem of 'Machine Gun'. Yet for a band with a nomadic moniker (inspired by Django Reinhardt), this is the sound of Hendrix running on the spot…

'Who Knows' (Jimi Hendrix)

Miles' incongruous scatting lends an unwelcome eccentricity, whilst the arrangement in general has Hendrix almost as a supporting – rather than driving – figure. Before the album's release, he'd remarked that he was happy for Miles to take over the vocals, as he felt his voice was 'right'. Miles' vocals are erratic, at times complementing the music well; at others, over-performing. Moreover, 'Who Knows' is the kind of song that would probably be more gripping to experience genuinely live, especially in terms of its controlled use of dynamics, but it seems to lack something in the recording. Honestly, if it wasn't labelled a Hendrix track, it might be more fairly received, but it's hard to not be a little frustrated at the back seat he's taking here, despite some interesting use of thirds. Hendrix is also employing a new version of the Octavia – specially crafted for the gig by Roger Mayer – and having some of the vocal pressure taken off him does allow for some startlingly inventive guitar work.

Eddie Kramer explained to John McDermott that the album's post-production proved to be problematic: 'Mixing the *Band of Gypsys* album was a challenge. It was like Jimi was really almost pressured into doing it. Hearing Buddy's vamping seemed to bother him. We were sitting there and he was like, "Oh, man, I wish Buddy would shut the fuck up."' Quite.

'Machine Gun' (Jimi Hendrix)

A tour de force. What could follow it? Well, four rather bland cuts, sadly. Yet this is a superb example of Hendrix's signature polyphony, moving between lead and rhythm as moving between an arsenal of weapons. David Stubbs insightfully compares it to Picasso's *Guernica*, as a visceral statement on the hell of war. This time there is no exulting in the violence or definite sense of domination, as in 'The Star-Spangled Banner', with Hendrix lamenting, 'Evil man make me kill you/Even though we're only families apart'.

It's the accident of nationality that pits soldiers against each other, which can also stand as a comment on racism. 'So let your bullets fly like rain' is heard in the guitar, and the machine gun is referred to as an axe (slang for a guitar), with Hendrix conflating both as weapons. A circumspect guitar tone opens the track; a low-key musing, then a sudden rattle like cocking a gun. The bass prowls behind in the undergrowth, not quite camouflaged, vulnerable yet concurrently threatening, and creating a humid atmosphere. Then the drum fills come like Gatling guns. The control of attack and decay throughout is masterly. In fact, the words are superfluous, the music itself lyrically conveying the tension of ambush and slaughter. The middle section is stealthy, building to the ballistic notes at the close. It's one of few Hendrix cuts to build and increase in might steadily, rather than bursting out of the speakers at once, and it's deeply unsettling with a feeling of attrition. The use of the Cry Baby pedal also heightens the mournful but poised, coiled texture. The track could unravel at any moment. Whereas 'The Star-Spangled Banner' is a guerrilla assault, 'Machine Gun' is a campaign of attrition and the definitive statement on Vietnam. Indeed, it's often praised as being the best song about this conflict. English singer-songwriter Kate Bush – who must've been influenced by it, alongside watching a documentary by an Australian cameraman – comes close with 'Pull Out The Pin', where she dares to sing from the Vietnamese point of view: 'They stink of the west.'

'Machine Gun' shows how the blues could evolve and still be the voice of America – from the killing floor to the killing fields, the blues was at once of the past and present. Hendrix's old compatriots, the Isley Brothers blended Neil Young's poignant 'Ohio' with 'Machine Gun' to unsettling effect on their 1971 album *Givin' It Back*, making it a potent opening track. On it, Ronald Isley intones, 'Jimi Hendrix would say…', and then does a great wailing vocal impression of his riffs, with some suitably Gatling drumming from George Moreland.

'Changes' (Buddy Miles)

Partly out of generosity and respect for his friend Buddy Miles, but also because Hendrix resented fulfilling his Chalpin contract, he made sure that Miles was given two tracks. This helped showcase Miles, but allowed Hendrix to keep some songs back for what he thought would be his next album.

'Changes' is a bouncy song with a zippy wah-wah riff, a strong vocal from Miles, and feels instantly more collaborative than the opening cut. The guitar-playing is controlled and slick, but breaks out for the energetic solo. Yet the audience involvement palls. Being encouraged to clap and sing along just doesn't fit somehow. Hendrix happens at the audience; singing along is like trying to sing along with a hurricane, and it tethers him. However, he was talking about his idea for an electric church, and there is a sense of the audience testifying here. Charles Shaar Murray quotes Hendrix as saying: '… we're making our music into electric church music – a new kind of Bible you can carry in your hearts, one that will give you a physical feeling. Our music is shock therapy to help them realise a little more of what their goals should be. We want them to realise that our music is just as spiritual as going to church.' 'Changes' is a manifestation of this.

Miles retitled the song as 'Them Changes', and used it as the opener on his 1970 album of the same name. The horns are efficient, but the more ponderous tempo doesn't work as well.

'Power To Love' (Jimi Hendrix)
This enjoyable funk-rock track, that's also known as 'Power Of Soul', looks forward to Deep Purple's album *Deep Purple In Rock.* But it's at about this point in the album when its faults become clear – it's shockingly conventional, albeit also grown-up, skilful and often professional. It balances some of the sloppier live tracks that lend weight to Hendrix's critics, who assert that his theatrics made up for a lack of basic proficiency, but it skates close to dull. Indeed, the listener does wonder what the intensity of Mitch Mitchell would bring. Miles Davis believed the Gypsys were 'perfect' for Hendrix because they were so 'solid'. They undeniably provide an unfailing canvas, but this can be lacking the shiver of danger that The Experience could evoke.

In John McDermott's notes for *Both Sides Of The Sky*, Cox revealed that the riff came from him playing Ray Charles' 'Mary Ann', and it does lend it a streamlined swagger.

'Message To Love' (Jimi Hendrix)
Another respectable (what an unexpected description of Hendrix's sound!) track, but a similar tempo and arrangement to what has passed previously, means the pieces are bleeding into each other. It's a monochrome sound, but the charging chromatic riff that announces it promises more. Hendrix rated the song enough to have it open his set at Woodstock. Perhaps it's more significant lyrically, building on the mirror motif that would reflect many of his late-career themes: 'I travel at the speed of a reborn man/I got a lot of love to give/From the mirrors of my hand/I sent a message of love'. Hendrix seems to be suggesting that his fame can be a way to foster clarity. The imagery continues with a woman now in 'chains', as Hendrix's consideration of freedom has become more political. John McDermott commented that a more carefree attitude 'had been replaced with a strident sense of self-examination'. The 'strident' doesn't quite fit. In fact, some of these tracks could benefit from a heightening of intensity, but lyrically, the message of self-determination is explicit.

An interesting alternative version is included on *The Jimi Hendrix Experience* box set, with some soulful backing vocals and a storming finish that propels an unequivocal message of hope.

'We Gotta Live Together' (Buddy Miles)
The second Miles-penned song – which takes inspiration from Sly and the Family Stone's 'Sing A Simple Song' – brings the album to a close, and it's a shame, because the band really seem to get going here, with Hendrix using the Octavia to create a powerful sustain that strengthens the feeble lyrics ('The old house dog if wagging his tail/Nobody loves him/He's dirty as hell'). As the track continues, the sound sharpens, and a jump in the tempo galvanises. The uncut track lasts around 15 minutes, and while that might be extreme, perhaps a longer mix would've lent the album a more potent resolution. The song was

performed in a medley with 'Voodoo Chile (Slight Return)', but stands better alone; the cocksure 'Voodoo Chile' doesn't seem to fit the vague message here.

For many acts, an album like *Band of Gypsys* would be an essential recording. But for Hendrix, with the exception of 'Machine Gun', it represents more of a sidestep than a stride forward. It's almost mainstream, probably his most conventional work since 'Hey Joe', complete with incongruous auxiliary vocals. There are a number of problems with the guitar tuning in performance, as Hendrix used light-gauge strings to enable precise manipulation, not to mention frequent use of the whammy bar, which would jerk him out of tune. In fact, Hendrix's strength – his mastery over the Fuzz Face and Uni-Vibe etc. – and his many innovations, often made it hard to stay in tune live, and sometimes even caused friction with the audience when this needed modifying.

The year leading up to the creation of Band of Gypsys certainly hadn't been conventional. From Handel to hostages, Hendrix was part of it. He began the year by moving into a building in Brook Street, London, that had also been the home and place of death of the German composer Handel: an ex-pat who also found acclaim in Britain. Mozart and Beethoven spoke of him as Eric Clapton and Jeff Beck would speak of Hendrix. Mozart divulged: 'Handel understands 'affect' better than any of us. When he chooses, he strikes like a thunder bolt.' Remind you of anyone?

Then The Experience briefly toured Europe, with the parting of the ways between Hendrix and Redding obvious leading up to The Experience playing their final show: in June at the Denver Pop Festival. Redding later claimed that Hendrix's mood was so low as The Experience faded out, that he slashed his wrists at one point.

It would be Gypsy Sun and Rainbows – or Band of Gypsys for short – who would play Woodstock in August, although this was a different line-up from the Fillmore recordings: Billy Cox, Larry Lee, Mitch Mitchell, Juma Sultan and Gerardo Velez. Nevertheless, they were introduced as The Experience, with Hendrix correcting this immediately, if somewhat apologetically. Despite performing some Experience numbers, there was a marked difference; indeed, this was the only live performance with another guitarist: Lee sometimes playing lead. Hendrix also deigned to do an encore: a rarity. Tellingly, the encore was 'Hey Joe'. The following month brought Hendrix rudely back to earth, and he endured a curious 'kidnapping', with him disappearing for a few days. Theories have ranged from a drug deal gone wrong, to an extended 'trip', to Mike Jeffery staging it to teach his wayward star a lesson. And all of this before a drug bust trial concluding in December, with Chas Chandler *as* a character witness, helping achieve an eventual not guilty verdict.

As 1969 drew to a close, Hendrix gave what was possibly his most famous interview: Sheila Weller's piece for *Rolling Stone* took Hendrix's assertion 'I Don't Want to be a Clown Anymore' as its title. On New Year's Day 1970, he began to wipe off the make-up. The shows with the Band of Gypsys are mature work: a pausing for breath. And even though the album would mark Hendrix's final release during his lifetime, there was much more spectacular – yet still grown-up – music to come.

The Jimi Hendrix Experience (Box set) (2000)

And the rocket's red glare, the bombs bursting in air

This is a gorgeously presented set, affordable too, and a must for any fan, as it contains rarities, alternate versions and live tracks. Its 2013 reissue saw bonus tracks added, including a performance of 'Burning Of The Midnight Lamp' from Simon Dee's *Dee Time* show, which had previously been thought to have been wiped. There's also 'The Stars That Play With Laughing Sam's Dice', 'Peace In Mississippi' and 'Like A Rolling Stone'. Explored below are the included tracks not previously collected on other releases.

'Killing Floor' (Chester Arthur Burnett)

This had been the track that curdled Cream – and indeed the hopes of other competitors – when Hendrix jammed with Jack Bruce and Ginger Baker as Clapton watched from the wings at the London Polytechnic in October 1966: Hendrix's first UK appearance. It had also been a moment of triumph during The Experience's tour of France supporting Johnny Hallyday, and was a song dear to Hendrix. Moreover, its composer Howlin' Wolf had befriended the novice Hendrix. Blues guitarists Hubert Sumlin – who played on 'Killing Floor', and whose experiments with distortion through his Wabash amp also influenced Hendrix – recollected to *Guitar World* in 1994:

> He (Hendrix) was just a little ol' dude living in England. It was before his band The Experience hit it big. We played in Liverpool, The Beatles' home, and in walked Jimi Hendrix: a little ol' hip guy wearing earrings and a bandanna. Wolf said, 'What the fuck is this guy? I ain't saying nothing to that motherfucker.' He came right up to Wolf and asked if he could play his guitar. Wolf nodded and Hendrix picked it up, turned it over, and played it with his teeth. (Laughs) He played the hell out of it. Wolf looked at him, big-eyed, and said, 'You hired, man, you hired!' He said, 'No thank you, Mr. Wolf. But I admire you and the blues. You guys are 100 per cent. Beautiful, man.'

Howlin' Wolf had recorded the song in 1964, and it was assumed the title was a reference to slaughterhouses, but Debra Devi interviewed Sumlin for her *The Language of the Blues: From Alcorub to Zuzu*, and he explained that it really referred to the time when Howlin' Wolf's wife shot him: making the killing floor image more literal than metaphorical!

Hendrix had performed it earlier in his career and at Café Wha?, upping the tempo and changing the bass to reflect the lyric's necessity of escape. This version from Paris' Olympia unveils The Experience on the cusp of stardom, and is victorious. Hendrix's vocals are confident with thoughtful and rhythmic phrasing; Redding thunders behind like the heartbeat of the universe, and Mitchell's intensity builds in perfect simpatico with Hendrix: astonishing for such an early performance by the trio. It would be the almighty certainty of this performance that they'd seek to recreate, many times.

'Title #3' (Jimi Hendrix)

This instrumental cut in April 1967 is the bridging sound between *Are You Experienced* and *Axis: Bold As Love*. There's a controlled fever about it, but also a palpable sense of band commitment as in the early versions of 'Killing Floor', whose influence can be heard in its riff, along with a shiver of 'I'm A Man'. Built around a basic riff, but including some impressive vibrato from Hendrix, it had the potential to have grown into a persuasive rocker.

'Taking Care Of No Business' (Jimi Hendrix)

Surprisingly, this track sees Hendrix taking a little inspiration from The Lovin' Spoonful's lazy take on trad jazz and 1930s vaudeville 'Daydream', but also Sopwith Camel's 'Hello Hello'. Bob Dylan's 'Rainy Day Women #12 & 35' is in a similar vein, and was recorded a month after 'Daydream''s release. As British music was looking backwards at Edwardian music hall, the more poppy psychedelic sounds of the US also took inspiration from earlier in the century. Furthermore, Hendrix's roots were in vaudeville, as his grandmother Zenora had danced in Lacy's Dixieland Band, and he might've felt nostalgic about its revival.

'Taking Care Of No Business' opens with a roadie pretending to be a barkeeper who's throwing out a rambunctious drunk. The lyrics tread the familiar 'nothing to my name but a guitar' path, and present an easy-come-easy-go 'Brother Can You Spare A Dime?' vibe with corny lines like 'I'm so broke I can't even pay attention'. It's a pleasant if inessential cut.

Hendrix vocally improvises a solo, by warbling and creating a sound not unlike that on 'Crosstown Traffic'. *Axis Outtakes* also shows that a version augmented by a wry saxophone was also produced.

'Like A Rolling Stone' (Bob Dylan)

Hendrix bled on his copy of *Highway 61 Revisited*, according to Larry Bartleet's *NME* article 'Inside Jimi Hendrix's Blood-Spattered Record Collection' – literal blood on the tracks after Hendrix pierced his hand on a shattered wine glass. Dylan was the artist most represented in his collection: *The Freewheelin' Bob Dylan; Blonde on Blonde; John Wesley Harding; Greatest Hits; Bringing it all Back Home; Nashville Skyline.* As Hendrix was insecure in his vocal abilities, he found Dylan reassuring, telling Chris Welch: 'When I first heard him, I thought, "You must admire that guy for having that much nerve to sing so out of key. Then I listened to the words."'

Hendrix performed 'Like A Rolling Stone' live several times, beginning with The Blue Flames, often excising the third verse – tellingly the one with the 'jugglers and the clowns': an echo of the iconography of 'The Wind Cries Mary', which was similarly imagistic in its lyrics.

Whilst many Dylan songs bear exquisite (indeed sometimes superior) covers, 'Like A Rolling Stone' has always seemed so bound up in the paradoxically intense – but also slightly offhand – delivery of Dylan, that interpretations of the song usually fall short. Hendrix's version is no different, and he suffers from being contained by its tight, purposefully repetitive – in fact, interminably rolling – structure. Charles Shaar Murray has pointed out the similarities between 'Wild Thing' and 'Like A Rolling Stone' in terms of their chord sequences, and both tracks rely on Hendrix's performance as a whole to hold the listener's attention. Yet Hendrix took a mediocre clichéd song in 'Wild Thing' and made it roar, but 'Like A Rolling Stone' was a rare thing for him: an interpretation that doesn't rival the original. This might possibly have been one of the tracks responsible for making Hendrix even more aware of the limitations of a three-piece, however potent they could be.

'Sgt. Pepper's Lonely Hearts Club Band' (John Lennon, Paul McCartney)

Performed live in Stockholm, this is a more relaxed version than the more famous Isle of Wight one, and slightly slower than The Beatles' cut. Hendrix sings it with much heart, and his guitar fills in well for the brass, with some controlled licks that don't stray too far from the root.

Paul McCartney was highly flattered by Hendrix choosing to open his 1967 Saville Theatre set with the song. Hendrix *almost* began his Isle of Wight set with it too, though strictly speaking, it followed a version of 'God Save The Queen' – juxtaposing two of England's most significant cultural artefacts, similar to how he would blend 'Voodoo Chile (Slight Return)' and 'The Star-Spangled Banner' to create something more representative of the US nation at that time.

In 2013, McCartney told *The Colbert Report* about the Saville Theatre performance:

> It's still obviously a shining memory for me because I admired him so much anyway, he was so accomplished. To think that that album had meant so much to him as to actually do it by the Sunday night, three days after the release. He must've been so into it, because normally it might take a day for rehearsal, and then you might wonder whether you'd put it in, but he just opened with it. It's a pretty major compliment in anyone's book. I put that down as one of the great honours of my career. I mean, I'm sure he wouldn't have thought of it as an honour, I'm sure he thought it was the other way round, but to me, that was like a great boost.

'Catfish Blues' (Jimi Hendrix)

This is a great blues by Hendrix, inspired by Muddy Waters, and it crackles with a dangerous energy – a feeling of something being kept just below the surface like a lurking catfish. When Hendrix's solo ruptures the surface, it's as though he's coming up for air.

He name-checks himself in the lyric, as a married woman entices him. But there's an unexpected pathos in 'Well there's two, two trains running/But there's not one, lord, that's goin' my way/You know there's-a one train runnin' at midnight', which quotes from Waters' 'Still A Fool' but also reminds us of Hendrix's sense of a spiritual homelessness, even as The Experience seemed to be coming home with this anniversary celebration: it was a year on from their triumph at the Olympia, and they had returned. Hendrix connects with the audience in this powerful performance, also making us aware of the 'Mannish Boy' influence as he begins to ask the audience to spell with him. The catfish imagery is said to have originated with Robert Petway: at once signifying freedom and also being a desirable man. Petway's blues is wistful, almost defeated, but Hendrix creates a rollicking sound to match his barbels. The audience greets Mitchell's drum solo rapturously, and there's some banter between Hendrix and Mitchell, building the anticipation, capped with Mitchell's 'Wait for this bit then'. The track then picks up speed and swims away: sadly, a little too soon.

Nevertheless, this is a glorious moment for The Experience. Hendrix introduces the track by asking the audience if they've heard of Mississippi, Muddy Waters and John Lee Hooker: each receiving a hearty cheer. He continues by stating that they will be playing the blues 'our kinda way'. Hendrix would develop this sound further when working on 'Voodoo Chile' and 'Voodoo Chile (Slight Return)': Petway's wishful fish evolved and now stalking on land.

'Somewhere' (Jimi Hendrix)

Using imagery from 'Up From The Skies', and looking ahead to 'Earth Blues', this is another song that imagines terrestrial difficulties from the point of view of aliens: 'I see weapons barkin' out the sting of death'. It's a convincing blues with some brooding guitar, yet the lyrics are tangled and incoherent. But the line about being 'wrapped in cellophane' so that the speaker can be sold, is incisive and recalls Hendrix's 'Letter To A Room Full Of Mirrors'.

Stephen Stills is on bass, with Mitch Mitchell having overdubbed Buddy Miles' drums in 1971. Miles' version is available on *People, Hell and Angels.*

'Gloria' (Van Morrison)

This is a riotous and raucous version of Them's 'Gloria', recorded at TTG Studios in Hollywood, and flaunting an unrestrained live atmosphere, with the trio blending garage rock and blues to create a simply thrilling noise. If it weren't for Hendrix's explicit extemporising about the various Glorias that Mitchell and Redding have 'known' (at the song's close, he teases, 'Wait until you hear the words in that!'), it would've made a sensational single. Some cover versions had watered down Van Morrison's lyrics – The Shadows of Knight changing the mild 'She comes to my room' to 'She calls out my name'. Hendrix amplifies the implied naughtiness and goes on to describe his time with Gloria as 'freaking, smoking and joking'.

'Peace In Mississippi' (Jimi Hendrix)

A rollicking instrumental that makes the title seem ironic, this piece graced the B-side of the 'Valleys Of Neptune' single. Also recorded in Hollywood, the piece is partly Hendrix's response to egregious racism – music publisher Bumps Blackwell had told Hendrix of the time when he'd worked for Little Richard and had sent out a black employee in a convertible to buy sandwiches. The employee was brought back by the police, but when a white employee explained the situation, they were called 'a nigger lover' and told to keep the black people out of Clarksdale, Mississippi. Upon hearing this, Hendrix changed the title of the track from 'Peace Alone' to 'Peace In Mississippi'. It's a both a hopeful cut and a most powerful and eloquent riposte to hatred.

'It's Too Bad' (Jimi Hendrix)

This is a moving blues with the guitar reverb lending a rich sincerity to Hendrix's thinking out loud. The lyric explores his relationship with his brother Leon, but also his brotherhood with the black community. It begins with some radiant blues licks, augmented by Duane Hitchings' doleful organ, evoking a continuation of 'Voodoo Chile', as if this is the under-confident confession of that glorious victor. Lyrically, it takes the '1983' line 'Well it's too bad that our friends can't be with us today', and extends this to Leon's drug addiction and the complexities of black militancy: 'Until you come back, completely black/Go back where you came from too'. Hendrix also refers to 'Room Full Of Mirrors', again suggesting that he's lamenting a part of himself too. Indeed, that song's insightful imagery informed many of Hendrix's later songs, and it might be interpreted that not only is the mirror symbolism pertinent to his own identity, but could also link to the effects of segregation.

'The Star-Spangled Banner' (Francis Scott Key, John Stafford Smith)

The crowd quietens at the urgings of the King …*Shhh*… Then Elvis politely asks them to be upstanding for the national anthem. Hundreds of teens rise; sorry the show has reached its end. But instead of being asked if they can see by the dawn's early light, they're castigated and cussed for being hound dogs. The kids are thrilled. Hendrix and his brother Leon are thrilled, and perhaps the seed for a later reworking of 'The Star-Spangled Banner' is born.

Of course, the anthem had taken on another significance during the 1968 Olympics, when the track and field athletes Tommie Smith and John Carlos gave the black-power salute as they stood on the winners' podium. By this point, the anthem was no longer a simple message of unthinking patriotism but a way of holding a nation to account. Smith later pointed out that all three athletes on the podium, including Peter Norman, wore badges symbolising human rights, making the protest much broader than might've previously been presumed. In the same year, Puerto Rican singer and guitarist José Feliciano performed the anthem for the Detroit Tigers. Listening now, it sounds inoffensive, but its Latin jazz flavours were then seen as subversive, and subsequently, his career took a knock.

Hendrix's version of Francis Scott Key and John Stafford Smith's American national anthem has been likened to *Guernica* – Picasso's black-and-white painting of the massacre of both humans and animals during the Spanish Civil War (although David Stubbs insightfully notes that 'Machine Gun' and *Guernica* are more analogous). Whilst that work is unequivocally anti-war, it's hard to assert the same here. In some ways, this piece exults in violence – a complicated violence – but this is in part the sound of invasion triumphant, and its ambiguity is the root of its power. Speaking to *Kick* magazine, Hendrix recalled:

> Did you send the Americans away when they landed in Normandy? That was also interference but that was concerning your own skin. The Americans are fighting in Vietnam for a completely free world. As soon as they move out, they will be at the mercy of the communists. For that matter, the yellow danger should not be underestimated. Of course, war is horrible, but at present, it's still the only guarantee of peace.

The pejorative epithet 'yellow danger', shows that racial insensitivity and prejudice are indeed complex, as is Hendrix unquestioningly accepting the domino theory: and as ex-military, feeling a sympathy with the army. However, his views on the conflict did become more nuanced in time. But simultaneously, Hendrix had an acute understanding of the culture he was in, describing the air in America as 'slightly static'. The Arbiter Fuzz Face helped him to recreate this brilliantly. He elaborated, on *The Dick Cavett Show* in 1969: 'Music is loud; the air is loud.' When Cavett asked about Hendrix's 'unorthodox' take on the anthem, he retaliated: 'It isn't unorthodox. I thought it was beautiful.' The audience applauded loudly.

Whilst beautiful doesn't seem apposite, Hendrix's use of feedback is devastating but controlled and meaningful; it's the screaming aftermath of assault and the most famous version is undoubtedly the Woodstock one. It's claimed that Hendrix had been up for three days before this performance, backed by Gypsy Sun and Rainbows, and this lends a further hysteria to the performance. Contrary to myth, he wasn't exactly playing at 'the dawn's early light' – more around 9 a.m., but nevertheless, there are parallels. Key wrote the lyrics the morning after a battle with the British – witnessed from his position aboard a neutral vessel, the flag flying above Fort McHenry, and therefore, the battle was subsequently known as The Defence of Fort McHenry. There was glory in the air. A morning-after victory song was almost perfect for the last bleary hours of Woodstock too. Furthermore, Key's poem was initially sung to the tune of a British drinking song, and so the *definitive* anthem is a reworking in itself. Hendrix had played traditional pieces at transformative moments in his past also: 'Auld Lang Syne' to usher in his reign in London, and then again to announce the tenure of The Band of Gypsys. This particular reworking was as the Summer of Love cooled.

But another reason for some of the hostile reactions to his interpretation might not only be to do with his style but could be more to do with how he ordered his setlist. He inserted the anthem into a medley that also included his 'Purple Haze' and 'Voodoo Chile (Slight Return)'. Hendrix had previously referred to 'Voodoo Chile' as a national anthem, and he was at once reclaiming the actual anthem, rejecting it, redesigning it and even changing the fabric of his own work in the process. Notwithstanding, Leon, who was in the army at the time, recalled being scorned because of his brother's defiling the nation's pride.

The chilly *The Jimi Hendrix Experience* box set version was recorded in New York in March 1969, and is said to be the first time Hendrix used a 16-track. It's astonishing. If lacking the danger of the more famous Woodstock performance, his guitar-playing has an iciness that sounds synthetic, to match the synthesizer work of Silver Apples: an experimental electronic band who guest-star here, and were admired by John Lennon. Legend has it that Robert Moog visited Silver Apples in the studio, as he was intrigued by their building their own synthesizer or 'oscillator'. Using this early synthesizer makes the American national anthem sound as it might to Martian ears: meticulous, but 'shrill and pointless'. There's a brittle gloss to it; a spangled tone. Coincidentally, Silver Apples were also intending to perform the anthem for a 4 July show.

'The Star-Spangled Banner' in any of Hendrix's incarnations remains a career-defining triumph; indeed, a defining artefact of the 20th century. Music critic Robert Christgau – who has said he's interested in 'where popular culture and avant-garde culture intersect' – didn't recognise where Hendrix's seemingly flashy or so-called pandering stagecraft was headed. It was shameful that he should describe Hendrix's performance at the crucial Monterey Pop Festival as an 'Uncle Tom' whose theatricality was a 'vulgar parody', whilst praising The Who's destruction as a 'defiant, lower-class stance'. If we manage to overlook the shocking double standard (indeed, Christgau did revise his opinion later), there's still a limited understanding of Hendrix's 'flamboyance'. It was leading to 'The Star-Spangled Banner': the moment when the popular and avant-garde ignited each other in a dreadful, honest stance.

The Who were inspired by Gustav Metzger's ideas of auto-destructive art – whereby everyday objects are broken – which he developed after World War I. This intensified after World War II, reflecting the development of sophisticated weaponry, with objects burned, shattered, obliterated. Hendrix and The Who were born during World War II; they were born *into* auto-destructive sound. Describing the appeal of the Marshall amp, Pete Townshend tellingly remarked in his autobiography *Who I Am*: '(it) screamed like a spitfire'. When Hans Keller said that the cacophony of pop music was 'a little bit of a regression to childhood', he wasn't wrong but was ignorant of how significant this is. This also links to The Move's notorious stage act, which involved their blitzing of Hitler effigies; their early ELO incarnation, blowing up cellos; the recreation of bomb raids and bomb sites. Furthermore, the Nazis saw expressionism and dissonance in music as degenerate, and we can detect a resistance to this in the war babies who went on to record the century's loudest and most discordant music so far.

But Hendrix went beyond smashing the guitar or amp, to taking the everyday object of the anthem, and slashing that to ribbons; it might also be said that the sabotaging of 'Hey Joe' was an example of auto-destructive art. And Hendrix's 'The Star-Spangled Banner' is *the* sound of the 20th century, not solely the sound of the US. From 'the war to end all wars', to the Russian Revolution, to blitzkrieg, to the cold war and on and on, the 20th century sounds like keening static with brief, tense silences.

Hendrix might also have been working on other versions of the anthem previously too. 'The Stars That Play With Laughing Sam's Dice' evokes the stars and stripes of a psychedelicised Uncle Sam. The influence goes further. Indeed, it's worth examining the 'The Star-Spangled Banner' lyric (or poem) in full, and noting several parallels with the Hendrix lexicon:

O say can you see, by the dawn's early light
What so proudly we hailed at the twilight's last gleaming
Whose broad stripes and bright stars through the perilous fight
O'er the ramparts we watched, were so gallantly streaming
And the rocket's red glare, the bombs bursting in air
Gave proof through the night that our flag was still there
O say does that star-spangled banner yet wave
O'er the land of the free and the home of the brave

Looking over the first verse, it's clear that Hendrix is recreating the 'rocket's red glare, the bombs bursting in the air' with his screaming Fender. The imagery even evokes that of the sci-fi novels Hendrix enjoyed so much. Hendrix had written countless songs in search or celebration 'of the land of the free'. Yet Francis Scott Key was a trusted confidant of Andrew Jackson, the slave-owning president, and Key himself – as a district attorney – prosecuted abolitionists, even executing some.

On the shore dimly seen through the mists of the deep
Where the foe's haughty host in dread silence reposes
What is that which the breeze, o'er the towering steep
As it fitfully blows, half conceals, half discloses?
Now it catches the gleam of the morning's first beam
In full glory reflected now shines in the stream
'Tis the star-spangled banner, O long may it wave
O'er the land of the free and the home of the brave

Here's the glory: the ambiguity in this protest. And its nationalism 'half conceals, half discloses' in Hendrix's interpretation's strafing. His guitar 'fitfully blows' in its recreations of war as elemental.

And where is that band who so vauntingly swore
That the havoc of war and the battle's confusion
A home and a country, should leave us no more?
Their blood has washed out their foul footsteps' pollution
No refuge could save the hireling and slave
From the terror of flight, or the gloom of the grave
And the star-spangled banner in triumph doth wave
O'er the land of the free and the home of the brave

For obvious reasons, this verse is now often excised, but the disturbing image 'Their blood has washed out their foul footsteps' pollution' is said to refer mostly to slaves who'd joined the British and were to be punished for their disloyalty.

O thus be it ever, when free men shall stand
Between their loved homes and the war's desolation
Blest with vict'ry and peace, may the Heav'n rescued land
Praise the power that hath made and preserved us a nation
Then conquer we must, when our cause it is just
And this be our motto: 'In God is our trust'
And the star-spangled banner in triumph shall wave
O'er the land of the free and the home of the brave

The more Key's words are examined, the plainer it becomes that perhaps what offended America about Hendrix's peerless rendition, wasn't that it was *subversive* at all. It was actually *traditional*: revelling in the glory of dominance. Hendrix could see indeed, and made the world hear.

Hendrix opened his Isle of Wight set with 'God Save The Queen', introducing it by saying, 'I think it would sound better if you stood up for your beliefs and started singing, but if you don't, fuck you.' There's a half-smile as he says it. And it's an almost respectful rendition, with the anthem turned more into a dignified blues than the noise orgy that 'The Star-Spangled Banner' became: suggesting it was less an act of subversion, than one of a qualified fondness. Alternatively, Keith Altham explained that it was Hendrix's canny attempt to get the fatigued audience standing; after all, it was 3 a.m. by the time he took to the stage. Interestingly, whilst Hendrix received death threats in America for his interpretation, his performance in England has barely received a mention over the years.

An interesting coda is recollected by Barry Miles in *London Calling; A Counter-Cultural History of London Since 1945:* 'On New Year's Eve, 1967,

Jimi played a 30-minute version of 'Auld Lang Syne' which reduced everyone to a stunned silence.' This performance at the Speakeasy was Hendrix taking another traditional ready-made, and remaking it with a satirical edge like French painter Marcel Duchamp did the Mona Lisa.

'Country Blues'

A relaxed jam with the Band of Gypsys and an unknown harmonica player, this track showcases some effortless guitar trills and runs. The slight wah-wah tone gives the piece a little edge too.

The Jimi Hendrix Experience box set is a superb artefact that testifies to the power of The Experience as both a live act and as masters of the studio. Essential.

First Rays of the New Rising Sun (1997)

The best love to have is the love of life

Personnel:
Jimi Hendrix: Guitar, vocals, bass, backing vocals
Mitch Mitchell, Buddy Miles, Jimmi Mayes: Drums
Billy Cox: Bass
Albert and Arthur Allen (The Ghetto Fighters), The Ronettes (Veronica Bennett, Estelle Bennett, Nedra Talley), Emmaretta Marks, Steve Winwood, Chris Wood: Backing vocals
Juma Sultan, Billy Armstrong: Percussion
Buzzy Linhart: Vibraphone
Kenny Pine: 12-string guitar
Stephen Stills: Piano
Paul Caruso: Harmonica
Recorded at Record Plant, Electric Lady, Sound Center
Producers: Jimi Hendrix, Eddie Kramer, Mitch Mitchell, John Jansen
Engineers: Eddie Kramer, Jack Adams, Tony Bongiovi, Bob Cotts, Jack Abrams, Bob Hughes, John Jansen
Chart placings: UK: 37, US: 49

It's a brave fan who delves into the complexities of Hendrix's posthumous releases, as these encompass the essential, the execrable and even the inauthentic, with some records that boast his name certainly not boasting the man himself. At the time of his death, Hendrix had been working on numerous tracks, but as far back as 1968, he'd been developing the themes of some of these and attempting to establish a new sound with some new players. The story of *First Rays Of The New Rising Sun* really begins with his work on 'Angel' in winter 1967, and ends with *The Cry Of Love* tour that would see Hendrix play his final concerts.

The Cry Of Love tour began in April 1970 in California, working across to Europe, then to the Isle of Wight and finishing in Germany. It was originally to have been a reforming of The Experience. In the end, Redding was replaced by Billy Cox, with Hendrix explaining that Cox's playing simply suited their sound better. He commented on The Experience: 'It's a ghost now – it's dead – like back pages in a diary. I'm into new things and I want to think about tomorrow, not yesterday'. Tomorrow was about *The Cry Of Love*: a name that was also going to be conferred on the band. This didn't happen, but even during the Experience days, the *band* was often introduced as 'Jimi Hendrix'.

The Cry Of Love did make it as the first posthumous studio album title, in 1971. Much of it was drawn from his most recent recordings: 'Freedom', 'Drifting', 'Ezy Ryder', 'Night Bird Flying', 'My Friend', 'Straight Ahead', 'Astro Man', 'Angel', 'In from the Storm' and 'Belly Button Window'. Whilst it was mostly well-received, with many remarking that it confirmed Hendrix's legacy, some were unhappy with Mike Jeffery's involvement as executive producer, and felt it was simply an unfinished work. Really, there's little to criticise in the songs themselves, but as a collection, it just doesn't have the wallop of *First Rays of the New Rising Sun,* and another dull album cover does Hendrix no favours. Furthermore, *The Cry Of Love* led to other releases of varying quality, such as the confusingly titled *Rainbow Bridge* (not the soundtrack to the film Hendrix performed in), which has an excellent A-side, but dilutes its power on the partially live B-side. The incoherent *War Heroes* has some interesting pieces, but doesn't work as a collection either.

But much worse was to come, such as *Crash Landing* from 1974 – produced by Alan Douglas, who used extra musicians to embellish and finish tracks, so much so that Douglas even gave himself a co-writing credit. Hendrix had been introduced to Douglas by Devon Wilson, and had worked on 'Izabella', 'Stepping Stone' and 'Room Full Of Mirrors' with him. However, nothing came of these sessions. In 1995, Douglas released *Voodoo Soup*, before Experience Hendrix (the company set up by Hendrix's family to safeguard his legacy) rounded up the best tracks from *Rainbow Bridge* and *War Heroes,* and *The Cry Of Love* in its entirety, to create *First Rays of the New Rising Sun*. Admittedly, it's a compilation album, but one put together carefully, with Eddie Kramer working from the original master tapes; not those 'cut' by Alan Douglas.

As early as pre-*Electric Ladyland*, Hendrix had been concerned about the effects of the stardom treadmill, telling *Melody Maker*: 'Pop slavery. I felt we were in danger of becoming the American version of Dave Dee, Dozy, Beaky, Mick and Tich,'. Therefore, even during his sessions with The Experience, he was thinking about his next direction, and it seemed that his first studio album after Band of Gypsys would need to be a double.

Between spring 1968 and prior to his death in 1970, Hendrix had spent hours and hours perfecting the album, which he'd first titled *People, Hell and Angels*: a neat way of summing up some of the challenges of recording it – not only was Electric Lady undergoing renovation, it was flooded out; the local mafia weren't pleased with Hendrix showing up on their previously obscure territory and paid him a visit to make their feelings plain; and tensions were increasing with Mike Jeffery. Yet, the sound captured is optimistic, light, almost a respite. Enriching his sound with other players is also much more successful this time, allowing his flavours to be sharper rather than muted. In fact, *First Rays* is a rousing listen, and it sounds as if Hendrix is loving every second of it. It's a little repetitive at times, but it's hard to know which tracks constitute him working out a theme etc., which he may have discarded, and which he would've decided on as the definitive statement. He did intend to release a double album, so it could've been that it was to be ordered eventually in the diptych manner of 'Voodoo Chile' and 'Voodoo Chile (Slight Return)' etc., with tracks revisiting but not repeating ideas.

Indeed, Hendrix's final live performance would reverse how he'd blazed into London at the close of 1966. Back in the UK, by September 1970, jamming with Eric Burdon at Ronnie Scott's (two days before Hendrix died), he played on John D. Loudermilk's 'Tobacco Road'. Its lyric is almost a potted history of Hendrix: 'I was born in a trunk/Mama died and my daddy got drunk', with the trunk being a symbol of his nomadism. The song continues 'Bring that dynamite and a crane/Blow it up, start all over again'. On 18 September at 12:45 p.m., Hendrix was pronounced dead. Much lurid speculation would follow regarding negligence, suicide and even murder, yet his death certificate records his demise as being caused by barbiturate intoxication and inhalation of vomit – open verdict.

What is without question is the ingenuity of his canon and the continued passion and interest it inspires. Indeed, despite critics usually being churlish about an artist's work being completed posthumously, the reviews were mostly favourable for *First Rays of the New Rising Sun*, with Robert Christgau redeeming himself a little by remarking that it's a 'powerful' work by an artist whose 'genius' was continuing to grow. Some critics remarked on the rhythm section being stronger than The Experience, but at times Redding's robustness is missed, as Billy Cox has an overly unobtrusive style sometimes, and even Mitchell's work is a little subdued on occasion. Nevertheless, the album at once illustrates Hendrix's promise, and consolidates his outstanding prowess.

'Freedom' (Jimi Hendrix)

'You got my heart/Speak electric water' is an example of many oblique and affecting lines in this track, which was one of the most complete before Hendrix's death. Kramer explains in the CD booklet that Hendrix had only intended to replace a few seconds of rhythm guitar, showing his perfectionism.

It was inevitable that he'd eventually write a song simply titled 'Freedom', as he'd been skirting around the theme since his debut, but here the motif has been developed. Hendrix now directs the song to a wider foe, not just lovers who want to tie him down. He even defends his wife and child in the lyric, seeking to fight back against some oppressive force. This is subverted later when he also mentions his girlfriend. The electric water evokes some chemical influence, and the later reference to a dagger – an object associated with his lover and heroin addict Devon Wilson – suggest this is a song about escaping the binds of addiction. Musically, however, it's joyous. Opening with a riff that seems to run in a circle (Cox says Hendrix had the riff first, and built the song from it), an abrupt clean, glistening lick breaks its hold. The bends on the notes are controlled and precise. This is a new sound for Hendrix – thinner, sharper, gleaming; a sound in contrast to the lyric's murky imagery. The song is an infectious groove all the way to the 'Keep on pushing, straight ahead' coda that lends it a triumphant climax. The fade-out also mimics the rush-hour buzz of 'Crosstown Traffic', but here Hendrix can charge ahead, leading towards the victorious, ascending closing chords: an aural path to liberty. He is also playing the slightly dissonant piano – quite low in the mix, it's almost a subliminal threat to his escape, but Miles' celebratory congas keep him 'pushing straight ahead'. Cox's descending bass line enhances this, recalling Hendrix's promise in 'House Burning Down' that 'The truth is straight ahead'. When commenting on this song, Mitchell remarked that this band 'was possibly the best band that we had'. 'Freedom' is testament to this.

The backing vocals are provided by The Ghetto Fighters – Arthur and Albert Allen – twin brothers who'd been friends with Hendrix since his New York days. They also sing on 'Dolly Dagger', 'Izabella' and 'Stepping Stone'. Hendrix had tried to return the favour by organising with the brothers a concert to aid Biafra, but this had fallen through. Ultimately, Hendrix played a benefit gig for the United Block Association instead.

Incidentally, Richie Havens also recorded a song named 'Freedom', and used it in the set that opened Woodstock. Havens visited Hendrix at his home, and played him his anti-war song 'Handsome Johnny', which may have helped make Hendrix more critical of the Vietnam conflict.

The early version of 'Freedom' on *The Jimi Hendrix Experience* box set has Hendrix still working out the lyrics, and is fairly lacklustre, repetitive and hindered by some uncertain drum parts, not really giving any hint of what it was to grow into.

'Izabella' (Jimi Hendrix)

Whilst the previous track seems to have been inspired by Devon Wilson, 'Izabella' had Monika Dannemann's name scribbled on the original handwritten lyric. Izabella comes from the root name Elizabeth, meaning 'God is my oath': a suitable switch for a song about vowing to fight on. At the time, Hendrix had been splitting his affections between Wilson and ice skater Dannemann, who would be the one to call the ambulance on the day of Hendrix's death.

The lyrics recount how the speaker's 'fighting a war' for Izabella and the children of the world, with Hendrix also suggesting 'Keep those dreams coming in strong' and hoping that 'Maybe one day I'll be holding you instead of these machine guns'. Izabella is another of those songs that works best in pairs, being a sort of companion to 'Machine Gun', now considering more of the civilian experience of war. The lyrics also partly reference what Hendrix had mooted as the album's title: 'Girl, here comes the rays of the rising sun'.

'Izabella' makes effective use of damping the strings to imply impatience, and there's a powerfully squalling solo. Hendrix was happy enough with the track to list it as complete, bar the mixing. Although it was released as the B-side of 'Stepping Stone', he nevertheless withdrew it because of his dissatisfaction with the mixing. The guitar sound here is dirtier than on 'Freedom', hinting at a licentiousness towards the pure saviour Izabella. The white Strat Hendrix played at Woodstock was said to be named Izabella too, and Hendrix debuted the track there. However, he was right to be dissatisfied – the backing vocals are strangely distracting, and the verses become a little repetitive with some faulty scansion. It's one track where there's a sense of straining to get at a sound that just isn't being fully captured.

'Night Bird Flying' (Jimi Hendrix)

In some ways, this is the closest Hendrix came to recording a country rock song. The theme is once again freedom, but now the speaker is aware of the need for release of his partner too: 'Well, she's flyin' down to me/But 'til tomorrow got to set her free'. Appropriately, its working title was 'Ships Passing In The Night', but the imagery in the finished version subverts that from 'Stone Free' and evokes 'Little Wing', as Hendrix celebrates the brief time he's allowed with the night bird. Ironically – or perhaps even in earnest – Hendrix had played snippets of 'Strangers In The Night' during live renditions of 'Purple Haze', and there's an echo of its themes in the lyrics. The track greatly benefits from multiple guitar overdubs, each one flying above the other, giving the impression of different aerial routes.

It was the first track recorded at Electric Lady Studios, and this lends it some *joie de vivre.* Kramer said it was one of the most complex to record; indeed, Hendrix never performed it live. The engineer said the extraordinary studio acoustics contributed to the track's clarity, and there's certainly something special about it. Also, there are four (at least!) different guitar parts – the rhythm, the high-pitched one like a bird cawing, and two guitars playing in the middle, layering like the troposphere to the exosphere. Mitchell's drum patterns are also elaborate and shifting, creating a feeling of velocity. The song passed the 30-take mark, and so it's remarkable its buoyancy didn't deflate at all. Rather, it has an indefatigable energy that makes it a delight, and achieves an extraordinary texture. Hendrix was again not content with music coming straight at the listener, but here it is swooping and soaring beautifully. Aside from the hint of a country feel, there's a whiff of boogie-woogie too, which grants it a real optimism: 'Until tomorrow no tears will be shed'. Even on the fade-out, a new, bassier and almost elastic riff begins to develop, but is too distant to really grasp like the night bird herself. It's a glorious song that can't fail to raise the spirit.

The work is likely an ode to WNEW New York DJ Alison Steele, who was known as The Nightbird. Not only playing the music of the counterculture, Steele also read poetry and esoteric texts, introducing her show with a lyrical description of the twilight skyline: 'The flutter of wings, the shadow across the moon, the sounds of the night…' She closed it by playing The Beatles' instrumental 'Flying' from *Magical Mystery Tour*. A sketch of a woman Hendrix drew resembling Steele was auctioned at Sotheby's. It also included some writing that may constitute a first draft of the 'Night Bird Flying' lyric:

Hello night bird
How was your day?
Did you visit the gods in the valleys far away?
What did you bring me in your visits from the sea?

Devon Wilson replied in pencil below: 'I brought you me!' signing it with her name.

The alternate version in the box set has more space, which means the power is lacking, but it does give one a chance to really hear Juma Sultan's percussion: a simple pattern remaining the clever constant in a continually shifting piece.

'Angel' (Jimi Hendrix)

Opening with rustling cymbals, languorous bass and splashing guitar, this is another secular gospel with a visceral, yearning depth. Musically and lyrically a sibling to 'Little Wing', its genesis dated back to 1967 when it was recorded under the name 'My Angel Catherina (Return Of Little Wing)'. This implies that Kathy Etchingham might've provided further inspiration, although it could also have been dedicated to Catharina Koch, but also shows that Hendrix was thinking in terms of developing existing material, as he would with 'Voodoo Chile' and 'Voodoo Chile (Slight Return)'. It's as though many of Hendrix's tracks have a parallel. At times, this could mean tired tropes dimly reflected in the lyrics, but could also lead to delicate beauty, as on 'Angel'. Furthermore, 'Night Bird Flying' has some lyrical resemblance, but is sonically opposed, with each part of the sound skilfully interwoven, whereas 'Angel''s strength is its use of space.

'Angel' was the first demo on which Hendrix worked out and played all the parts ready for the studio, shortly after completing *Axis.* An early lyric had the lines 'Angel came down from heaven yesterday/She stays long enough to rescue me' originally as 'She stayed long enough for afternoon tea': perhaps further evidence that the angel is, in part, Etchingham. The December 1967 version, known as 'Sweet Angel' on *The Jimi Hendrix Experience* box set, has Hendrix on bass as well as guitar and vocals, and it opens evocatively with a gliding riff, and *in medias res* lyrically. Beginning with 'About the sweet love between the moon and the deep blue sea', it bestows an immediate (albeit unintentional) otherworldliness. Hendrix uses a drum machine, but the track is still effective with his guitar notes stitching flight patterns in the air. It may not have the polish of some other tracks, but it's simply lovely, with an unselfconscious tenderness, and is often, justifiably, favoured over the *First Rays* version.

Hendrix recounted that he'd dreamed of his mother's death shortly before writing this song, and he took much of the lyric imagery from it, meaning it shares a number of tropes with '1983'. Returning to the *First Rays* version, there's a gorgeous chromatic run linking it to *Axis,* but quite different in effect from 'Spanish Castle Magic', as here it's full of potential rather than foreboding. Cox claimed in John McDermott's liner notes that his bass part was inspired by 'Cherry Pie': 'That gave the record the feel of those great 1950s R&B ballads'. However, the notes credit 'Cherry Pie' to Skip and Flip (also technically not from the 1950s, being released in 1960), but this is a much frothier cover of Marvin and Johnny's slower, more hankering doo-wop-flavoured original, which also includes some bluesy licks.

'Angel' is a gorgeous blend of anticipation and wonder as the music swells and falls. The increasing intensity at the close creates a sense of elevation, with the riff sounding more like a piano, echoing the percussive riffs of 'Little Wing'. The lingering bass of Billy Cox is melodic, and at times provides more of the hook than the guitar, whilst the guitar tone is almost wet with the drums rushing and shushing like tides, illustrating the merging of the moon and the sea. The final exhale of the cymbal meeting the guitar at the end, comes as a poignant full stop; the sound fading back in like an ascent to heaven. Mitchell overdubbed the drum parts after Hendrix's death, in an attempt to enrich the piece, and it's some of his most responsive and sensitive playing, showing a tenderness lacking in his earlier performances. The underdeveloped vocal lets the track down a little, though it's unfair to judge these songs in terms of polish. But this song can lay claim to being a Hendrix standard, with covers by Rod Stewart to Lulu to Jeff Healey attesting to its appeal.

'Room Full Of Mirrors' (Jimi Hendrix)

This song – here riotously performed by Band of Gypsys – began life in a much slower version, but this more fleeting cut is more urgent and rousing. Its lyric speaks of an epiphany:

> I used to live in a room full of mirrors
> All I could see was me
> Then I take my spirit and I smash my mirrors
> And now the whole world is here for me to see

On the surface, some of the lyrics might seem too fragmentary, and at other times too verbose for the melody, but the fragments certainly fit the song's theme. 'A broken glass was solving my brain' shows that a shattered false image is actually an awakening for the speaker.

The intro has Hendrix using his guitar in a similar way to the studio version of 'The Star-Spangled Banner', with its tones almost like a synthesizer and the futuristic bleating of lasers. It's a rousing performance, but one wonders what this would've sounded like with Hendrix employing backwards guitar to depict the altered state of consciousness. However, having the guitar lines mimic or reflect the verse vocals is a clever detail, and the bass is smashing and crashing all the while. The song has a glam feel with its intergalactic sounds, and employs another false ending with a surprise fade-in, as if Hendrix just doesn't want to stop. Incidentally, Sharon Lawrence recalled Hendrix admiring Elvis's 'Suspicious Minds', on which producer Felton Jarvis developed a false ending in order to recreate the excitement of a live performance; though this had already been used to more disorienting effect on The Beatles' 'Helter Skelter', and previously on 'Bold As Love' of course. But there are a number of false endings on this album, perhaps to imbue a live feel.

The Jimi Hendrix Experience box set has a potent 'Room Full Of Mirrors' with some assured and responsive bass from Billy Cox on his first recording session with Hendrix. Rocky Isaac's drums have an unobtrusive potency, and

Hendrix coaches him at the start: 'Whatever you do, get that boom boom; the bass will be kicking right with you'. The band has a strong cohesion, with Hendrix seeming to relish playing with fresh musicians. However, Al Marks, who played percussion, recollected to the *Experience Hendrix* website:

> We recorded 'Room Full Of Mirrors', and it took forever because Rocky couldn't keep the beat on drums. Midway through the session, Jimi turned to him and said something to the effect of, 'Man, do you know how to play drums? What's going on?' I had been banging one of the maracas against my leg for three and a half hours, and my leg was black and blue. I told Rocky quietly that he'd better get things right because I couldn't walk!

It was worth it, as Hendrix paid him three times the union standard for the session.

'Dolly Dagger' (Jimi Hendrix)

Hendrix watched amused as his lover Devon Wilson sucked the blood from Mick Jagger's cut finger: 'She drinks her blood from a jagged edge…'

The hesitant and innocent Dolly Mae of 'Wait Until Tomorrow' is now the vampiric and experienced 'Dolly Dagger'. The lyric is visceral and supernatural, with allusions to witchcraft, bringing to mind the John's Children song 'Desdemona'. Although 'Dolly Dagger' has been linked mostly to Devon Wilson – who was in the studio at the time of its recording – Linda Keith revealed to Philip Norman that Hendrix had insisted on them being 'blood brothers', so they cut their wrists to mingle their blood. The line 'Her love so heavy gonna make you stagger' may make the song's inspiration broader than Wilson too. Understandably, Keith and Hendrix were close, but many biographies attest to the power struggles between Etchingham and Keith, then Wilson and Monika Dannemann, and several other complex relationships that might've made Hendrix feel like a prize, with him as a 'burnt-out superman'. Yet Hendrix's desire to love, or use, then to cut and run, is also evident in his harking back to 'Highway Chile', with 'Better get in some highway and clear outta town'. However, he does directly refer to Wilson in the fade-out: 'That's right Devon/ Give me a little bit of that dagger'.

The track was issued as a single in 1971, backed with 'The Star-Spangled Banner' – quite a dynamic pairing of catchy funk-pop and avant-garde aural assault. Kramer commented that 'Dolly Dagger' is the best snapshot of Hendrix's sound at the time, explaining how Hendrix layered different guitar tones from his original demo, but kept his solo: testifying to how diligently he'd worked it out previously. Mitchell and Cox provide a pulsating backing, and this track attests that not only was Hendrix developing his sound, but Mitchell was adding funk rhythm to his jazz sensibilities. Cox's bass isn't amplified but plugged straight into the console to create a fuzzier, even jagged sound. Cox told *Classic Rock* about the track's musical inspiration:

'I'd put some new strings on, and I'm playing doo-doo-dum-dum, the chime of Big Ben. Jimi's room was right above, and the window flew open. He said, 'Hold it! Keep playing that, don't stop!' He comes down in his undershorts and grabs his guitar, then he completes the riff. That was the formation of 'Dolly Dagger'.

If we return to the lines 'Yeah, look at old burnt out superman/Tryin' to shoot his dust on the sun', it's not the last time that the superhero will be linked to a kind of impotence in Hendrix's lyrics, and this track also includes some uncomfortable sexual politics: 'She drinks the blood from the jagged edge/You better watch out baby/Here comes your master, alright'.

However, this might be a more subtle allusion again to Mick Jagger, whose queasily sleazy 'Brown Sugar' fetishises women of colour and includes descriptions of a 'scarred old slaver' whipping women at midnight. Whilst 'Brown Sugar' wasn't officially released until 1971, it had been recorded in 1969, and was already notorious for its earlier and even more explicit and brutal lyrics. Hendrix's Dolly – who has 'got a bullwhip just as long as your life/Her tongue can even scratch the soul out of the Devil's wife' – might be a riposte to the salacious and almost salivating 'Brown Sugar', thereby making the master image mocking.

And speaking of the satirical, Alice Cooper would echo the opening riff on their swaggering 'Elected' – a rewrite of 'Reflected' from their debut 1969 album *Pretties for You* – that builds on the innate arrogance of the tone.

'Ezy Ryder' (Jimi Hendrix)

Returning the favour after 'If 6 Was 9' was included on the *Easy Rider* soundtrack, Hendrix celebrates the spirit of the film on this song. Band of Gypsys performed it at the Fillmore, but it wasn't on the original live album as Hendrix was intending it for his next release. At that point, the lyrics were still undecided, with Hendrix not sure what to title the song when introducing it to the audience, joking that it had '20 verses'. It's a superb performance, showing the strength of the Band of Gypsys much more than most of their official album. Indeed, it could be their theme tune.

The *First Rays* version is compelling too, with the drums kick-starting the track and igniting the engine with flanging guitar, creating a sense of speed, like hearing the buzzy whine of a motorbike after it has flashed past. Hendrix's desire to create 3D music is particularly evident towards the close, where the riffs rev and zoom in a circle, and the guitar delay allows a hum of anticipation: a tour de force. Hendrix's vocals are rhythmic, but less forced than on earlier recordings, with secure control of tone and sustain matching his guitar mastery.

The freedom theme is continued, but with some interesting variations. 'He says the free world takes him higher' is looking beyond personal freedom to more political freedom, but there are also some surprises as Hendrix sings:

In a cloud of angel dust
I think I see me a freak
Hey motorcycle mama
You gonna marry me?

'Highway Chile' would never have proposed marriage! Hendrix also uses his trademark 'Ha! Ha!' to inject a sense of irony, but the 'Ezy Rider' is really 'dyin' to be loved' now as much as he wants to be unshackled.

The Band of Gypsys are joined by Steve Winwood and Chris Wood, who provide the energetic backing vocals. The alternate version in the box set has a dreamier fade-out with these higher in the mix, which perhaps should've been retained for this cut. The final swell that rounds off the track was said to have been the result of two pratfalls by Kramer and co-engineer Kim King, who tumbled off their chairs before one of them hit the fader: a lovely piece of serendipity that was kept in the final mix.

(See also 'Lullaby For The Summer' on *Valleys of Neptune.*)

'Drifting' (Jimi Hendrix)

One of the quickest tracks to record, 'Drifting' is a reflective ballad that makes use of the Leslie speaker to evoke a sensation of moving through clouds, although Hendrix mentions floating on 'a sea of forgotten tears'. His vocal comes in after a gentle intro pauses, and the backing flows in again like a tide. A subtle but poignant moment on the album, it's a delicate tune, given a hint of might by some shimmering chromatic runs and hazy backwards guitar. The guitar tone in the main sounds like 'Little Wing', before it gets fuzzier at the close, suggesting something moving further away and becoming blurred, drifting out, as Cox's bass fluctuates like waves: a gorgeous detail.

Mitchell's drums are controlled, the rhythm rising and ebbing – a dry sound that complements the flowing guitar like the sea meeting the shore, meeting the mountains. Two months after Hendrix's death, Buzzy Linhart – who'd played with Buffy Sainte-Marie and Richie Havens – contributed vibraphone, prettily twinkling through the chromatic runs like light on water.

'Drifting' is effortlessly beautiful, and it's like a slow exhale after the holding-breath excitement of the previous tracks.

'Beginnings' (Jimi Hendrix)

An instrumental that has some interesting time signature and tempo changes and a little of the fade-out riff that's heard on 'Angel', 'Beginnings' started life as 'Jam Back At The House'. This was performed at Woodstock but was reworked often in later jam sessions.

The snapping riff becomes jazzier in the middle, but the bass repeats it before the drums also mimic it. It has the swagger of 'Voodoo Chile (Slight Return)', and one wonders how Hendrix might've interpreted the piece lyrically. Nevertheless, it's a potent work without words, with a proto-metal atmosphere.

'Stepping Stone' (Jimi Hendrix)

This track can be heard in the Woodstock version of 'Voodoo Chile (Slight Return)', but lyrically is much less of a macho brag, confessing, 'I'm a man, at least I'm trying to be', and speaking of a lover who only wants 'a ticket to ride'.

Opening with the spoken 'I sure got the blues this morning, baby/Yeah, and I'm here to tell you about it', it proceeds with a gallop, but its sense of attack is more successfully realised elsewhere on the album. Nevertheless, the howling coda notes rejuvenate it before it's brought to a smashing stop.

'Stepping Stone' was released as a single, but Hendrix withdrew it, dissatisfied. Although, other reports suggest it was pulled to stop affecting sales of the *Band of Gypsys* album. Whatever the reason, Hendrix and Mitchell subsequently overdubbed new parts. But it's almost Hendrix by numbers, and in many ways, is the most regressive track on *First Rays*. But the version on *Both Sides Of The Sky* really compensates, imbuing it with a visceral verve.

Did Hendrix recall The Monkees' song 'Stepping Stone' from their shared tour? When *Melody Maker* asked him about the fabricated group (admittedly before the tour was even a glimmer in Mike Jeffery's eye), Hendrix commented: 'Oh God, I hate them! Dishwater! You can't knock anybody for making it, but people like The Monkees?' Yet, supporting them on tour was certainly a stepping stone for Hendrix, who managed eight dates before wearying of shouts for 'Davy!' from the audience.

'My Friend' (Jimi Hendrix)

An apt title for a track that included many of Hendrix's Greenwich Village buddies, 'My Friend' is at once a celebration of his past, but also of his new Village-situated studio. Paul Caruso plays harmonica, with The Fugs' Ken Pine on guitar, singer Joey Dee from the Starliters, Jimmi Mayes on drums, and a smattering of Stephen Stills on piano.

The lyrics are a sub-Dylan collage, but nevertheless, inexplicable images are affecting: 'A stagecoach full of feathers and footprints' seems to be addressing Hendrix's heritage. 'I combed his breath right out of my hair' is an imaginative way for Hendrix to depict his quest for freedom, whilst 'Just got out of a Scandinavian jail/And I'm on my way straight home to you' refers to his immediate past: an arrest in Sweden for trashing a hotel room (perhaps a room of mirrors). There are differing accounts of why Hendrix became destructive that night, with simple and more obvious explanations linked to drugs, frustration and boredom. But Redding stated in his autobiography that a male groupie had encouraged Hendrix to make a pass at him. Redding and Hendrix's relationship became increasingly fractious as the music became more complex, and also as the effects of harder drugs began to follow them into the studio. Hendrix and Redding were rumoured to have fought physically on occasion and a sense of bitterness is tangible in the *Classic Albums Electric Ladyland* documentary when Redding constantly refers to his bandmate as 'Hendrix', whilst Mitchell, Kramer and Chandler refer to him as 'Jimi'.

The track looks at the complexity of friendships, with Hendrix's isolation apparent in the lines, 'And-eh, sometimes it's not so easy, baby/Especially when your only friend talks, sees, looks and feels like you'.

'My Friend' is a languid blues track with a hint of 'Taking Care Of No Business' that was probably more fun to have played on than to listen to.

'Straight Ahead' (Jimi Hendrix)

When Keith Altham asked Hendrix about his political views, he was noncommittal, eschewing any particular belief, but he did refer to 'Straight Ahead' as an expression of his philosophy. In some ways, it returns to his original manifesto: 'Stone Free'. 'Keep on pushing, straight ahead' becomes almost a litany in the coda, and coheres it to the album's opening track 'Freedom'. 'Straight Ahead' also includes a couplet that summarises Hendrix's ethos: 'Woman and child and man and wife/The best love to have is the love of life'.

The song was created in the studio and demonstrates the best and worst of *First Rays* as an album. It opens – like too many of the tracks – with an impatient riff, and suffers from being too long, with the verses grinding on, almost formulaic. Yet that will be the case with unfinished work. Notwithstanding, the ascending guitar and bass lines at the 'straight ahead' chorus ramp up the excitement, with the circular riff at the end like being caught in a whirlwind.

'Hey Baby (New Rising Sun)' (Jimi Hendrix)

This includes Hendrix's first live take of his singing as no final vocal was ever recorded, yet it's a potently atmospheric song. The chord sequence recalls 'All Along The Watchtower', but here is less ominously portentous and more suggestive of a coming change.

The song opens in an almost prog fashion, having three intros or short movements. The first has the guitar notes circling like the sun as Mitchell's drums mimic this when their sound fans out. Then come the arpeggios, brightening the sunrise, and the last part of the intro is a pensive guitar lick, combining Hendrix's two most famous cover versions – 'Hey Joe' and 'All Along The Watchtower' – implying that the old rays of the rising sun have been completely eschewed. As befits a song of rebirth, there are many innovative guitar touches. The first solo manages to imply a rich sustain, and yet each note is distinct and simultaneously short and crisp, having a travelling panoramic feel that uncovers the landscape, like light itself, with striking glissando. The second solo creates a flamenco feel, bestowing a sultry air. Hendrix is again returning to his desire to originate 3D sounds, and now he's trying to create a sensation of light in his work.

The lyrics had previously been used on the earlier track '(Hey) Gypsy Boy', and recount a meeting between the speaker and a woman who's possibly an alien. The speaker wants to travel with the alien: 'And she said, "I'm coming from the land of new rising sun"/And I said, "Hey baby, where you tryin' to go to?"' It's a sort of rewrite of 'Hey Joe, where you going with that gun in your hand?', even keeping the 'Hey'. Now instead of a gun, there is a message of intergalactic peace. The sense of relief and release is heightened when the track goes from the 'May I come along?' minor refrain into its repetition then in the major: a musical rising of the sun.

It's a fascinating track, as it illustrates where Hendrix has come from as well as the direction he was headed, moving off into the sunrise.

'Earth Blues' (Jimi Hendrix)

The Ronettes and Buddy Miles provide backing vocals on this sort of 'Freedom' rewrite: 'Everybody can hear the sound of freedom's beating heart'.

When asked about the future of his music, Hendrix told the *New York Post*: 'Earth, man, earth… I want to bring it down to earth. I want to get back to the blues, man, because that's what I am.'

In 'Earth Blues', Hendrix elaborated on the conflict between a terrestrial awareness and a sense of otherworldly aspiration, as in, 'My head in the cloud, my feet on the pavement': a fitting summary of his intergalactic blues. The line 'Tell the child to bury daddy's old clothes', is a striking image of disavowal. Lyrically, it's a strong song, emboldened by the gospel shift in the 'Help me' section: again implying a rising optimism.

'Astro Man' (Jimi Hendrix)

Opening with a superhero theme parody that recalls *Mighty Mouse* – 'Here I come to save the day!' – there is then something of the 1970s New Wave about its intro proper, before it shifts into a more conventional rock blues. This is an ode to Hendrix's love of superhero comics, featuring some expectedly childish lyrics, but also unfortunate lines: 'And he's called the Astro Man/And he's flyin' higher than that old faggot superman'. However, Hendrix was often cast as the superhero/alter ego himself, with rock photographer Herbie Worthington telling John Einarson: 'Arthur (Lee) once said that Jimi was Clark Kent until he put his guitar on. Then he became Superman.' Superman has already been used to symbolise emasculation, as in 'Dolly Dagger', and perhaps Hendrix is drawing parallels between the costumed pop performer and the superhero.

Billy Cox recalled that he and Hendrix would often watch cartoons like *Mighty Mouse* together, and when Hendrix was a child, he identified so much with *Flash Gordon* (or, interestingly, Buster Crabbe, the actor who played him), that he insisted on being called Buster, as revealed earlier. But however revealing it might be psychologically, in truth, 'Astro Man' is messy and a little irritating – a distraction from the album rather than an enhancement.

'In From The Storm' (Jimi Hendrix)

With a lumbering riff reminiscent of Deep Purple's tracks on *In Rock*, this is a song of being able to escape 'the crying blue rain': a line that would become the title of another Hendrix song. This song developed in part from a jam around 'Cherokee Mist' with Cox and Mitchell, and here Emmaretta Marks from *Hair* supplies backing vocals. The track is boosted by an exciting solo that sounds backwards even though it's not, and lacerating wah-wah supported by strongly controlled drums that compete with the supremacy of the guitar tone.

'Belly Button Window' (Jimi Hendrix)

Narrated from the point of view of an unborn child (like Kate Bush's 'Breathing'), this is a reflection on existence. Mitchell and his wife Lynn were expecting a child, and this is said to have given Hendrix the idea of looking at the world *in utero;* a return to innocence. We've come full circle from the experience of Hendrix's debut to the final track on, arguably, his *final album*. But this is an aware child:

> Because you know if you don't want me this time around
> Yeah, I'll be glad to go back to spirit land
> And even take a longer rest
> Before a-comin' down the shoot again
> Man I sure remember the last time, baby
> They were still talkin' about me then
> So if you don't want me now
> Make up your mind

It's hard not to think this isn't also a belated message to Lucille. Moreover, Hendrix had received a number of paternity claims against him, confessing to Sharon Lawrence that he'd definitely fathered a little girl. He'd planned to meet her but never did.

As well as being lyrically imaginative, the guitar has a liquid, reverberating tone, as if being heard as embedded in a womb, and there's an ironic – or hopeful, or even protesting – echo of 'I'm A Man'. This child's identity, like Hendrix's, is tied to the blues, and the track is a poignant epilogue not only to *First Rays*' exploration of dawns both false and true, but to Hendrix's career as a whole.

In some ways, *First Rays* cannot help but be inadequate, as it's cursed to remain an impression of what might've been. Like all posthumous releases, it's a glimmer, sometimes a shadow, sometimes a sketch of what was originally intended. Hendrix was planning a double album, but this version isn't quite a single or a double, and would have benefited from dropping at least three songs as there's a receptive sagging from 'Stepping Stone' onwards.

But what makes *First Rays* unique is its joy. Whilst there are innovations in the blend of funk, rock and jazz inflections, the album does link back to *Axis* for its atmosphere of unalloyed delight. 'Spanish Castle Magic' is the template for the hard rock numbers, with 'Little Wing' setting the wistfulness of the ballads, and 'Wait Until Tomorrow' informing the more poppy R&B feel. The track order is sensitively considered, minimising as much as possible the effects of repeated tempos, keys and extended instrumental fade-outs that proliferate. And as posthumous releases go, it's dignified and pretty close to essential. Indeed, this *joie de vivre* here is more often to be found on debut albums: the glorious noise of someone rejoicing in their own skill. Whilst *Are You Experienced* is at times angst-ridden and self-doubting, *First Rays of the New Rising Sun* really is the dawning of a new contentment.

South Saturn Delta (1997)

I travel at the speed of a reborn man

Personnel:
Jimi Hendrix: Guitar, vocals, bass
Mitch Mitchell, Rocky Isaac: Drums
Noel Redding: Bass
Billy Cox: Bass, backing vocals
Brian Jones, Juma Sultan, Jerry Velez: Percussion
Larry Lee: guitar
Dave Mason: 12-string guitar
Buddy Miles: Drums, backing vocals
Recorded at TTG Studios, Olympic, Record Plant, Electric Lady, Mayfair, Olmstead
Compilation producers: Eddie Kramer, John McDermott, Janie Hendrix
Engineers: Eddie Kramer, John Seymour

Comprising five songs that didn't make *First Rays* but had been included on *Rainbow Bridge* and *War Heroes* ('Look Over Yonder', 'Tax Free', 'Midnight', 'Bleeding Heart' and 'Pali Gap'), along with some alternate takes, *South Saturn Delta* is less successful than its predecessor, but does span tracks from 1967 to 1970, and is an enthralling overview of Hendrix's progression. The Experience, the Woodstock Gypsys line-up and Band of Gypsys are all represented.

'Look Over Yonder' (Jimi Hendrix)

This song from 1968 was originally considered for *Axis*, and is a reworking of 'Mr. Bad Luck': a song that Hendrix performed back when he was Jimmy James. It's a high-energy opener from The Experience, with Hendrix coaxing a playful riff. The falsetto backing vocals raise the excitement, and the drop in intensity near the close helps to keep the attention.

'Little Wing' (Jimi Hendrix)

This is in fact, not 'Little Wing', but an embryonic version of 'Angel' from autumn 1967, showing the symbiosis between the two songs. Although, it's rockier and less soulful than the track would become. In a sense, 'Little Wing' and 'Angel' are twins – there's a strong resemblance, but some difference in how the tracks harness an unearthly power. Mitchell is on drums and would eventually overdub parts onto the definitive *First Rays* version: poignantly, in the wake of Hendrix's death.

'Here He Comes (Lover Man)' (Jimi Hendrix)

A full-bodied 1968 version of one of Hendrix's favourite tracks. John McDermott noted in the *South Saturn Delta* liner notes that Hendrix performed this song with all of his bands from The Experience onwards, making it almost talismanic.

Inspired by the B.B. King songs 'Lover Man' and 'Rock Me Baby', this is proof that the power trio of The Experience were still a storming force. The controlled solo and precise bends strengthen the piece's muscularity, as does Mitchell's tight timing, and Redding is hand in hand with them all the way. And Hendrix's (sort of) scatting at the close is much less grating than Buddy Miles'!

'South Saturn Delta' (Jimi Hendrix)

Larry Fallon helped Hendrix with the horn arrangement on this intriguing cocktail of jazz, blues and funk. Fallon's talents had been used on Van Morrison's *Astral Weeks* and Jimmy Cliff's *Wonderful World, Beautiful People,* and would be heard on The Stones' menacing 'Gimme Shelter'. Hendrix had long wanted to not only augment his work with horns, but to compose a piece to showcase how they and the guitar could work more innovatively together. This collaboration from summer 1968 presented the opportunity, and it's an inviting glimpse of a possible future Hendrix sound. Fallon told a writer for the official Hendrix website, Steven C. Pesant in 2010:

> It was a very interesting track. We really had a lot of fun doing that. He wanted to experiment with something, and then we were going to do a whole album in that particular kind of concept. Of course, the record companies came in and said that the album wouldn't be commercial enough and so forth, you know, that's how it goes. I understood it. That's what business is about. So they just put the track aside. I was very happy with that track, it sounded really good, very inventive.

When Pesant asked Fallon about what type of musician Hendrix was, Fallon replied:

> Ohhh, I don't know how to categorise Jimi. Jimi is like in a class of his own. He's not a mainstream jazz, he wasn't a commercial jazz artist, he wasn't a rock 'n' roll jazz artist, he was a blues… I would say maybe, a very hip blues-jazz artist, in that kind of artist. That's where his heart was, and his roots were really there. I guess he maybe never really had the chance to do the things that he really wanted to do in that particular world of music. And, he was kinda quite excited about what we did, and so was I. I thought we had a situation happening where, I think Michael, or something, the record company doesn't think it's commercial enough for an album in this direction. It was a real disappointment, but that's business.

The track opens with a nag of guitar – Hendrix playing a 1950s Les Paul Special – then a rustle of drums, and some low-key but funky licks take over before the horns begin to punctuate as the licks develop into a propelling riff. Hendrix's jazz fills are gleaming, and anticipate a change in rhythm before the track suddenly falls back into the opening licks. Some critics have argued that the brass really doesn't add anything, but it's as if Hendrix is testing out a new medium. Also, it seems more collaborative than much of the *Band of Gypsys* album, with Mitchell and Hendrix responding to each other sensitively and the horn syncopation lending a ruminative atmosphere. On the fade-out, Hendrix breaks out, beginning to chase his sharp licks with something fuzzier. Keith Shadwick perceptively remarks that this piece might've been Hendrix endeavouring to produce a response to 'Tax Free'. Certainly, Hendrix had been developing his understanding of countermelody, and he'd been experimenting by layering guitars on different tracks to sculpt the sound more. He also plays bass here.

Whilst it's a track of promise rather than realisation, the title is a neat encapsulation of Hendrix's blending of blues with more exploratory and innovative sounds. Perhaps the horns here add little to Hendrix's palette, but jazz guitarist Mike Stern (who paid tribute to Hendrix with live performances of his work) told *Jazz Times*: 'Jimi was definitely a legato player. He started a movement among guitar players with his long, sustaining legato lines. He sounded more like a horn player than anyone before him.' This perceptive observation means that Hendrix was always going to incorporate them into his sound at some point, whilst, paradoxically, not really requiring their embellishment.

'Power Of Soul' (Jimi Hendrix)

More arresting than the Band of Gypsys' *official* version, the guitar here is slinkier, dirtier, with some shining drum fills by Miles. It's a seemingly effortless performance, highly polished and much preferable to the previous Gypsys release. However, this is an abridged version of the master, after an even shorter version was released on *Crash Landing* – the posthumous and contentious Alan Douglas production – which included input from session musicians, and Douglas augmenting so much that he felt the need to give himself a co-writing credit for some tracks. Kramer remixed 'Power Of Soul' from the multitrack master, but the complete piece was only made available on *Both Sides Of The Sky*.

'Message To The Universe (Message To Love)' (Jimi Hendrix)

By the time the Gypsys performed it, it had changed its title to 'Message To Love' and lost some of its potency. Gypsy Sun and Rainbows – performing a week after their Woodstock debut – create intriguing flavours, with Hendrix using arabesques (as in 'Hey Baby') to lend it a nuance of Eastern music.

'Tax Free' (Bo Hansson, Janne Carlsson)

A lesser-known track by Swedish duo Bo Hansson and Jan Carlsson, with whom Hendrix had jammed in Stockholm. It became a live favourite of his. Hansson became more famous for his prog rock albums, including an interpretation of *Lord of the Rings*. The duo's version is Hammond organ drenched with hints of 'Voodoo Chile', but is too circuitous to be as powerful as it could be, and Hendrix's interpretations would sometimes follow suit, extending to 15 minutes with no direction home.

'Tax Free' was initially considered for *Electric Ladyland* (Brian Jones is on percussion as on 'All Along The Watchtower', as they were recorded at a similar time), but 'Voodoo Chile' is the centrepiece of that album, and 'Tax Free' would've tipped the collection into something of a torpor.

'All Along The Watchtower' (Bob Dylan)

An unreleased mix from January 1968, which shows that Chandler did a sterling job on the last songs he produced for *Electric Ladyland*. But Hendrix understood that something was missing, and added to the track on and off over the summer of 1968: moving from 4-track to 12-track and then 16-track. The toiling was worth it, as this version is simply good. What was to come, is superb.

'The Stars That Play With Laughing Sam's Dice' (Jimi Hendrix)

An unfortunately murky sound plagues this wonderfully idiosyncratic track. It recalls 'Third Stone From The Sun' in its unselfconscious delirious imaginings. Opening like a conventional rocker before taking off into space and becoming an interstellar 'Magical Mystery Tour', the track often makes the best ever psychedelic songs lists. Hendrix is our tour guide around the galaxy: 'The milky way express is loaded, all aboard', 'No throwing cigarette butts out the window/Now if you look to your right, you'll see Saturn'. The raucous passengers who provide sound effects and backing vocals are rumoured to include Frank Zappa, who gifted Hendrix a Strat in 1968.

But it's not just the lyrics that create a cosmic ether. Hendrix uses an Octavia, which has his guitar howling like the rushing of asteroids, invoking a purple haze in the atmosphere. The journey ends with a passenger slipping through the rocket's doors – possibly an apposite metaphor for drug casualties, which the title initials also hint at: STP and LSD.

The song had previously been available on *Jimi Hendrix Smash Hits*, but in an inferior mix.

'Midnight' (Jimi Hendrix)

A brooding track from 1969, with a lighter middle section, as if caught between night and day. It was previously called 'Midnight Lightning', hinting at this blending of light and dark. The guitar tone has a forked, flashing feel about it, and The Experience provide an implacable backing, with Redding's bass a gloomy cloud behind the streaking riffs.

'Sweet Angel (Angel)' (Jimi Hendrix)

See 'Angel' on *First Rays of the New Rising Sun*.

'Bleeding Heart' (Elmore James)

This is a fine version of the Elmore James song. James' cut from 1961 (released in 1965) is slower, with some lamenting saxophones, but Hendrix speeds it up and lets the riff gush rather than bleed. He would also sometimes change the lyrics: ad-libbing about the blues coming for him. Lithofayne Pridgon recollected that Hendrix loved Elmore James (who was known as the King of Slide), specifically his 'The Sky is Crying' and 'It Hurts Me Too'. James' slide implies a sobbing and sighing that Hendrix often conjures in *his* sound, too (particularly on 'Crying Blue Rain'), but he made the tone on 'Bleeding Heart' drier and more defiant.

A drunken and lewd Jim Morrison joined for a *performance* of this track with The Experience at the Scene Club in 1968: a slight but disastrous episode known as The Night of the Kings. Legend has Morrison stumbling about the stage, rambling pornographically, then attempting to fellate Hendrix before Janis Joplin punched him. 'Morrison's Lament' is a bootlegged jam that captures Hendrix's (suspiciously?) crystal tones and Morrison's almost inaudible mumblings.

Before the release of this track as a single (b/w 'Peace In Mississippi'), Kramer remarked to Toronto's *The Globe and Mail*: 'It's certainly a nice little jaunt for Jimi. Anytime he felt he could take off in a wild direction, within reason, he would do it – not so much to prove a point, but to stretch the boundaries.' This sums up Hendrix's approach to many other tracks too.

Julien Temple directed the single's video, inserting Hendrix into a *modern* festival, complete with Kate Moss watching from the wings. It has the unfortunate atmosphere of those little films they show between the acts on the Eurovision Song Contest.

See also the *Valleys of Neptune* version.

'Pali Gap' (Jimi Hendrix)

Developing from an instrumental jam following a rehearsal of 'Dolly Dagger', this track lacked a title. Therefore, Mike Jeffery named it to provide an opportunistic link to the Hawaii-set film *Rainbow Bridge* and its subsequent soundtrack, both of which featured Hendrix. Pali is Hawaiian for 'cliff', and the dizzying wind of notes that Hendrix plays disorients like vertigo. Opening with the sounds of Martian seagulls, there follows a coiling riff with an initially wet tone that becomes sharper as Cox picks out a determined, mountainous bass line behind it. It's an atmospheric piece that could've provided an extended coda to 'Dolly Dagger', emphasising a supernatural, predatory quality that the music of that track plays down.

'Drifter's Escape' (Bob Dylan)

This is another cover from Dylan's *John Wesley Harding*. Like 'All Along The Watchtower', it opens with dialogue from an outsider: 'Oh, help me in my weakness/I heard the drifter say'. The song was partly inspired by

Kafka's novel *The Trial*: about the accused Josef K, whose crime is never disclosed.

Hendrix's sympathy with liberty and escape had been made apparent on a number of songs, and again it returns us to 'Hey Joe' as well as Hendrix's first original composition 'Stone Free'. Musically, it transforms Dylan's rustic lament into a proto-funk rocker, backed by Cox and Mitchell. The track begins with its jumpy bass line, before the siren wail of the guitar begins to hunt the drifter. Hendrix's vocals are sincere, with an effecting tremor when he takes on the drifter's role. Once again, it surpasses Dylan's original. The final line describes lightning taking out the courthouse and allowing the drifter to break free; the music crackles and suddenly stops as if also struck.

'Midnight Lightning' (Jimi Hendrix)

With shivers of Robert Johnson, this is unique among Hendrix recordings for its stripped-back tone and only him appearing on it. Building on 'Midnight', and foreshadowed by the lightning imagery of the previous song, it has an end-of-days feel: 'Church bells ring mad against the night'. The blues chords are augmented by some uncanny runs that give a shiver of the Devil's interval, making this not just a powerful blues, but one of Hendrix's *purples* – an innovative hybrid of blues, psychedelia and rock; indeed, of innocence and experience. It's undoubtedly a superior finale.

South Saturn Delta is a varied palette of rainbow blues that enhances an understanding of Hendrix's evolution, whilst providing a coherent and satisfying listening experience. Stephen Thomas Erlewine from *AllMusic* described it as 'an alternate history'. Certainly, facets of Hendrix's sound that weren't as listened to or explored before are richly represented.

Valleys of Neptune (2010)

> Feel my heart kind of runnin' hot/That's when I've got to move before I get caught…

Personnel:
Jimi Hendrix: Guitar, vocals, bass
Mitch Mitchell, Rocky Isaac: Drums
Noel Redding: Bass
Billy Cox: Bass, backing vocals
Rocky Dzidzornu, Juma Sultan: Percussion
Roger Chapman, Andy Fairweather Low: backing vocals
Chris Grimes: Tambourine
Al Marks: Maracas
Recorded at: Olympic, Record Plant, AIR
Producers: Jimi Hendrix, Eddie Kramer
Engineers: George Chkiantz, Gary Kellgren, Jack Adams

Time magazine's Man of the Year in 1967 – the year of the first Hendrix album – was Lyndon B. Johnson: the US president associated with civil rights acts, the voting act, the Apollo space programme, the war on poverty and the escalation of the Vietnam War. The year of the *Valleys of Neptune* release would see *Time*'s Person of the Year named as Mark Zuckerberg: the founder of Facebook. Whilst signifying the future of communication, Facebook is an inherently nostalgic medium. And releasing alternate and unfinished versions from Hendrix's back pages could also have been an exercise in nostalgia akin to gazing at the holiday snaps of someone you half-remember. That *Valleys of Neptune* was one of the most vital releases of the year, in many ways, said more about the state of contemporary music than Hendrix's legacy. Yet the album is full of thrilling details that attest to how Hendrix's offcuts could be heart-stopping in a way that the many new releases couldn't provoke. The period just after *Electric Ladyland* is often described as being something of the 'wilderness years' for Hendrix. But if the songs don't represent a new age exactly, they are a taking stock of where he had been and was, and the album reflects a kind of clear thinking.

The album artwork is also poignant: a shot by Linda McCartney is combined with a watercolour Hendrix did at school. Al said it was one of many that he kept: an unexpectedly tender gesture from Hendrix's undemonstrative father.

'Stone Free' (Jimi Hendrix)

It's believed that Hendrix was inspired to revisit this song after his Toronto drugs bust in 1969, although the dates don't bear this out, with his arrest coming in May 1969 and the recording being from April. Whatever the reason for its revival, it doesn't compete with the original, but the line 'Woman here, woman there, try to keep me in plastic cage' is now '*Women* here, *women* there', perhaps making this version more concerned with personal relationships than the 1966/67 cut. It also sounds like Hendrix sings not 'My heart kind of runnin' hot', but explaining instead that 'When I feel my heart kinda getting hard' is what makes him want to run. Whilst some accusations of sexism or even misogyny seemed somewhat strong when directed at the original, the shift here is not merely apparent lyrically, but in Hendrix's behaviour, which changed not only towards women but to many of those around him, with Paul Caruso and Noel Redding being on the receiving end of Hendrix's aggression. Yet, violent outbursts towards women were also witnessed by Eric Burdon, and one girlfriend claimed that Hendrix's hitherto vanilla sexual inclinations had tilted towards the sadomasochistic. In some ways, re-recording 'Stone Free' seemed to be about reconnecting with an older self as much as lamenting newer restrictions.

But, ironically, Hendrix's freedom appeared to be threatened mostly by those not considered to be part of the Establishment. The Toronto bust offers some insight – Hendrix is said to have been gifted the drugs by a fan (small amounts of cannabis and heroin were discovered in his luggage, which did seem to be a genuine surprise to him), and he didn't take notice of what he was given. Of course, he was using drugs, and whilst the drugs were definitely in his possession, it couldn't be proven that he was aware of this, therefore, he was acquitted. However, the trial occurred in December, and its threat darkened the rest of the year for him – though it does have to be noted that his mugshots are almost classy portraits, with him looking more serene, sardonic and stately than most of his album artwork!

Returning to 'Stone Free', the backing vocals by Andy Fairweather Low and Roger Chapman shout less than the original and are more… stoned sounding à la 'Purple Haze', implying a tantalising freedom beyond, but Hendrix's almost scatting 'Got to be free' over the solo irritates, and then dilutes this hope. However, the gentler melodic fade-out – as opposed to the original's twitchy running riff – is a twist, making the close more of a relaxed stroll away and less of a desperate bolt.

'Valleys Of Neptune' (Jimi Hendrix)

Opening similarly to 'Angel' with a gentle drum murmur and a sunrise of cymbal, this track takes us through water instead of air. The lyrics are almost a patchwork of Hendrix motifs: colours, planets, sun, sand, birds. The song's first title was 'Gypsy Blood', and there's a mosaic feel to the lyrics, which keep the landscape shifting, but the themes of Atlantis and escape are more successfully realised in '1983… (A Merman I Should Turn To Be)'. The track was released as a single backed with the promising instrumental 'Cat Talkin' To Me'. The video moves through this landscape too, with images of Hendrix manifesting from the ether and then dissolving. Then there's the usual kaleidoscopic patterns: the typical visual representation of Hendrix's soundscapes. But the song meanders a little too long through this soundscape before a sudden fade-out.

It's clear Hendrix is going to take the track somewhere worthwhile, but the version left behind isn't it. Nevertheless, the rhythm-playing lends a swaying quality that's skilfully augmented by some precise licks, illustrating how 'The wind make love to all/The ocean'.

It's thought that 'Valleys Of Neptune' was one of the first songs Hendrix and Mitchell worked on after Redding left The Experience. The version on *Valleys of Neptune* includes take five with Cox and Mitchell as the rhythm section, but other versions include Buddy Miles on drums, Stephen Stills on piano, and both Stills and The Lovin' Spoonful's John Sebastian on guitar.

'Bleeding Heart' (Jimi Hendrix)

This is a pounding version of the Elmore James classic, with a solo that sounds more like 1970s heavy rock than the blues, and is testament to Hendrix's power to reinvigorate the traditional. Towards the end of the solo, the notes blur together like a rundown of piano scales in an astonishing moment of virtuosity. His flip between blues metal shredding and controlled jazz-like trills is superb too. Cox's bass-playing is also excellent, beginning with its jittery rhythm like a broken heart beating, before bouncing out defiantly all over the place as Rocky Isaac's drums stutter, stunned by it all. A gem of a track.

See also *South Saturn Delta.*

'Hear My Train A Comin'' (Jimi Hendrix)

This is a demo featuring The Experience, and even in this early form, it's evident why Hendrix frequently revisited the song. Of particular note is the moment about four minutes in when his shredding and Mitchell's fills swell together like a locomotive storming through the song. All the while, the bass keeps on rumbling, providing the solid train track for the licks to gambol on.

However, the acoustic version in Joe Boyd's *Jimi Hendrix* documentary (filmed between 1967 and 1970 but released in 1973) is the best. Showing his mastery of acoustic-playing too (a Zemaitis 12-string), it also reflects his exacting standards, as he winces at a note and then asks to begin again. His voice is unforced and doleful, and his harmonic execution is just as seamless when playing organically.

Returning to this album's cut, a playful little 'All aboard' just after the band have finished, is an unexpectedly wry detail after a superbly earnest performance.

See also *People, Hell and Angels*

'Mr. Bad Luck' (Jimi Hendrix)

Originating in 1966, this is a version of 'Look Over Yonder', first performed with The Blue Flames. Indeed, The Flames' second guitarist Randy California would produce a faithful cover with Spirit on their 1996 album *California Blues*, which also included their live version of 'Red House' – a decent cover spoiled by over-egging the punchline: 'I know, I know-ow-ow-ow, her sister will!'.

'The fools and their rules' are bringing the blues to Hendrix, who notes: 'You're sittin' here with your violins/Hittin' wrong notes', instead of the violin calling him in 'Are You Experienced'. The lyrics and some of the verse melody would be used in 'House Burning Down' too.

The intro was later reworked for Vivian Stanshall's sort of blues tribute 'King Kripple': the opening track on his 1981 album *Teddy Boys Don't Knit*. In Hendrix's London record collection was a copy of The Bonzo Dog Doo-Dah Band's *The Doughnut in Granny's Greenhouse*, which included the satirical 'Can Blue Men Sing the Whites':

> And now it's getting near the time, I gotta make the scene
> I change out my dark grey mohair suit, put on my dirty jeans
> The band comes 'round to pick me up, I holler, 'Hello boys'
> I gotta mess my hair up, I'm gonna make some noise brrr
> Can blue men sing the whites?
> Or are they hypocrites for singing woo, woo, wooh?

As they frequently did, The Bonzos made the wrangling over cultural appropriation and authenticity moot. Incidentally, that album title was inspired by a Michael Palin joke. Hendrix was also a *Monty Python* fan, and enjoyed Stanshall's humour and company. Stanshall told Geoffrey Giuliano in *Calypso to Collapso: The Resurrection of Vivian Stanshall*: 'Jimi Hendrix stayed at my place quite a bit. Jim was very courteous and a gentleman. The stories of him turning up at clubs at the height of his fame and just wanting to sit in with the band humbly, are quite true.' Stanshall sometimes jammed with him on the banjo or ukulele.

'Sunshine Of Your Love' (Jack Bruce, Eric Clapton, Pete Brown)

Cream's Hendrix tribute is developed around a Jack Bruce bass riff that follows a traditional blues progression. Eric Clapton added the chorus part, with the lyrics supplied by frequent Cream collaborator Pete Brown. Clapton used his Gibson SG to play the 'Blue Moon'-inspired solo, lending his performance a sly humour, and Hendrix also often played the track on an SG. In David Hepworth's highly enjoyable *A Fabulous Creation: How the LP Saved Our Lives*, he says that Ginger Baker initially floundered when it came to working out the drum part. Eventually, The Shadows' 'Apache' (with drumming by Tony Meehan) was suggested as a template. Baker played tom-toms on the downbeat, giving 'Sunshine Of Your Love' its distinctive and almost imposing rhythm.

But Cream were not initially as warm towards Hendrix as their tribute indicates. When Hendrix asked to jam with them, there was some reluctance. Ginger Baker told *Classic Rock*:

> We – Cream – were doing a gig in a theatre in London, and Jimi turned up to sit in with the band at the Central London Polytechnic. I was totally against it.

> I didn't want him to sit in at all because I didn't think it appropriate. We were fine without him. I didn't know who he was or anything, and when he did sit in, I was not at all impressed: he was doing all that playing guitar with his teeth and rolling about. I really don't know if Eric and Jack were impressed. I know Eric liked him. To me, he was being the big showman, whereas Eric just stood there and played. He was a great player.'

Jack Bruce told *Classic Rock*:

> I was just having a pre-gig pint in a pub across the road, and in comes this guy who turns out to be Jimi Hendrix. Now, we had already heard about Jimi on the grapevine. Jimi came up to me and said, 'Hi. I would like to sit in with the band.' I said it was fine with me, but he'd obviously have to check it out with Eric and Ginger. So we went across to the gig and Eric immediately said yes, and Ginger said, 'Oh, dunno about that.' So he came on and plugged into my bass amp, and as far as I can remember, he just blew us all away.

The most famous Hendrix version of 'Sunshine Of Your Love' is the fragment from *A Happening for Lulu*. The Experience had played 'Voodoo Chile (Slight Return)', and then were to close with the two-year-old 'Hey Joe' before being joined by Lulu for the last part of the song. However, Hendrix notoriously sabotaged the performance: 'We'd like to stop playing this rubbish, and dedicate a song to the Cream, regardless of what kind of group they may be in. We dedicate this to Eric Clapton, Ginger Baker and Jack Bruce.'

Whilst Hendrix definitely wanted to honour Cream – whose final album would be released the following month – it's also rumoured that he wanted to avoid duetting with Lulu in such a contrived fashion. Another theory is that Lulu was going to sing 'To Sir With Love' as a duet, and possibly Hendrix felt this was exploitative, as the film is concerned with a black teacher being accepted at an inner-city school in London's East End. Neither Redding nor Mitchell knew of his plans for rebellion, suggesting it was a response to something that had happened recently, so avoiding the duet seems more likely. Interestingly, Hendrix chose not to sing the lyrics of the song either, turning it into a savage instrumental. His most subversive moments often revolve around his reconstructing/deconstructing others' work, and this interpretation ranks high amongst them. Lulu didn't hold it against him, as The Experience visited her and Maurice Gibb's home after the show.

The instrumental version on *Valleys of Neptune* opens with a fast take on the famous riff, with some splashier drums before moving into a loose section where the rhythm alters to a samba. (The percussion is provided by Rocky Dzidzornu, whose distinctive conga-playing can be heard on The Rolling Stones' 'Sympathy For The Devil'.) There's a superb bass solo as Hendrix damps his strings behind it, before the drums return with an almost military-style fill; the track builds until Hendrix's guitar is once again blazing into an ascending run before arriving at the central riff: now fattened with some trills and lambent notes between. The fizzy cymbals remind us of the line 'when the stars start falling'. There's a flavour of Alexis Korner's CCS about the piece, and also of the middle section of Iron Butterfly's 'In-A-Gadda-Da-Vida', making this a unique piece in Hendrix's canon. Does it rival the original? Of course!

'Lover Man' (Jimi Hendrix)

Hendrix is the lover quitting the house before being caught by his lover's other man. It's a rollicking blues – played by The Experience – that was inspired by B.B. King's fertile 'Rock Me Baby'. Despite passing the four-minute mark, its intensity is such that it always feels too short. Band of Gypsys also recorded the song, and it can be found on *Both Sides Of The Sky*.

'Ships Passing Through The Night' (Jimi Hendrix)

This embryonic version of 'Night Bird Flying' was lost for a time but is a very interesting discovery. The tempo is slower here, with a feeling of The Move's 'Brontosaurus' in the bass riff, and some sudden pauses and shifts in rhythm not troubling the rhythm section at all. Different guitar licks pass each other like those ships, and the Leslie cabinet gives the guitar the timbre of gulls or even a ship's foghorn.

This track holds much of the promise of the jubilant 'Night Bird Flying', but is captivating in its own right. It also shows that Hendrix could probably have taken The Experience sound further.

'Fire' (Jimi Hendrix)

Fast, fun, furious – this version is the sound of The Experience getting on like… well, a house on fire, despite it now being 1969 and Redding and Hendrix's relationship becoming incendiary for all the wrong reasons. The solo is a little too long, and the backing vocals are immature against Hendrix's seductive cajoling, and there's a palpable excitement about playing one of their *old* songs.

'Red House' (Jimi Hendrix)

The tracks that The Experience recut as part of their rehearsals at Olympic are some of their finest and bring it home what a loss it was that they ended. The tempo is taken down, lending a further gravitas. It makes the intro a little faltering, but Hendrix's jazz-like trills more than make up for this. It's simply a great blues band performance.

'Lullaby For The Summer' (Jimi Hendrix)

The Experience recorded this embryonic version of 'Ezy Ryder' in New York. At this point it's an instrumental that takes some inspiration from 'Fire' in terms of its rhythm, as well as the call and response between bass and guitar, with Redding's bass looking ahead to Billy Cox's work in Band of Gypsys.

It's notable for the guitar distortion – created by the Octavia – which is getting close in parts to the synth sound from the studio version of 'The Star-Spangled Banner'. The track is a fruitful blend of R&B rhythms and phrasing, with a range of rock trilling and bending on the lead guitar licks that thread over one another in true Hendrix fashion: there are at least three different tones, from the thin to the blurry. Sadly, the track comes to a sudden end, but some of the magic that will be woven into 'Ezy Ryder' has already been invoked here.

'Crying Blue Rain' (Jimi Hendrix)

Valleys of Neptune comes adrift a little towards the end, in part because of the instrumentals that close it. But they can be seen as companion pieces in a sense, with 'Crying Blue Rain' being a cool riposte to the heat of 'Lullaby For The Summer'. Strictly speaking, Hendrix sings a little, but it's merely 'yeah yeah' here and there.

Opening a little similarly to 'Voodoo Chile', the rhythm then shifts to something more syncopated that creates a sense of anticipation. The guitar tone is fatter, matched by Mitchell's fills creating the sibilance of wheels through water. The tempo abruptly increases in the second half, and the backing struggle to lock in with this, the drums stammering and lagging somewhat. But it's an atmospheric piece showing that The Experience were far from moribund at this time.

Bonus tracks

'Trash Man' (Jimi Hendrix)

A sort of 'Purple Haze' without the psychedelic trappings, this is an electrifying instrumental with some wild but simultaneously controlled guitar, and a shift in the second half to a dreamier refrain and slower tempo.

'Slow Version' (Jimi Hendrix)

A very Hendrix-like jam with some sharp turns in the riff, and a contrasting steady bass with stormy, rustling drums.

Valleys of Neptune doesn't come across as a cohesive album in the way that *First Rays* mostly manages, but is essential listening. Opening with the later version of 'Stone Free' sans Redding, by the album's close, the power trio of The Experience have become indispensable. The Olympia recordings are simply excellent. It's easy to hear *Electric Ladyland* and not feel the loss of the trio in the awe-inspiring arrangement of textures, licks and tasteful, apposite guest stars (not always the way!), and then hear 'Machine Gun' and conclude that The Experience were spent. But *Valleys of Neptune* offers an alternative narrative. The work of Billy Cox also is so much richer than on *Band of Gypsys,* and it's regrettable that The Experience couldn't have continued in an augmented or more fluid form.

People, Hell and Angels (2013)

Well, everybody can hear the sound of freedom's beating heart…

Personnel:
Jimi Hendrix: Guitar, vocals, bass
Mitch Mitchell, Buddy Miles, Rocky Isaac: Drums
Billy Cox, Stephen Stills: Bass
Juma Sultan, Jerry Velez: Congas
Larry Lee: Rhythm guitar
Lonnie Youngblood: Vocals, saxophone
Al Marks: Percussion
Albert Allen: Vocals
James Booker: Piano
Gerry Sack: Triangle and mime vocal
Recorded at Record Plant, Hit Factory, Sound Centre, Electric Lady
Producers: Jimi Hendrix, Eddie Kramer
Engineers: Eddie Kramer
UK: 30, US: 2

As *Valleys of Neptune* gave a glimpse into The Experience shortly after *Electric Ladyland, People, Hell and Angels* represents more of the development of Band of Gypsys.

'Earth Blues' (Jimi Hendrix)

Lacking the power of the *First Rays* version, this is still an interesting take, with the backing vocals of Cox and Miles (instead of The Ronettes) giving it more of a rock feel. It does attest to an assurance in Hendrix's playing and vocals. As tumultuous as 1969 was – court cases, infighting, political turmoil etc. – Hendrix seemed to be ending the year in a secure place, at least musically.

'Somewhere' (Jimi Hendrix)

One of the album's strongest tracks, this might've made a better album opener than 'Earth Blues', and was released as the album's only single. Indeed, in *Two Riders Were Approaching: The Life and Death of Jimi Hendrix*, Eddie Kramer remarked to Mick Wall that it was his favourite track from this collection. Kramer also felt that Stephen Stills' bass was a vital ingredient. Indeed, there's a great atmosphere to the song with Miles on drums and Hendrix's guitar snarling. This is a sort of bridging sound between The Experience and The Gypsys, being recorded in March 1968. Mitch Mitchell later attempted to overdub drums on the track, but despite Kramer's praise, Stills' bass line was said to be off on that take, making an already tricky task even more difficult. Mitchell's attempt is available on *The Jimi Hendrix Experience* box set.

'Hear My Train A Comin'' (Jimi Hendrix)
The Experience had worked on this track previously, but here's an early take from the Band of Gypsys during their first-ever recording session in spring 1969. Hendrix often referred to it as 'Getting My Heart Back Together Again', and indeed it became a touchstone to which he frequently returned.
See also *Valleys of Neptune.*

'Bleeding Heart' (Jimi Hendrix)
According to John McDermott's liner notes for *People, Hell and Angels*, Hendrix was experimenting with a range of rhythm for this Elmore James song. Like with 'Hear My Train A Comin'', The Experience had previously recorded a version, but Hendrix was most pleased with this cut.
See also *Valleys of Neptune.*

'Let Me Move You' (Jimi Hendrix)
This is an exciting collaboration showing that Hendrix could be a tour de force – even when not being the main man, and even when someone else was singing a song he'd written. Here, Lonnie Youngblood takes the vocal, but it doesn't suffer like some of the Band of Gypsys cuts where Hendrix skates on the edge of anonymity. There's a thick sound to this one-off band, in which Hendrix's guitar seems to cry even louder. Hank Anderson is on bass, with John Winfield on organ, and drummer Jimmi Mayes of the Starliters and later Marvin Gaye's backing band. John McDermott notes that the group was assembled as a kind of celebration because they were able to work on a 16-track for the first time. There's certainly something triumphant about it.

'Izabella' (Jimi Hendrix)
Both a lesser and a greater version than the *First Rays* one, the rhythm is more compelling, with Hendrix's vocals smooth and his guitar almost nonchalantly funky. But therein lies the problem, as the music lacks the intensity that the lyrical content requires. Musically preferable, perhaps Hendrix should've reworked the lyric to reflect this. However, old friend Larry Lee – who's on rhythm guitar and would go on to play with Al Green and Albert King – had recently returned from Vietnam: lending the lyrics more weight, and possibly inspiring the content in the first place.
See also *First Rays of the Rising Sun.*

'Easy Blues' (Jimi Hendrix)
Featuring the same line-up as the previous track, this instrumental showcases some great playing by Cox and Mitchell's jazz-like fills are tightly controlled, with Hendrix's playing a squalling rhythm attack, and then behind that, some buzzing licks.

'Crash Landing' (Jimi Hendrix)

This is Hendrix working through the ideas for what would become 'Freedom'. Some falsetto singing from him is effective. Isaac's drumming has a nervous energy about it and it's clear it'll burst into something, but it's not there yet. The organ – uncredited – bleats in to try and vary the track, but it becomes momentous.

'Inside Out' (Jimi Hendrix)

Again using the Leslie speaker to invoke a more 3D sound, this is an extraordinary piece, with only Hendrix and Mitchell. Their experiments in this rhythm pattern would flower on 'Ezy Ryder'. There's a whiff of Fleetwood Mac's 'Oh Well' in some of the licks (although that song was still to come) and it has a pleasing propulsion with a lacing of menace.

'Hey Gypsy Boy' (Jimi Hendrix)

A version of 'Hey Baby (New Rising Sun)', and even whilst still in skeletal form, Hendrix's guitar is almost lachrymose, exhibiting such precision and sensitivity in the playing. In the middle, the guitar tone recalls 'Little Wing', before the wah-wah soaks into the piece, lending a dreamy off-balance feeling. Hendrix's use of the whammy bar is also exemplary here, conveying light travelling across a landscape. There's been some mystery about who's on bass. But on the same day, Hank Anderson had played bass on 'Let Me Move You', so he might be here too.

See also *First Rays of the Rising Sun*.

'Mojo Man' (Albert Allen, Arthur Allen)

Written by TaharQa and Tunde Ra Aleem (also known as Arthur and Albert Allen), with vocals by Albert, 'Mojo Man' has Hendrix overdubbing two guitar parts. It's always fascinating to hear him play with a horn section, as this is quite rare and never fully realised on any of those tracks. But Hendrix's sustain howls behind the vocals that speak of keeping away bad luck because they're 'a mojo man'. It continues with 'Can't love electric flames/Though it can fuck with me/Cause I'm, I'm a Mojo Man'. Despite the mojo being a good luck charm, there's something unclear in Allen's message with his being got at. But he also alludes to 'voodoo ingenuity', and this, combined with the fire imagery, evokes Hendrix as a kind of high priest. It might be expected that the fire *couldn't* 'fuck' with a man of power, and yet this isn't part of this song's brag: implying the mojo man's impotence.

James Booker – who'd worked with Fats Domino and was sometimes nicknamed 'the black Liberace' – is on organ.

'Villanova Junction Blues' (Jimi Hendrix)

This is a snippet of the piece that Hendrix would play at Woodstock, backed by the Band of Gypsys. It's a fragment that rounds off the album almost casually. For Hendrix, it *was* this easy.

People, Hell and Angels offers some interesting cuts, but doesn't illuminate quite as much as the previous albums, and seems to suggest there was little of real value left in the vaults. However, the following *Both Sides Of The Sky* would be a surprise.

Both Sides Of The Sky (2018)

So he goes on the road to be a Voodoo Child, come back to be a Magic Boy…

Personnel:
Jimi Hendrix: Guitar, vocals, bass
Mitch Mitchell, Buddy Miles: Drums
Noel Redding, Billy Cox: Bass
Stephen Stills: Vocal, organ
Johnny Winter: Guitar
Lonnie Youngblood: Vocals, saxophone
Recorded at Olympic, Record Plant
Producers: Jimi Hendrix, Eddie Kramer
Engineers: George Chkiantz, Gary Kellgren, Jack Adams

The last official release from the Legacy deal, *Both Sides Of The Sky* is a mature (mostly) blues album that works well as a collection, with Hendrix's own compositions slotting naturally into the blues canon *proper*, asserting his authentic voice in this genre. The guest stars (including Lonnie Youngblood and Stephen Stills) enhance rather than detract as can sometimes be case, and instead of this being a last option for a bored or jaded performer, Hendrix seems to be taking something away from each player, to feed his development.

'Mannish Boy' (Muddy Waters)

As Charles Shaar Murray pointed out, Muddy Waters' 'Mannish Boy' from 1955 is much more than a macho brag, with the racist overtone of the term 'boy' being implicitly addressed here. Waters built on Bo Diddley's 'I'm A Man' (also from 1955), with both songs spelling out their humanity – M, A, N – regardless of race. Diddly's opens with:

> Now when I was a little boy
> At the age of five
> I had somethin' in my pocket
> Keep a lot of folks alive

Whereas Waters' gambit is:

> Everything gonna be alright this mornin'
> Now, when I was a young boy
> At the age of five
> My mother said I was gonna be
> The greatest man alive

This shift from sexual bragging and innuendo is an acknowledgement of the halted potential of people of colour. Furthermore, Waters also adds that he's 'a rolling stone', in defiance of vagrancy laws. Not that Waters eschews the libidinous completely, and he would sometimes enhance the song's performance by using a beer bottle as a phallus. And if we can detect Hendrix's stagecraft also being inspired by Waters, it was mutual, as Waters was to employ fuzz tone on his 1968 *Electric Mud* album.

Hendrix's version is certainly an adult interpretation, with a change to the tempo that lends a self-assured power. Indeed, this is a poised performance; it isn't at all obvious that it's from the Gypsy's first session, with a strongly controlled vocal from Hendrix and some unironic falsetto that adds a pure joy to his proclamation. The drum fills after the 'I'm a man' refrain seem to applaud him; the muscular bass flexing and rallying behind. Unfortunately, the take ends suddenly: something of an anticlimax.

The Experience also performed 'Hoochie Coochie Man' (also made famous by Muddy Waters, but written by Willie Dixon), and its stop-time riff became the inspiration for 'I'm A Man'. Their slick version for the BBC programme *Rhythm and Blues* – with Alexis Korner on slide guitar and Redding on his muscular 8-string bass – is available on *The Jimi Hendrix Experience BBC Sessions.*

'Lover Man' (Jimi Hendrix)

Hendrix kept returning to this song but never found what he sought, as no definitive version was made. After trying it with The Experience, he attempted it again with Band of Gypsys. It's a fiery piece with an effortlessly controlled solo that segues into the *Batman* theme, adding a sly humour and again merging the 'mojo man' of the blues with the cartoon superhero. This is continued towards the end, when there's a shift, and a new riff emerges, seeming to announce the lover man cometh.

'Hear My Train A Comin'' (Jimi Hendrix)

This version is The Experience in April 1969, and its atmosphere is coolly controlled, sounding like a blues classic that has already been around for at least a decade.

See also *Valleys of Neptune* and *South Saturn Delta.*

'Stepping Stone' (Jimi Hendrix)

This more rousing version than the one from *First Rays* opens with that train-track rhythm, reminding us of the previous cut and linking it back to *Are You Experienced*. The pace is sustained by Cox's wired bass and Hendrix's guitar lines mirroring his confident vocals: the scolding lines after 'You're a woman/ At least you say you are' are particularly striking. The bass also steps across Hendrix's solo: a clever allusion to the lyric's theme. The song was originally known as 'I'm A Man': Hendrix's own riff on freedom and movement as inspired by Waters and Diddley. This seems to be Hendrix's answer in the tradition of blues songs answering previous blues songs, and once again, the heightened performance and the committed company around it makes this seem like an authentic Chicago blues classic.

'$20 Fine' (Stephen Stills)

A Stephen Stills composition with some effective flares of organ, this song demonstrates the band working as one. As well as Stills on vocals and organ, there's Duane Hitchings from The Buddy Miles Express (best known for co-writing Rod Stewart's 'Da Ya Think I'm Sexy?') on piano and Mitchell on drums. But, surprisingly, the weak link is Hendrix: his licks and solo are almost pedestrian, as though he's struggling for ideas. This isn't aided by him forgoing his usual mastery of sustain, and playing a series of short notes around some repetitive licks that can't help but be sunk by the organ. This is rectified towards the end when the damping, scratchy strumming and note bends spring alive. Also, there's an ear-catching opening riff – a Hendrix trademark of course – with prints of 'Under My Thumb'. Indeed, the song has some melodic resemblance to The Rolling Stones' 'Tumbling Dice', so they must've taken back the inspiration. Overall, the song is fairly engaging and has a memorable chorus hook, but it fails as a Hendrix collaboration. Nevertheless, the lyrics are in similar territory to 'Hear My Train A Comin'': 'And I know my time is comin'/Everything we want is just around the corner/ Carry it all'.

Hendrix later played guitar on 'Old Times, Good Times' from Stephen Stills' eponymous 1970 debut album, which Stills dedicated to Hendrix's memory. In another link to Hendrix, the album also includes the love song 'Cherokee' – said to be regarding Stills' relationship with Rita Coolidge, who'd sung backing vocals for Hendrix. Hendrix admired Stills and considered offering him a permanent post in the band. Stills told *Record Collector*:

> I also played bass a lot of the time when we were jamming, which I was pretty good at. I read in Mitch Mitchell's book (*Jimi Hendrix: Inside The Experience*) that I was in Hawaii with a cast on my left hand, just sitting there, and Jimi's office was desperately trying to find me because he and Noel Redding had had a falling out and they wanted me to play on this one more tour. And David Geffen just said, 'I don't know where he is.' Y'know, he owned the franchise, and what a complication it would have been for them if Jimi and I had started another franchise! So that was that. I'd heard rumours down the years, which I didn't believe, because I thought, 'Aw, they'd never do that to me.' But 20 years later, Mitch writes a book, and there it is. God bless him.

Stills would also collaborate with Hendrix on the controversially titled 'White Nigger', which is sometimes billed as 'No Name Jam'. The cut has a Stones feel, with some spidery licks from Hendrix.

'Power Of Soul' (Jimi Hendrix)

Hendrix almost has his guitar gargling on this preferable version of 'Power Of Soul' recorded early in 1970. It's strangely effective and more powerful than the Fillmore cut. It seems that almost all of the other Gypsy recordings are in some ways superior to that album. Yet the clichéd chorus (both lyrically and melodically) weakens the track, although it's saved by the smooth backing vocals and how they cohere at the close.

This is the full unedited piece from which the shorter *South Saturn Delta* version is cut.

'Jungle' (Jimi Hendrix)

Only Hendrix and Buddy Miles appear on this initially laid-back instrumental. Rustling cymbals highlight a gently picked riff with some precise Uni-Vibe effects, and it has the feel of a nocturnal animal slinking low in the undergrowth.

Miles' drumming shifts to a more native feel before the second half picks up speed with a scratchier riff that fades out too quickly. This is another fine example of Hendrix creating evocative soundscapes that didn't need to be delineated by lyrics.

'Things I Used To Do' (Guitar Slim)

Hendrix was inspired by Guitar Slim's distortion innovations, and Slim in turn had been influenced by another Hendrix favourite: T-Bone Walker. Hendrix's interpretation is less weary and resigned than the original and is a very grown-up, measured blues. He also includes a snippet from Bo Diddley's 'Before You Accuse Me' in the 'Try my love one more time' verse. Cleverly, it complicates the lyric, developing the wrongdoing on both parts.

Johnny Winter joins on astute slide guitar, along with Crosby, Stills & Nash drummer Dallas Taylor. Winter spoke of his time with Hendrix in the introduction to his biography *Raisin' Cain: The Wild and Raucous Story of Johnny Winter* by Mary Lou Sullivan:

> I usually gave him the reins pretty much, I mostly played rhythm. But on the song we recorded – 'The Things That I Used to Do' – we traded off: I played slide guitar and he played regular guitar. It came out really well. I believe that was the only song that was recorded. I played with him about ten times maybe, and thought he was the best guitar player around.

Winter has another less illustrious connection to Hendrix – Winter's debut album was partly produced by Eddie Kramer, but Kramer was sacked, with Winter remarking that the producer spent too much time outside trying to record sound effects.

Winter would go on to produce Muddy Waters' later re-recording of 'Mannish Boy' for his 1977 album *Hard Working*.

'Georgia Blues' (Jimi Hendrix)

Opening with slinking bass and sauntering licks, this is a casually cool blues with Lonnie Youngblood from Curtis Knight and the Squires on vocals, grieving for a lost love. Hendrix's guitar weeps, wails and whimpers throughout this standout track. Admittedly, Youngblood's saxophone is sometimes a little ill-conceived, and its quacking tone ruptures the atmosphere, but in the main, its rancorous whimper is woeful. It also highlights how tasteful Hendrix's improvisations are and how *elastic* his tone is. Youngblood recounts his misery, and asks for help from his mama and God, as his little girl and all of his friends have let him down. Albeit, they are the most clichéd of blues lyrics, but are given a resonance and pathos through the superior backing. Jimmi Mayes of the Starliters is on drums, with the Squires' Hank Anderson (sometimes known as Napoleon Anderson) on bass and John Winfield on organ. Little seems to be known about the mysterious John Winfield.

Hendrix had previously duetted with Lonnie Youngblood on 'Wipe The Sweat' – one of the more Hendrix-sounding early tracks – with some smoky blues licks in the first section, and, in 'Part 3' (another track with multiple parts), Hendrix telling us he's dancing with 'Miss Lucy Mae', who would become Dolly Mae for 'Wait Until Tomorrow'. Lenny Howard reused the backing track for 'Keep The Faith, Baby' in 1966.

Youngblood later unsuccessfully sued filmmaker Martin Scorsese and the Hendrix estate for including this track without permission on the fine collection *Martin Scorsese Presents the Blues*: which also boasts 'Red House'.

'Sweet Angel' (Jimi Hendrix)

This is an early performance of 'Angel' with just Hendrix and Mitchell; the former taking on bass and vibraphone too. It's much more affecting than the one on *First Rays,* as the music thoughtfully implies the rise and rise of the angel, and also of Hendrix's spirit. The muscular bass contrasts gorgeously with the evanescent vibraphone, and lends a salvational strength that surpasses the other versions. This track and 'Cherokee Mist' show that Hendrix may well have been moving towards more symbolist works. Although his vocals are a crucial feature of his sound – and more skilful than he ever believed – as his music advanced, they were needed less. The guitar punctuation and the arrangement of the whole piece was taking on the greater nuances of a complete language, and 'Sweet Angel' is this in bud.

'Woodstock' (Joni Mitchell)

This has Stephen Stills on vocals and organ, and Hendrix on bass. The song doesn't gain much from being reworked as a straight-up rock track – some of Stills' phrasing suffers, and the organ jam at the end is rather dull with Hendrix's bass cocking impatiently behind it. Stills told Joe Bosso at *MusicRadar* about his recollections of Hendrix:

> Not much taller than me. A little wisp of a guy. Very soft-spoken. I wouldn't be able to hear him today – my ears are so bad, even with these. But he was funny, and he taught me a great deal about playing lead. I remember he was showing me something, and I said, 'Jimi, Jimi… put your hand up.' So he held his hand up, and I put mine next to his, and I said, 'That's Wilt Chamberlain. This is me. Your thumb is longer than mine. I can't do what you're doing.' So he went, 'Oh yeah,' and he figured out a way to show me the same thing. Jimi was astonishing. Very dear, a dear soul. We'd decompress, and talked for hours and hours.

Sadly, in the same interview, Stills also scotched rumours of their being a lost album with Hendrix. But he did confirm some unreleased recorded jams that didn't really go anywhere.

CSN's admiration for Joni Mitchell is widely known, and they would also record their own version of 'Woodstock' for their *Déjà Vu* album. Less well known is how Hendrix was also a big fan of Joni Mitchell, even asking if he could record one of her gigs in Ottawa. Mitchell agreed, and Hendrix crouched by the stage with his recorder for her entire performance. The tapes were later stolen, but were miraculously unearthed 50 years later, with Hendrix's recording being included on *Joni Mitchell Archives Vol. 2: The Reprise Years (1968–1971)*.

'Send My Love To Linda' (Jimi Hendrix)

Thought to be a paean to Linda Keith – the woman who recommended Hendrix to Chandler, and who probably inspired The Rolling Stones' elegiac 'Ruby Tuesday' – this is a unique track in the Hendrix canon, owing to its lo-fi atmosphere.

Though Keith and Hendrix initially had a strong friendship, there was also conflict between them. Keith told *The Observer* that trouble began when '…he smashed up a white guitar. I was beside myself. I'd lent him a guitar belonging to my boyfriend (Keith Richards), and there he was smashing one up on stage! I was absolutely livid with Jimi because to me, that's the most uncool thing to do.'

In the same interview, she continues: 'I was still the one he came to when the chips were really down. And before his death, he made contact again. He wrote saying he'd written a new track, "See Me Linda, Hear Me, I'm Playing The Blues". I always loved his blues playing, but then, most of his songs do sound like the blues.'

Hendrix's sound had thrilled Keith when she saw him performing at the Café Wha? and she was bemused by how little attention it was receiving. But not everyone was as happy about Hendrix as she was, with Keith Richards describing him to Linda Keith's father as a 'black junkie' – a gobsmacking act of hypocrisy regarding both drug abuse and African American culture (part of it was paying Richards' bills after all). It's also rumoured that even Keith Moon remarked disapprovingly that Hendrix was 'savage'. This contradicts the idea that Hendrix was welcomed with the widest of embraces on British soil, and Linda Keith's loyalty and belief in him was precious indeed. Nevertheless, some sources say that Linda Keith was superseded by Kathy Etchingham, and Keith became resentful and disappointed in how Hendrix seemed to cast her aside. Nevertheless, the lyrics offer a belated gratitude and a worrying fatalism: 'She lit a fire way down inside/She made the sun shine in my eye/God, let me hold her once more before I die'. The first half of the song is the sound of the fire sputtering, whilst the latter is its second coming.

Opening with a classical guitar flourish, this marks a change in tone for the album, with some critics feeling that the track had a 1990s grunge tone. Hendrix uses the body of his guitar as a percussive instrument, and initially there's minimal accompaniment. His vocal is sincere, if a little muted. Then the drum pattern quickens, breaking the suspense, and a walking bass line propels the message as Hendrix excels on an undeniably widdly guitar solo – but in such sharp contrast to the song's first half, it's like the passion he wants to send is escaping into the ether. Again, it fades out too suddenly and demands to be repeated.

Hendrix had recorded another song to a previously lost love in a comparable tone before: *The West Coast Seattle Boy* version of '1983' has a similar air, and one wonders if 'Send My Love To Linda' would've retained its lo-fi feel if it had been reworked.

'Cherokee Mist' (Jimi Hendrix)

This title was also mooted as the title of a forthcoming Hendrix album during his lifetime. Hendrix plays the electric sitar – a new invention pioneered by Danelectro with session guitarist Vinnie Bell, which had been designed to be played more easily than a traditional sitar, as its fretboard was more like that of a standard guitar. Eric Burdon and The Animals are often credited with its first use on their track 'Monterey', but it graces Stevie Wonder's 'I Was Made To Love Her' from five months earlier (a song which The Experience and Wonder were to jam on together at the BBC). On Cherokee Mist it's played by The Funk Brothers' guitarist Eddie Willis.

Musically, Hendrix worked out the rhythm first, jamming around it with Cox and Mitchell in early versions before it clarified into the piece on *Both Sides Of The Sky*. Opening with a tribal drum rhythm, this is a fascinating track with multiple guitar tones. One mimics a buzzard's scream, one glints like chips of starlight, and another is a spiral of mist; then there's the red heat of white sands. The sitar-like tone adds a contemporary feel, as Hendrix added to the traditional tones of 'Voodoo Chile'. Mitchell's drumming is sensitive, and Redding's bass is the constant in the landscape that the mist obscures, reveals, redefines. It's an extraordinary piece, and shows there was much territory left to explore for The Experience.

Hendrix's paternal grandmother Zenora – known as Nora – was a quarter Cherokee, and this heritage was very important to him. It's rumoured that

Lucille once told Hendrix that Al wasn't his father. The two men bear an undeniable likeness, but doubt over the fatherhood of Lucille's children was often a source of contention for Al. Indeed, Al suspected that Hendrix's father was a man named John: leading him to change Hendrix's name to Allen. If Al wasn't Hendrix's father, then that would've also meant that his Native American legacy was being denied to him, although Lucille is said to have had a similar heritage. Yet, Hendrix would be shorn of his paternal grandmother and her links to the stage as well. In Philip Norman's biography, he recounts how Hendrix stared into his father's face several times before boarding the plane that would take him back to London and his premature death. Perhaps Hendrix was looking for proof of his providence, or reflecting on an older version of his face that would never stare back at him in the room full of mirrors. 'Cherokee Mist' – as essentially the *last* Hendrix track, and the final one on what is mostly a blues collection – makes a compelling statement about his heritage.

Both Sides Of The Sky is a much better coda than many had anticipated. Indeed, its final tracks ('Send My Love To Linda' and 'Cherokee Mist') are amongst Hendrix's most intriguing and accomplished, each signifying a sonic leap.

Live Roundup

Hendrix live is best explicated by Roger Mayer, as told to *The Observer*'s Ed Vulliamy:

> When you listen to Hendrix, you are listening to music in its pure form... The input from the player projects forward the equivalent of electronic shadow-dancing, so that what happens derives from the original sound and modifies what is being played. But nothing can be predictive... if you throw a pebble into a lake, you have no way of predicting the ripples. It depends how you throw the stone, or the wind.

Here is the strength and weakness of his live work: moments of genius, happy accidents, spontaneous communication. But it also hints at the lack of control or discipline that could infect his performances.

BBC Sessions

This includes Hendrix's only recorded version of Bob Dylan's 1965 single 'Can You Please Crawl Out Your Window?', recorded for *Rhythm and Blues* and introduced by Alexis Korner, who followed the performance with 'And that's to show that you can never predict what's gonna happen on the BBC World Service!' It's not a particularly noteworthy cut in truth, but The Experience also excellently perform Willie Dixon's '(I'm Your) Hoochie Coochie Man', (an influence on 'Voodoo Chile') with Korner on feathery slide and Redding on the 8-string bass. In *Hear My Train A' Comin': The Songs of Jimi Hendrix*, Kevin Le Gendre remarks that the 8-string bass had a personal significance for Hendrix, as he played it on his Curtis Knight recordings from 1965: but, in Hendrix's opinion, unsuccessfully. He'd been looking for the right song, and with its swaggering sound complemented by Korner's sensitive slide, it creates a seductive tone. Hendrix had first met Alexis Korner at a jam he organised at the club Les Cousins at 49 Greek Street. Hendrix paid admission like any other punter, then joined in with an all-night jam, gobsmacking everyone. The Experience conclude the programme with the catchy Curtis Knight instrumental 'Driving South', and this is also revisited for *Top Gear* which also boasts a lively take on Leiber and Stoller's 'Hound Dog', complete with doggy backing vocals. Stevie Wonder happened to be recording another programme at the same time, so ended up drumming (badly!) on the meandering 'Jammin'', where his timekeeping suffers from trying to keep up with the mercurial Hendrix. He's also on 'I Was Made To Love Her', but here Hendrix struggles and isn't really playing the right song at all!

But Hendrix *must* have enjoyed his radio session, because he even writes a jingle. The affectionate piss-take 'Radio One' grants the station a hard-rocking theme with a flavour of 'Wild Thing'. An ebullient 'Day Tripper' opens with a snippet of the riff from The Beatles 'I Want To Tell You', and then has Redding taking the lead vocal. It's said some believed this was really John Lennon sneaking a cameo, but the vocals – whilst pleasing – are not of his quality. From *Top of the Pops*, there's a storming 'Purple Haze', and Hendrix makes some revealing comments when chatting to Brian Matthew on *Saturday Club,* when he explains that The Experience and Cream are not really alike, as what he's doing has more feeling. In another snippet of conversation, he also states that he prefers playing live to being in the studio: a sentiment that wouldn't last much longer.

Live at Monterey (recorded in 1967; released in 2007) has The Experience being introduced by Brian Jones, who's one of few MCs to remember that the band isn't called Jimi Hendrix. A lethally good 'Killing Floor' opens the set, with another highlight being a furious 'Rock Me Baby'. In *Forever Changes*, Arthur Lee recalled that guitarist Nooney Rickett told Hendrix he sounded like B.B. King: 'If looks could kill, I think Nooney would have died on the spot.' Nevertheless, Hendrix's tone is as fluid as King's. There's also a version of 'Can You See Me' that makes its debt to Cream more evident than the album cut. 'The Wind Cries Mary' seems a little jarring in the other company, even though it's a fine version.

Then the set blazes out with The Troggs' 'Wild Thing' (written by Chip Taylor), and Hendrix includes flurries of Frank Sinatra's 'Strangers In The Night'. As a track, it's much less exciting without being able to see the performance, too, of course. Hendrix told *Melody Maker*: 'The Troggs and that scene just aren't solid. A group like them will never really get any respect.' John Lennon was said to have been thrilled by Hendrix's version. Indeed, *Live at Monterey* is probably the definitive artefact of the early live Experience.

Miami Pop Festival (recorded in 1968; released in 2013) opens with an unrecognisable 'Hey Joe' that takes the squalling triumph of 'The Star-Spangled Banner' to stun the audience before the familiar swagger of the intro takes over. It's followed by another crowd-pleaser: 'Foxy Lady'. 'Tax Free' might seem a little overwrought, but the crowd's reaction to it belies this, and the drumming is superb. Although this set has a reputation for being lacklustre, The Experience rarely sag.

Hendrix In The West (including cuts from 1969 and 1970; released in 1972) includes some spirited performances of rock 'n' roll standards, like a cocksure 'Johnny B. Goode' and a blues-funk interpretation of 'Blue Suede Shoes'. It also includes 'God Save The Queen' – billed here as 'The Queen' – which is missed off the first release of the Isle of Wight concert.

Woodstock (recorded in 1969; released in 1994) has a fine 'Red House', and the apocalyptic and, of course, most famous version of 'The Star-Spangled Banner'. But an inertia hangs over much of the set: particularly the tracks from the Experience years. 'Message To Love' crawls along before a stinging solo slaps the band to life. 'Woodstock Improvisation' has flamenco touches and the air of Hendrix duelling with himself. Interestingly, he makes a point of introducing his band first – naming each player, making a definite comment on this being Gypsy Sun and Rainbows, and *not* The Jimi Hendrix Experience as the MC had billed them.

*Live in Maui (*recorded in 1970; released in 2020) collects the two sets from the scrappy *Rainbow Bridge* film, and shows off the superb medley of 'Hey Baby'/'In From The Storm'. The music's muscularity is simply thrilling, even if Hendrix's vocals sound as though he's singing through a blanket – or if we're being kind, through a storm. 'Voodoo Chile (Slight Return)', though slightly faster, stays on the right side of brash, and Cox and Mitchell complete an impressive power trio that at times rival The Experience.

Blue Wild Angel: Live at the Isle of Wight (recorded in 1970; released in 2002) is an interesting artefact of the Cox and Mitchell rhythm section, showing a magic touch from Cox on Experience material as well as new cuts. The gig's title comes from Hendrix wanting to be introduced as a blue wild angel, but instead, he was billed with the comparatively anticlimactic The man with the guitar'. The live 'All Along The Watchtower' lays out much of Hendrix's new direction: multiple solos of different textures; lulls and surges in dynamics etc.

But a recurrent gripe about many of Hendrix's live recordings are the muted vocals, and *Isle of Wight* is no different. It includes Hendrix's take on 'God Save The Queen', a strident 'Sgt. Pepper's Lonely Hearts Club Band' and an interminable 'Machine Gun' (admittedly, the sound quality is abysmal, with the security guards' radio messages intruding) that lacks the ammunition of the Band of Gypsys' triumph – mostly because it loses its own atmosphere by alluding to 'Voodoo Chile' and having rather monotonous long/short note patterns. Yet the set is nowhere near as incoherent as some have suggested. Indeed, it's said that protesters were trying to set the stage roof alight as Hendrix kept his cool and played! They should've done 'Fire'! But the previous release from this set (*Isle of Wight* (1971)) includes the best tracks from this concert – 'Midnight Lightning', 'Foxy Lady', 'Lover Man', 'Freedom', 'All Along The Watchtower', 'In from The Storm' – and also boasts a different mix.

Live at the Fillmore East (recorded in 1970; released in 1999) presents the tracks cut from the 1970 *Band of Gypsys* album, and is an excellent – even superior – collection. 'Auld Lang Syne' is the opener, with 'Wild Thing' providing the finale. There's also the epic blues 'Burning Desire', and a version of Howard Tate's 'Stop' (written by Jerry Ragovoy and Mort Shuman) that has the band in top form. However, the album was superseded by *Songs for Groovy Children: The Fillmore East Concerts*, rounding up most of the unreleased tracks, including longer versions of others, and an aimless version of Jimmy Hughes' 'Steal Away' with Miles on lead vocal.
Freedom: Atlanta Pop Festival (recorded in 1970; released in 2015), ironically, has a less-than-potent 'Freedom' suffering from a lack of attesting backing vocals. There's a slight hollowness about the entire set; something missing in the sound that might be a lack of overall mastering compression, making each cut seem chilly and remote, even affecting usually unassailable tracks like 'Spanish Castle Magic'.

Compilations

Smash Hits is a round-up of hits and B-sides that was released in the spring of 1968: being the only best of-style compilation available during Hendrix's lifetime. The UK version is preferable, as it rounds up the early work of The Experience, including 'The Stars That Play with Laughing Sam's Dice', whereas the US one replaces that song with 'All Along The Watchtower', bringing in the sound of Act Two and muddying the album's atmosphere.

This works better on *Experience Hendrix: The Best of Jimi Hendrix* from 1997, which is a fine overview with an effectively ordered tracklist, although some feel short-changed that it doesn't include '...Laughing Sam...', or 'Third Stone From The Sun' which is often seen as an essential cut. Moreover, the album includes tracks from *First Rays*, but misses out on any official Band of Gypsys tracks altogether. Nevertheless, it's a superb collection showcasing the full wingspan of Hendrix's creativity. Many must agree, as the album's gone platinum in the UK and US.

A definitive overview can be found on the excellent *West Coast Seattle Boy: The Jimi Hendrix Anthology*. This collects his significant early recordings, many of which were discussed in the introduction to this book. There's another Little Richard cut: the catchy 'Dancing All Around The World', with sparing guitar from Hendrix. Frank Howard and the Commanders perform Billy Cox's Motown-sounding 'I'm So Glad', with Hendrix's slightly fuzzy riffing working well against the clear brass. His flashing licks and bent notes are more evident on the predictable R&B of Jimmy Norman's 'That Little Old Groovemaker'. Billy Lamont's 'Sweet Thang' is another generic cut, showing that Hendrix was often to be found backing sub-'Land Of 1000 Dances' works, that meant his playing sometimes bordered on anonymous. And King Curtis' 'Instant Groove' is a reworking of the backing track to Ray Sharpe's 'Help Me'. But Hendrix and Curtis had recorded together in 1966, resulting in the unreleased 'Linda Lou', 'Baby How About You' and 'I Can't Take It'.

Rosa Lee Brooks' contentious 'My Diary' is collected here as well. Brooks met Hendrix back in his Little Richard days, and she was a girlfriend of both him and Arthur Lee. She told author Kevin Grace that she and Hendrix wrote the song together on New Year's Day, and that Arthur Lee had no involvement in composing it, despite his claims to the contrary. Hendrix described his playing on the track as 'love notes', and Brooks felt the song was a deeply personal moment between the two of them, referring to Lee's later appropriation as 'grave robbing'. Lee did produce the song and explained he wanted someone who could play like Curtis Mayfield, and so sought out Hendrix. The line '... love sicken image I turned out to be' is arresting, but musically, it's a fairly generic soul, lifted by the committed vocal and memorable brass refrain. Again, Hendrix's playing is restrained; merely Mayfield-lite. Another Rosa Lee Brooks track – 'Utee' – is a dance song augmented by a Hendrix solo of frenetic notes, then some experimentation with sustain before progressing to bassier – Hendrix's signature – sounds.

The collection also includes live cuts, unreleased versions, rarities and a fascinating documentary. Of the unreleased tracks, 'Calling All The Devil's Children' is an icy-cool rocker with a feel of 'Purple Haze''s diabolic mode. The track simmers down as voices and applause swell, and Hendrix becomes a rabble-rousing MC. 'Hear My Freedom' has some 'Voodoo Chile' organ, and grows around a twitchy bass riff, before the organ breaks out in Ray Manzarek fashion. It's nearly three minutes before Hendrix begins to sing, describing his favourite theme: freedom. 'Messenger' has some interesting ascending and descending chord patterns combined with gentle piano trills, creating an effective blend of rock and lounge that ends with Hendrix giggling and declaring, 'We're going to have to keep that one!'.

'Untitled Basic Track' is less inspired and 'Ezy Rider' would achieve its defiant dynamism much more successfully. 'Young/Hendrix' was titled by Alan Douglas, and references organist Larry Young, originally appearing on 'Nine To The Universe'. Clocking in at around 20 minutes, this monster jam showcases some of Hendrix's most jazz-like playing against Young's judicious flurries. The change to a boogie-woogie rhythm in the middle keeps the ear entertained in what could be a test of the listener's stamina. Nevertheless, it's an extraordinary testament to two towering musicians. 'Mastermind' features a lead vocal from Larry Lee: a track he performed at Woodstock. Hendrix's guitar has an almost acoustic tone in the short but arresting solo. It seems to chime. 'Burning Desire' is another *First Rays*-style rocker with some clean, lucid playing, and the guitar effects are tastefully used, as on 'All God's Children', which distinguishes itself with a little Spanish heat highlighting its flourishes. 'Lonely Avenue' is the Doc Pomus song made famous by Ray Charles, and benefits from Hendrix's lachrymose riffing after the 'I'm cryin, I'm crying' refrain. 'Peter Gunn/Catastrophe' is a more Dick-Dale-esque version of the theme song, before Hendrix breaks off to snarl a little of the 'Lover Man' opening and then improvises around an overdramatic repetition of the word 'catastrophe'. The (likely) Brian Jones collaboration 'Little One' also appears: it's a lost gem and should've been taken further. 'Cat Talking To Me' has an effective rhythm, and chords reminiscent of The Kinks' 'Big Sky'.

'Tears Of Rage' is a cover to be found on Dylan and The Band's *The Basement Tapes*. Indeed, Paul Caruso – who provides backing vocals and harmonica – has a quavering, gravelly Dylan vocal timbre. It's a sensitive, semi-acoustic performance. 'Bolero' is an instrumental that recalls the softer tracks by Love, e.g. 'She Comes In Colours', before galloping away into a tightly controlled rock that's not really a bolero and has more of a Mexican than Cuban feel. Part of its sound can also be found on 'Send My Love To Linda'. Hendrix may have taken some inspiration from Jeff Beck's 'Beck's Bolero' (the B-side (though superior, of course!) to 'Hi Ho Silver Lining'): a track he rated highly. 'Hound Dog Blues' – based on the Leiber and Stoller song – has touches of

'Lover Man' in its unrestrained intro and ringing solo. 'New Rising Sun' takes the second part of '1983' further, and is gentler than the previously released version, evocatively implying the movement of light in its delicate guitar lines and shimmering tremolo tone; the track swelling gradually like a sunrise. Its pausing and moments of stasis are taken from 'Little Wing' and 'Angel'. In contrast, 'Suddenly November Morning' mourns for the loss of warmth – 'But it seems like years ago/Since I felt the warm glow of the sun/Lately things seem a little colder' – and this mood is continued in the shivery strumming of an acoustic guitar. The imagery also returns us to *Are You Experienced*, with the wind having moved on and taken his love with it, and every day now being like November. Hendrix was born towards the end of this month, and there's an ironic twist here. The song then shifts into 'Drifting', and it has the atmosphere of some of the *White Album* Marrakesh outtakes.

West Coast Seattle Boy is a superb collection, where the alternative versions really do offer something different. Indispensable.

Although compiled by Alan Douglas in 1994, *Blues* has remained a fan favourite that evokes an after-hours jam atmosphere, collects fascinating versions of Hendrix and blues classics, and showcases his astonishing versatility. The instrumental version of 'Born Under A Bad Sign' – made famous by Albert King – is magnificently moody, whilst 'Once I Had A Woman' backed by Band of Gypsys is a lean, slinky lament that combines the atmosphere of 'Red House' with the lacerating guitar tone of 'Voodoo Chile (Slight Return). The album also includes two worthwhile jams – 'Jelly 292' and 'Electric Church Red House' – featuring Lee Michaels on organ.

Guest Appearances

Predictably, Hendrix's prowess was much sought by other musicians, and he appeared on several tracks as a guest star.

The Curtis Knight songs that were said to be recorded in 1967, are rounded up on *The Summer of Love Sessions*, although some of these recordings could be from earlier. A haze hangs over exactly when Hendrix laid them down, as some skulduggery regarding management and record company red tape has been cited. Included among these tracks is 'My Best Friend' showing some interesting experimentation with wah-wah and fuzz tone.

Hendrix played restless bass on Robert Wyatt's jazzy 'Slow Walkin' Talk', which was finally released in 1994 on Wyatt's *Flotsam Jetsam,* but is also available on his 2013 release *'68.*

Hendrix produced the 1969 album *Sunrise* by Northern Ireland's Eire Apparent, with him lending gleaming guitar to the spirited opener 'Yes, I Needed Someone'; psychedelic scribbles to the creepy 'The Clown'; melancholy chords to 'Mr. Guy Fawkes' ('Got one love and she is dynamite…'); flashing trills to 'Someone Is Sure To (Want You)' and 'Morning Glory'; gliding riffs for 'Magic Carpet'; sardonic wah-wah to 'Captive In The Sun', and triumphant licks to 'Let Me Stay'. It's one of those curious and beautiful forgotten albums that the 1960s keeps on revealing à la July or even The Idle Race. There's also the tang of Marmalade about this album and Hendrix being able to indulge his love of British pop. In fact, he had cited Marmalade's 'I See The Rain' as the best single of 1967. Eire Apparent – featuring guitarist Henry McCullough (later of Spooky Tooth and Wings), often evokes its bittersweet melodicism.

In 1968, Hendrix played on McGough and McGear's eponymous album: that is Mike McCartney and Roger McGough from The Scaffold. 'So Much' is breezy in the best 1960s pop tradition, and sounds more like a Redding cut than a Hendrix composition, but is good fun.

Not sounding much like the 1960s is Lightnin' Rod & The Last Poets' 'Doriella Du Fontaine' from 1984. It has some cool blues by Hendrix, with a rap over the top.

Although he recorded pop, rock and blues for other acts, Hendrix's playing is always responsive to the needs of the piece, and is more restrained than in his own work. Those years as a session player instilled a discipline he could use at will.

See also the Arthur Lee and Love collaborations under 'Spanish Castle Magic' on *Axis: Bold As Love.*

Afterword

Where would Hendrix have gone next? The obligatory question. He'd mentioned wanting to use strings to *Melody Maker*, but not in a classical way, and how he'd achieve 'extreme and opposite musical textures'. He'd already done that with his combining of fire and water; air and earth; the psychedelic with the rootsy blues. And anyway, much better to *really* listen to what he *did*, than speculate.

The next thing Hendrix writers *have* to do is list the legacy of his influence. Someone as dynamic, unique and simply thrilling as Hendrix couldn't fail to influence all who heard him. We can list Tony Iommi, Marc Bolan, Nile Rodgers (who, as a 16-year-old, jammed with Hendrix in Greenwich Village), Prince, Slash, Lenny Kravitz and John Frusciante, and of course, there's the impact Hendrix had on his contemporaries. But let's not dwell too long on this either. Whilst looking at who and what an artist influenced can be revealing, it's also like judging any of us by the children we have – not always what was intended; not always a fair measure of the value of someone's work. We don't do this as much with novelists or painters or actors either. Hendrix told *The Mirror*: 'Now that is what the world is all about… having kids. Like planting flowers.' He certainly planted flowers with his impact on blues, funk, fusion, hip hop, heavy metal and rock. But the most important are the ones he grew himself: they're still peaking over 60 years on. Perhaps the flowers of those he inspired might wither sooner. And anyway, we were lucky enough to hear Hendrix's future in his present. That's what all the best music does. It looks ahead; it time travels…

One of the most poignant moments when writing this book was looking at a copy of Hendrix's death certificate: his occupation is listed as 'musician'. Nothing surprising about this, and yet the single defining word says it all; says nothing. At Hendrix's funeral, there was none of his music, but the following hymns were sung – 'His Eye Is On The Sparrow' with the very Hendrix line 'I sing because I'm free', 'The Angels Keep Watch Over Me' and 'Just A Closer Walk With Thee'. Angels, music and movement. Not his music, but certainly sharing a spirit. Hendrix had said he didn't want hymns, but these show that his lexicon might have been more on the side of innocence after all.

Regrettably, Hendrix was denied a truly great album cover, but he deserved a masterwork evoking the sublime. Caspar David Friedrich's *Wanderer Above the Sea of Fog,* in psychedelic colours, would have been perfect – Hendrix on the precipice, guitar strap across his back like a bandolier: Wanderer Above the Purple Haze…

On Track series

Alan Parsons Project – Steve Swift 978-1-78952-154-2
Tori Amos – Lisa Torem 978-1-78952-142-9
Asia – Peter Braidis 978-1-78952-099-6
Badfinger – Robert Day-Webb 978-1-878952-176-4
Barclay James Harvest – Keith and Monica Domone 978-1-78952-067-5
The Beatles – Andrew Wild 978-1-78952-009-5
The Beatles Solo 1969-1980 – Andrew Wild 978-1-78952-030-9
Blue Oyster Cult – Jacob Holm-Lupo 978-1-78952-007-1
Blur – Matt Bishop 978-178952-164-1
Marc Bolan and T.Rex – Peter Gallagher 978-1-78952-124-5
Kate Bush – Bill Thomas 978-1-78952-097-2
Camel – Hamish Kuzminski 978-1-78952-040-8
Caravan – Andy Boot 978-1-78952-127-6
Cardiacs – Eric Benac 978-1-78952-131-3
Eric Clapton Solo – Andrew Wild 978-1-78952-141-2
The Clash – Nick Assirati 978-1-78952-077-4
Crosby, Stills and Nash – Andrew Wild 978-1-78952-039-2
The Damned – Morgan Brown 978-1-78952-136-8
Deep Purple and Rainbow 1968-79 – Steve Pilkington 978-1-78952-002-6
Dire Straits – Andrew Wild 978-1-78952-044-6
The Doors – Tony Thompson 978-1-78952-137-5
Dream Theater – Jordan Blum 978-1-78952-050-7
Electric Light Orchestra – Barry Delve 978-1-78952-152-8
Elvis Costello and The Attractions – Georg Purvis 978-1-78952-129-0
Emerson Lake and Palmer – Mike Goode 978-1-78952-000-2
Fairport Convention – Kevan Furbank 978-1-78952-051-4
Peter Gabriel – Graeme Scarfe 978-1-78952-138-2
Genesis – Stuart MacFarlane 978-1-78952-005-7
Gentle Giant – Gary Steel 978-1-78952-058-3
Gong – Kevan Furbank 978-1-78952-082-8
Hall and Oates – Ian Abrahams 978-1-78952-167-2
Hawkwind – Duncan Harris 978-1-78952-052-1
Peter Hammill – Richard Rees Jones 978-1-78952-163-4
Roy Harper – Opher Goodwin 978-1-78952-130-6
Jimi Hendrix – Emma Stott 978-1-78952-175-7
The Hollies – Andrew Darlington 978-1-78952-159-7
Iron Maiden – Steve Pilkington 978-1-78952-061-3
Jefferson Airplane – Richard Butterworth 978-1-78952-143-6
Jethro Tull – Jordan Blum 978-1-78952-016-3
Elton John in the 1970s – Peter Kearns 978-1-78952-034-7
The Incredible String Band – Tim Moon 978-1-78952-107-8
Iron Maiden – Steve Pilkington 978-1-78952-061-3
Judas Priest – John Tucker 978-1-78952-018-7
Kansas – Kevin Cummings 978-1-78952-057-6
The Kinks – Martin Hutchinson 978-1-78952-172-6
Korn – Matt Karpe 978-1-78952-153-5
Led Zeppelin – Steve Pilkington 978-1-78952-151-1
Level 42 – Matt Philips 978-1-78952-102-3
Little Feat – 978-1-78952-168-9
Aimee Mann – Jez Rowden 978-1-78952-036-1
Joni Mitchell – Peter Kearns 978-1-78952-081-1
The Moody Blues – Geoffrey Feakes 978-1-78952-042-2
Motorhead – Duncan Harris 978-1-78952-173-3
Mike Oldfield – Ryan Yard 978-1-78952-060-6
Opeth – Jordan Blum 978-1-78-952-166-5
Tom Petty – Richard James 978-1-78952-128-3
Porcupine Tree – Nick Holmes 978-1-78952-144-3
Queen – Andrew Wild 978-1-78952-003-3
Radiohead – William Allen 978-1-78952-149-8
Renaissance – David Detmer 978-1-78952-062-0
The Rolling Stones 1963-80 – Steve Pilkington 978-1-78952-017-0
The Smiths and Morrissey – Tommy Gunnarsson 978-1-78952-140-5
Status Quo the Frantic Four Years – Richard James 978-1-78952-160-3
Steely Dan – Jez Rowden 978-1-78952-043-9
Steve Hackett – Geoffrey Feakes 978-1-78952-098-9
Thin Lizzy – Graeme Stroud 978-1-78952-064-4
Toto – Jacob Holm-Lupo 978-1-78952-019-4
U2 – Eoghan Lyng 978-1-78952-078-1
UFO – Richard James 978-1-78952-073-6
The Who – Geoffrey Feakes 978-1-78952-076-7

Roy Wood and the Move – James R Turner
978-1-78952-008-8
Van Der Graaf Generator – Dan Coffey
978-1-78952-031-6
Yes – Stephen Lambe 978-1-78952-001-9
Frank Zappa 1966 to 1979 – Eric Benac
978-1-78952-033-0
Warren Zevon – Peter Gallagher
978-1-78952-170-2
10CC – Peter Kearns 978-1-78952-054-5

Decades Series

The Bee Gees in the 1960s –
Andrew Mon Hughes et al 978-1-78952-148-1
The Bee Gees in the 1970s –
Andrew Mon Hughes et al 978-1-78952-179-5
Black Sabbath in the 1970s – Chris Sutton
978-1-78952-171-9
Britpop – Peter Richard Adams and Matt Pooler
978-1-78952-169-6
Alice Cooper in the 1970s – Chris Sutton
978-1-78952-104-7
Curved Air in the 1970s – Laura Shenton
978-1-78952-069-9
Bob Dylan in the 1980s – Don Klees
978-1-78952-157-3
Fleetwood Mac in the 1970s – Andrew Wild
978-1-78952-105-4
Focus in the 1970s – Stephen Lambe
978-1-78952-079-8
Free and Bad Company in the 1970s –
John Van der Kiste 978-1-78952-178-8
Genesis in the 1970s – Bill Thomas
978178952-146-7
George Harrison in the 1970s – Eoghan Lyng
978-1-78952-174-0
Marillion in the 1980s – Nathaniel Webb
978-1-78952-065-1
Mott the Hoople and Ian Hunter in the 1970s –
John Van der Kiste 978-1-78-952-162-7
Pink Floyd In The 1970s – Georg Purvis
978-1-78952-072-9
Tangerine Dream in the 1970s –
Stephen Palmer 978-1-78952-161-0
The Sweet in the 1970s – Darren Johnson
978-1-78952-139-9
Uriah Heep in the 1970s – Steve Pilkington
978-1-78952-103-0
Yes in the 1980s – Stephen Lambe with David
Watkinson 978-1-78952-125-2

On Screen series

Carry On… – Stephen Lambe 978-1-78952-004-0
David Cronenberg – Patrick Chapman
978-1-78952-071-2
Doctor Who: The David Tennant Years –
Jamie Hailstone 978-1-78952-066-8
James Bond – Andrew Wild –
978-1-78952-010-1
Monty Python – Steve Pilkington
978-1-78952-047-7
Seinfeld Seasons 1 to 5 – Stephen Lambe
978-1-78952-012-5

Other Books

1967: A Year In Psychedelic Rock – Kevan Furbank
978-1-78952-155-9
1970: A Year In Rock – John Van der Kiste
978-1-78952-147-4
1973: The Golden Year of Progressive Rock
978-1-78952-165-8
Babysitting A Band On The Rocks –
G.D. Praetorius 978-1-78952-106-1
Eric Clapton Sessions – Andrew Wild
978-1-78952-177-1
Derek Taylor: For Your Radioactive Children –
Andrew Darlington 978-1-78952-038-5
The Golden Road: The Recording History of The
Grateful Dead –
John Kilbride 978-1-78952-156-6
Iggy and The Stooges On Stage 1967-1974 –
Per Nilsen 978-1-78952-101-6
Jon Anderson and the Warriors – the road to Yes –
David Watkinson 978-1-78952-059-0
Nu Metal: A Definitive Guide – Matt Karpe
978-1-78952-063-7
Tommy Bolin: In and Out of Deep Purple –
Laura Shenton 978-1-78952-070-5
Maximum Darkness – Deke Leonard
978-1-78952-048-4
Maybe I Should've Stayed In Bed –
Deke Leonard 978-1-78952-053-8
The Twang Dynasty – Deke Leonard
978-1-78952-049-1

and many more to come!